Come
to
the
Edge

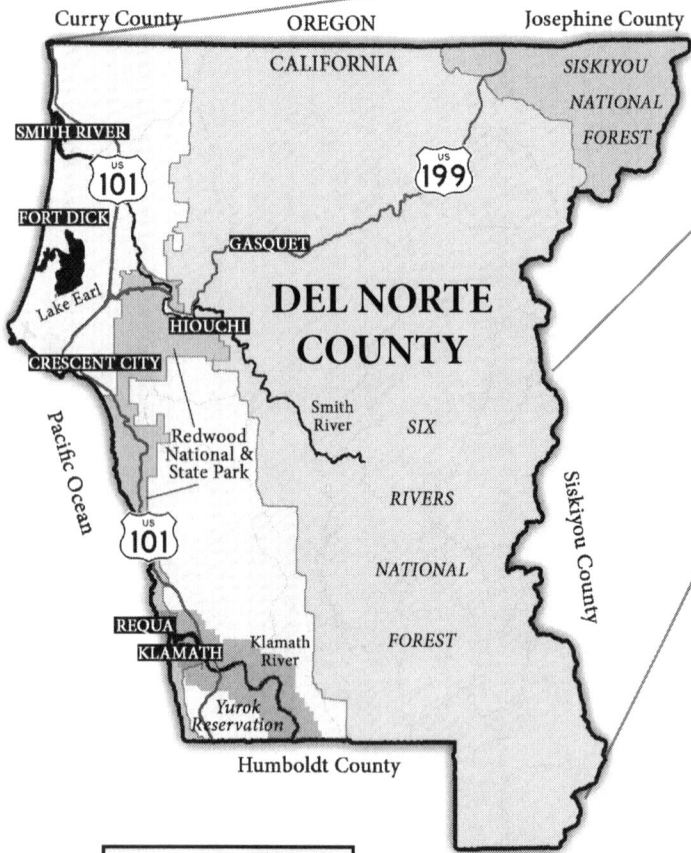

Curry County — OREGON — Josephine County

CALIFORNIA

SISKIYOU

NATIONAL

FOREST

SMITH RIVER

US 101

FORT DICK

GASQUET

US 199

Lake Earl

HIOUCHI

**DEL NORTE COUNTY**

CRESCENT CITY

Smith River

SIX

Pacific Ocean

Redwood National & State Park

RIVERS

NATIONAL

Siskiyou County

US 101

REQUA

KLAMATH

Klamath River

FOREST

Yurok Reservation

Humboldt County

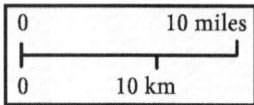

| 0 | 10 miles |
|---|----------|
| 0 | 10 km |

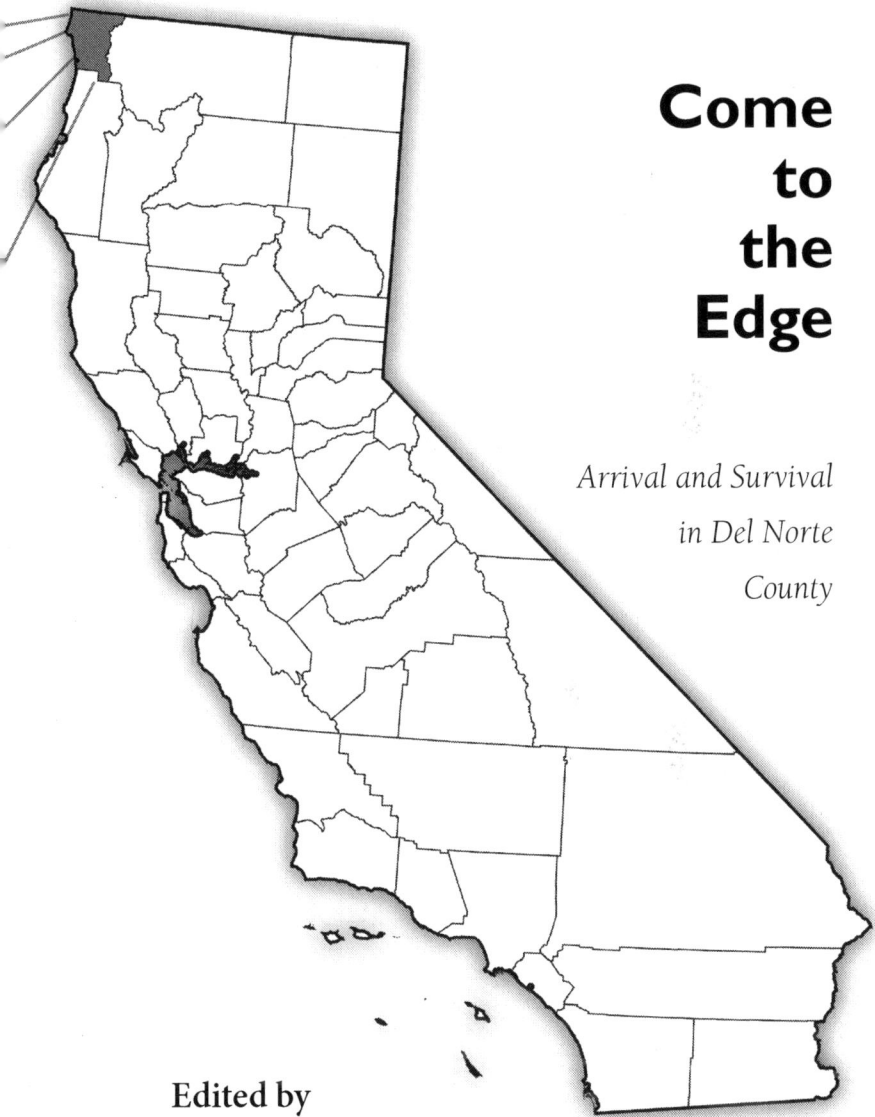

# Come
# to
# the
# Edge

*Arrival and Survival*
*in Del Norte*
*County*

**Edited by**
**Ruth Rhodes**

# Contents

## Part 1: Justice

*What feels fair? What feels unfair?*

## Part II: Resources

*Where do we feel abundance? Where do we sense scarcity?*

# Part III: Belonging

*When do we feel like outsiders? When do we feel we belong?*

# Part IV: Values

*When do our values clash with those around us? How do we find common ground?*

# Come to the Edge

Come to the edge.
We might fall.
Come to the edge.
It's too high!
COME TO THE EDGE!
And they came,
and he pushed,
And they flew.


*- Christopher Logue*

*Ruth Rhodes with two of her children,*
*visiting the edge of Del Norte County.*

# Preface
## by Ruth Rhodes

IN ONE OF MY MOST VIVID MEMORIES of Del Norte County, my husband Lathrop is standing on the edge of a dramatic cliff at the tip of Point St. George, arms spread, looking towards the sea. It is 2003. We have just moved to Crescent City, and this is the first time we've ever seen the view at the end of Pebble Beach Drive.

"I can't believe we live here!" Lathrop shouts over the sound of the wind and waves.

We had truly come to the edge—and in more ways than we could fully understand at that moment.

Del Norte is *literally* on the edge of the sea and on the northern edge of California. On our west flank is the Pacific Ocean. On a sunny day, if you look out over the water, you see a few sea stacks, maybe small fishing boats, but the dominant view is the fullness of a vast, blue ocean, the horizon, and the curve of the earth itself.

If you turn around and look east, you face mountains. Running up them, dense redwood forests. In the protected places where old growth still stands, you find the tallest trees in the world. These giants grow largest on the alluvial flats of the watershed, on Redwood Creek, the mighty Klamath, and the small but pristine Smith. These rivers, ribbons of seemingly endless water, serve as ancient highways for salmon which return regularly to feed whole communities, cultures and ecosystems. Despite a range of environmental impacts, the land and water here still burst with life.

As many residents have put it, Del Norte is "God's Country." Those less inclined to use religious language call it "breathtaking" and "serene."

But we also live on another sort of edge here. Del Norte is isolated. Only a few long, winding roads connect us to the outside world. We are cut off geographically from the rest of the nation in a way that's hard to understand until you actually get in a vehicle and make the journey yourself.

While our isolation has its advantages, it comes with unique challenges, too. Despite living in the great outdoors, despite clean air and abundant water, despite the recent growth and expansion of organic, family-run farms, and despite the perception that, as contributor Joan Buhler puts it, "people pull together here," we have one of the highest early death rates in the state. *People die sooner* here than in nearby counties. According to the Centers for Disease Control, the average life expectancy in Marin County is 81. Here, the average is just under 75.

But early death rates only show us part of the picture. According to the Robert Wood Johnson Foundation's Community Health Rankings, Del Norte has higher rates of teen pregnancy, drug abuse, child abuse, and domestic violence than most other places *in the country*. We are poorer, as a whole, and less educated than most other Americans.

Health rankings, of course, have a way of limiting the scope of our imagination. They don't show us the texture of life here. They don't tell us the full story. The only real experts are the residents of Del Norte County themselves. This book is about letting them speak—in turn—about what it's like to live here.

In August, 2017, I started interviewing Del Norters to get their stories—stories about themselves, their community, and their place in it. I asked how they came to live in Del Norte County. Sometimes *that* was the story. But I also asked about justice: What feels fair here? What feels unfair? I asked about resources. Where do they feel abundance? Where do they feel scarcity? When have they felt they really belonged? When have they felt like outsiders? I also asked them about their values: When did their belief systems clash with those around them? When did they connect?

I interviewed people from all walks of life, people of different ages, races, and ethnicities. Some were prominent citizens, but most were not. The interviewees came from different economic backgrounds, sexual orientations, gender identities, and legal statuses. I talked to people with different work histories, too, and sought out people who could offer alternative perspectives on subjects that kept coming up in other interviews—like law enforcement, health care, and land management.

The interviews were transcribed, and each interviewee had a chance to edit their piece, to add what they wished they had said but didn't, delete what they regretted saying, and change wording and details that didn't come out quite right. The contributors needed to feel they could stand by their words.

There were about fifty interviews in all. Not all the interviews are included. A few folks withdrew from the project. Not everyone was comfortable with what they had said or trusted that their words would not be used against them somehow. This speaks of the times we live in. But forty-two Del Norters did want to contribute. That speaks to their individual courage.

This book is not trying to present a scientific sample of the average Del Norter's experience. As you'll see, there is nothing average about these contributors. Nor is this a formal study. In fact, it is not a study at all. It is a collection of stories from diverse and interesting people who have something to say about living here.

It's also a collection full of contradictions. That's what many readers may find most captivating. The interviews reveal a great deal about our community's history and the varied experiences people have of it. But they also reveal the way people live in different worlds—different realities.

For example, white people tend to report that we have very little racism here. People don't see color. Everyone gets along. But people of color report a much different story, one of interpersonal pain, but also structural racism—systems stacked against certain sectors of our community. This dual-reality exists beyond racial divides, into economic, cultural, and generational ones. People in power say that most things are fair and institutions are doing a pretty good job. But ask people on the margins, people outside the circles of power and influence in our community about what's fair and what's unfair. They tell you a different story. And while many older contributors despair the laziness of youth, many younger contributors report that they have very few adults in their lives whom they can trust or rely on, and little or no opportunity to find meaningful work here.

Each story, on its own, is precious. It's a life, distilled down, from the expert who lived it. But together, these stories have a way of talking to one another, as if the contributors were in the same room. In fact, the essays are arranged in "rooms" of conversational themes. If you listen carefully, you can hear the contributors surfacing gaps in understanding, revealing contradictions, and calling out deep disparities when it comes to the experiences of living here.

What we do with these gifts—these stories—what we learn from them—is up to us. If we want to form communities where we all really do "pull together," then we must come together in a real and honest way, with open eyes. We must stand where our neighbor stands—and get right up to the edge—so we can see what our neighbor sees.

*Geneva Wiki with two of her children and her grandmother Lavina Bowers.*

# Introduction
## by Geneva Wiki

I WAS ASKED TO WRITE THE INTRODUCTION to *Come to the Edge* because of my involvement in community development here in Del Norte County and my professional understanding of the challenges we face, living in such an isolated and unique place. But I was also asked to start as each contributor starts—with myself and my own story of arrival and survival here—so that's how I'll begin.

My dad says the line between heaven and earth is the thinnest at Requa. It is the place where the Klamath River spills into the Pacific Ocean on the far northwest coast of California, in Del Norte County. Yurok people, my people, have lived here since the beginning of time.

My earliest memories are with my great grandparents at Requa. I remember checking on salmon in the smoke house with my Grandpa Mattz, the thin strips of fish hanging from racks and the smell of burning alder wood. As a toddler, the first full sentence I ever spoke was at their dining room table, standing on my chair, hands on my hips, asking, "More eels, please." Summers meant gill-net fishing on the Klamath River, playing at the beach below my grandmother's house, dancing in Brush dance ceremonies. We never took a family vacation to somewhere exotic. Holidays were always spent going "home" to Requa.

So Requa was always my spiritual and cultural home. But my brother and I didn't grow up here. My parents raised us in Oregon, close enough to drive for a weekend visit, but the love and appreciation we had for Requa did not extend beyond the reservation to the rest of Del Norte County. When I was about ten, I remember driving through a neighborhood in Crescent City on the way back to Oregon and commenting that I could imagine living there when I grew up. My mother clearly told me that living in Crescent City was not the dream. "This place is depressing, and you will not live here," she told me.

My mom had good reason to feel this way. Del Norte County often boasts the worst social and health outcomes in California. No one in my family had ever successfully graduated from Del Norte High School and completed university. Good jobs were scarce. Racism felt pervasive.

But regardless of where I lived and how much fun I was having in cities around the country, my heart was always homesick for Requa, and in 2003, after graduate school, I moved home to live with my Grandma at the home my great-grandmother's grandfather built. And later, I moved to Crescent City itself, and bought a house in town with my husband.

In 2009, The California Endowment, a private health foundation, chose Del Norte County and the Yurok reservation as one of 14 communities across the state to engage in a 10-year and $1 billion experiment: the Building Healthy Communities Initiative. I was asked to facilitate the process of creating a community plan, which asked the question: *What must be true for Del Norte to truly be a healthy community?*

In 2010, we held many meetings throughout the Del Norte County and across the Yurok reservation, talking through challenges, reviewing data, dreaming about what was possible. In meetings with Hmong neighbors in Crescent City, Tolowas in Smith River, Yuroks in Klamath, white folks in Fort Dick, the message across the county was clear: *Our young people have no hope.*

This, in part, is why *Come to the Edge: Arrival and Survival in Del Norte County* is so important today. In the wake of the 2016 election, our nation struggles to understand the psyche of the rural United States.

Del Norte County is a place that is simultaneously breathtaking in its natural beauty and heartbreaking in its abject poverty. Each fall, hundreds of people will turn out to celebrate Del Norte High School football homecoming games, but only 20% of high school graduates are prepared to enter a state college. Each summer, hundreds of thousands of tourists come to visit our redwood forests, but our rates of children living in poverty are still the highest in the state.

Policy makers and public health officials are working hard to understand why rural whites without college degrees are dying prematurely from suicide, alcohol and drugs at shocking rates. This book gives us insights directly from the people on the front lines—my neighbors of rural Del Norte County, California—about the conditions that contribute to those alarming statistics.

*Come to the Edge* turns a dramatic cast of real people into published authors. As I read these stories, I am struck by how each voice tells a story I know to be true.

The most striking contradiction in these stories is the new narrative told by the Del Norte young adults. Unlike a decade ago, when the message of young people was one of hopelessness, in these stories we now hear glimmers of a new story of what it means to grow up and come from this place. These young people now have dreams, and those dreams feel like our collective responsibility.

Taking on that responsibility is one of the many ways we here in Del Norte now approach the edge—the edge of empowerment and change.

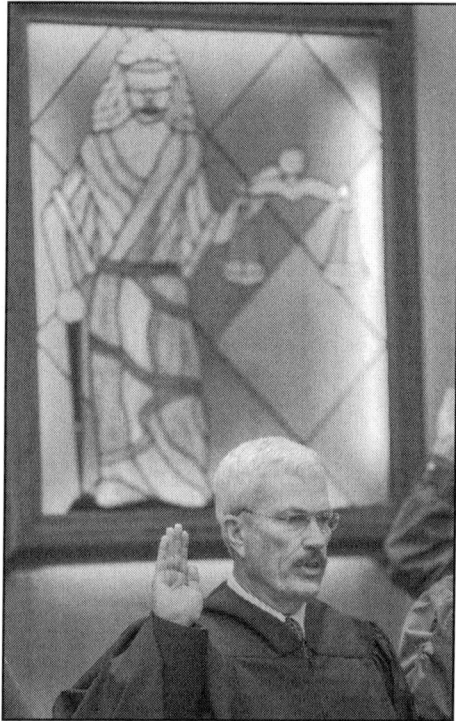

*Superior Court Judge William Follett
swears an oath before a stained glass depiction
of the scales of justice.*

# PART I:
# JUSTICE

*What feels fair?*
*What feels unfair?*

# Lavina Bowers

"My classmates called us 'black' and 'squaw' and used other derogatory words and expressions. But mostly, they just stopped talking to us. I think they were taking their cues from the adults in town. White grown-ups never talked to us in public."

*Lavina Bowers is an elder in the Yurok Tribe. In this interview, she bears witness to her family's experiences of "termination era" politics and their assertion of their rights in the infamous Fish Wars. She also recounts her personal growth, from a shy and withdrawn girl to a more outspoken woman, cognizant of the need to do what is right. Notably, this interview took place at the Requa Inn, which overlooks one of the family's traditional fishing spots on the Klamath River. Her daughter's family recently acquired it as part of a lifelong dream to re-establish the family here.*

I WAS BORN IN 1935 at Knapp Hospital—Seaside Hospital—in Crescent City. My brothers and sisters and I grew up as upriver Indians. Our house was right across from Brooks' Riffle on the Klamath River. An Indian boy lived next door to us, and across the river there were a lot of Indian kids coming from probably four or five families living there. We saw very few white people.

We didn't go to town very often. It was a big deal. But to get to our place from town, I remember, we went by car, and we had to walk a ways. Then we went by boat across the river, and then walked up the hill to our place. Later, Simpson Timber Company made a road, but that was after we had moved.

There was one white man and woman who lived up there. I think the man's name was Max Barber. It's crazy I would remember that. They were lovely. She always had cookies for us when we came by. But my experience with white people wasn't always positive in those early days.

My parents were wonderful people. My mama was raised in Requa by her grandparents and at an early age went to Chemawa, an Indian Boarding School in Salem, Oregon. She stayed there until she was sixteen. A lot of her generation did. They had to. The government made children go back then. Mama was lonely there, she told me. She missed her grandmother terribly.

Her grandmother had pretty much raised her, you see. What happened to my mama's mother, Martha Reuben, is a long story. When she was just a girl, Martha was bought by my great-grandparents in the Indian way. Martha came from Orleans, from a dance family, and my great-grandparents paid regalia for her. She lived in Requa with them for two or three years before she married their son, James Brooks, who lived in Crescent City.

When my great-grandma and great-grandpa told their son James that they'd bought him a wife and brought her to Requa, he was mad.

He said, "Why did you do that? I already have a girlfriend!"

But it was too late. It didn't matter. They'd paid for her, and she was there. She stayed at Requa until they got married. They had three children, including my mom, Geneva Brooks.

Geneva was two when her daddy died. Her grandparents sent her mom, Martha, home to Orleans after that. That was the tradition when a bought wife's husband died. Because they fully paid for her, she wasn't allowed to take her babies. I guess they let her take one—but mama never said who it was. Anyway, Martha was so lonesome, she asked to come back to be with the kids. They let her, but they made her get married to her *wetchger*—a relation of her late husband who was single. That's another part of the tradition. Martha moved clear up to Crescent when she did that, and although she did get to visit her kids, she didn't live with them. That's why when my mom, Geneva, went to boarding school at Chemawa, she complained about missing her grandma. That's who she was most attached to.

Mom was small, so in Chemawa, even though she had no family and was terribly lonely, she said the older girls took care of her and treated her alright. She learned a lot of housekeeping skills at the school and caught on very quickly. The teachers taught the girls how to keep things clean, set tables, wash and iron and fold white linen, things like that. They were being trained for domestic service, to work in the houses of white people. But my mom would use all those skills running her own home after she married.

When my mom finished at Chemawa, she went back to Requa. Shortly after that, at age seventeen, she met my dad, Emery Mattz. He was twenty-one. They met in a dance hall that used to be just down from the Requa Inn. There were a lot of dance halls in the area. They played popular music. Everyone from Klamath came on the weekends. It was very social.

My grandmother said that if a man really likes you, he'll swim the Klamath River for you. My dad didn't have to do that. But he did ride a horse part way from Crescent and walked the rest. Mom loved to dance, and she liked him despite the fact that he wasn't a very good dancer. He danced like a stick—with stiff arms and legs. Between them, Mama and Daddy had ten children. The first five were mostly grown up when I came along.

Life upriver was wonderful for us kids. Mom had a flower garden—a huge garden—nothing but roses. She had a catalogue and sent away for every kind of rose you could find. She had a vegetable garden, too, and she and my daddy grew everything. Tomatoes, corn, string beans, bush beans. I remember they picked the bush beans and laid them out on a big tarp, dried them, shelled them, and gave huge amounts away to relatives at the end of the summer, in big mason jars. Dad used to say he was like Henny Penny, giving it all away and doing all the work.

I remember we had to water the garden when it was hot. Each plant got a little bucketful. But we didn't have running water. We packed it in from a stream. Daddy carried four buckets with one of those carriers that went over his shoulders. Mama carried two buckets. Each of us kids had a bucket. Sometimes, we'd take the horse and the sled and carry water back in a barrel.

We raised pigs. My sister and I used to visit the pigs and kind of made pets of them. So we didn't eat any of the pork until later in the year, after we forgot the meat used to be our friends. We also had a couple of cows and a horse. We had everything we needed. Our shelves were always plumb full. So many good things, it's hard to remember it all.

The only thing I didn't like growing up was taking my cod liver oil. I used to take a big spoonful every morning. Mama would give us a very small piece of orange and a very small piece of apple to take with it. That was the only thing I can complain about. Otherwise, life was so good. Mama took us swimming every day in the summer. We always had breakfast, lunch, and dinner at the same time every day. When Dad came home, she always put dinner right on the table.

My dad worked across the river cutting trees. When the road was being built, he worked on that as a powder monkey, doing the blasting. Mama worked hard, too. Mondays we packed all the dirty clothes up and she scrubbed them with a washing board up at the stream. I remember it so clearly because we played at the stream. Tuesdays she ironed. She ironed everything. I don't know why she did—we lived up there all by ourselves. No one ever saw us! Wednesdays she baked. Every week it was like that. Once a month maybe, they went to town.

I don't remember going to town very much. Indian people were mostly all I knew. We came out Christmas times and other holidays. We visited my Grandma, Agnes Mattz. Sometimes we went to her sister's in Trinidad. She was a wonderful woman. Her dad's brother, who married a Hoopa woman, would come. It was all our own family out at Elk Valley and other places. I really felt like I belonged, sitting at a big table outside, eating together with all those relations.

The first white man I remember seeing was here at Requa. Red Knutzson was the owner of a little store down here. My mom always shopped there. I went in with her one time—I was maybe five—and I saw some gum. My mother had never bought me any, and so you know what I did? I just took it and came out of the store. My mother saw it and asked me about it. When I told her the truth, she marched me right back in that store and I had to tell Mr. Knutzson that I'd taken it. I don't know how I knew to be embarrassed at so young an age, but my face got so hot.

He looked me in the eye and said, "Thank you for bringing this back in."

"My mama made me bring it back," I told him.

"Then thank your mama," he said. He added, "Someday I will give you a piece of gum. But not today."

For years and years, because of that, I had the feeling I should never steal. I was with a bunch of girls in town one time trying to steal something, and I told them I could never do it. I don't remember Mr. Knutson ever giving me a piece of gum, though!

My childhood really was very good, even though there were some sad parts. We moved to Grants Pass when my older sister came down with tuberculosis. They said the hot weather would be good for her, but she died there, at seventeen. After that, instead of moving back to the river, we moved to Crescent City.

I was eight years old when I started at Crescent Elk. My teacher there was Bessie Maxwell. She was a big woman with a very pink tongue that seemed to stick out a lot when she talked. I can't say she was a prejudiced teacher because she never said anything to me, but I can't say I either liked or disliked her. I don't think she paid much attention to me, actually.

I do remember she was very hard on a white boy named Lester Cook and an Indian boy named Eddie John. She would hit them over and over again on the sides of their head. Poor kids. They would flinch as she said, "I'll give you something to duck for!"

I was shocked when I moved home later as an adult that they'd named a school after her. I didn't think of her as a particularly kind or good teacher.

One thing I remember was how around sixth grade, the white kids started separating themselves from us. It's like that was when they figured we were different. Girls I used to be friends with stopped socializing with me. It was very hurtful.

A lot of the Indian kids left for Chemawa then, too. Some of them went there because they didn't like the way they were being treated in the Del Norte schools. But my brothers and sisters never went there. My mom never said why she didn't send us, but I think she didn't want us to be lonely. So we stayed in the school system even though there weren't so many other Indians left.

My classmates called us "black" and "squaw" and used other derogatory words and expressions. But mostly, they just stopped talking to us. I think they were taking their cues from the adults in town. White grown-ups never talked to us in public. The shop workers would watch us in stores as if we were criminals and wait on us last if any white people were in there, but otherwise we were invisible. They mostly just ignored us.

I was very shy as a child. I almost never talked. I think it had something to do with the way I was treated and the way I saw other people treated. It made me feel so bad. Yes, this was something that made me feel like I didn't belong.

I had a girlfriend in my class named Katie Pleasant, and we were close for a while. But one day, I got a letter in typing class, just left on my desk. It was nearly a page long, and it described all the reasons you shouldn't trust Indians and shouldn't be friends with them. Things like that. I cried all the way home. I showed it to Mama, and she told me to show it to the typing teacher, so I did.

The typing teacher had a plan. She told our class we were going to do something different that day. She would speak, and we would type her words. So we did. She used the word "friend" a couple of times, and we all typed it.

Afterwards, the typing teacher showed me that in the letter I'd received, the "f" in the word "friend" was out of place. The person who'd written the letter used a typewriter where the "f" was a little off. It turned out the typewriter used was Katie Pleasant's. I thought she was my friend, but she'd written it. I was heartbroken. We didn't really talk after that, of course.

Another girlfriend, Dee Spanz, also stopped speaking to me. Recently, my daughter Sue met her and asked her what she remembered about me. Dee recalled that we were good friends, but she forgot about how she stopped talking to me. Sue made me go visit Dee and talk to her about it. I told her how she'd treated me. I also reminded her that her mother didn't like Indians, and would say so. Her mother had even written several letters to the paper, saying ugly things about Indians. Dee didn't know about that, and she had no memory of how she'd abandoned our friendship.

Some people easily forget the things they've said and done. But you know, the people they hurt don't forget so easily. Maybe that's why so many white people don't think there is any racism here in Del Norte County, but so many brown people can tell you they've experienced it.

Overall, I don't think life for my siblings and me was quite as rough as it was for other Indians, though, because of who my mama and daddy were. We were known as good people. My dad was Portuguese, Yurok, and Smith River Indian, so he wasn't as dark as others, and my mother always dressed well. My parents had a lot of white friends who came to our house. The man who owned the Benbow Inn, Principal Thuning, and some others visited. But we almost never went to their houses. We weren't invited.

When I was twelve, I made up my mind to marry a white man. That way, I thought, I wouldn't get treated so bad.

And you know, I did marry a white man. When I was in high school, I met an Air Force guy who worked at the base at the top of Requa. He was shipping out and asked me to go with him. I said I didn't know if Mama and Daddy would let me go since I'd have to drop out of school, but he went up the hill and talked to them. We had a fast wedding.

We moved up to Prince George, British Columbia. It was only the second time I'd been out of the county. I was so lonely for my family. And pretty soon I wasn't even sure if I liked the guy.

The first time my brother called me up there, I was so upset, I couldn't even speak. I could only sob. On the other end of the line,

I heard him say, "I can hear sound but she's not saying anything. It must be the telephone," and he hung up.

Probably three or four hours later, they called again, and we got to talk. They said, "What can we send you up there?" I said, "Send me a Three Musketeers bar." I didn't know what I was saying. I tried it after I came home, and I didn't even like it.

The Canada Indians had it even worse up there than here, if you can imagine. The kids there couldn't go to school with white kids. My husband and I talked about moving somewhere like Japan, but by then, I was having a baby every year. So we stayed, but I made it so that I could come home once or twice a year with the kids to be with my family.

Eventually, we moved to Corvallis, Oregon, where we raised our kids. After I had my children, I learned to get over my fear of talking, and soon I could communicate with just about anybody. Their teachers needed to know I was going to help my kids in school when they needed it, and that I would be an advocate for them. So I sort of came out of my shell.

I changed. I became more of a talker. My husband used to say, "I liked her the way she used to be, when she didn't talk so much."

We stayed married twenty-three years. He drank a lot, and he gambled. I always seemed to have an upset stomach and a headache, but I focused on the kids. I worked two jobs, including the late shift, so I wasn't home all day, but I made sure all those kids were taken care of and all went to college.

In 1972, my daddy had a heart attack. The kids were grown and out of the house, so I moved back to Klamath without my husband. The time I came home, I remember it was beautiful weather. I hadn't remembered it being so warm. People were wearing shorts. We'd never done that when I was a kid. I said to everyone, "It's so beautiful!" I knew I was home, then. I felt like I really belonged.

They laughed at me and said, "We're in the middle of a drought, Lavina!"

You know, I stopped having those stomach problems and headaches when I came home. I filed for divorce a few years later.

You asked about things that were fair and unfair. One thing that was unfair was how Indians were treated, and a big example of that relates to traditional fishing, or gill netting. It was something that Yurok people had always done. It was how we survived. It was who we were. Who we are even now.

But there were many ways white people tried to take this right away from us, many times over. In my family, my mother remembered a time when a judge came to see my great-grandpa Brooks. My great-grandpa had sold the timber on his land up the hill here in Requa. After he'd signed the papers and sold the timber, this judge named Bowie came to my dad's house with another white man. My mom didn't know who he was.

Judge Bowie said, "You know, Mr. Brooks, you sold timber to the white man. That means you're no longer an Indian."

My mama said she saw the muscles on grandpa's jaw go back and forth.

"What do you mean, I'm no longer an Indian?" he said.

"You took money for your timber. That means you're not an Indian. You can no longer fish on the river like Indians do," the judge said, meaning he no longer had fishing rights.

They had words then. My great-grandpa used to work for Mr. DeMartin—who came from somewhere else and had an accent from wherever he came from—and great-grandpa learned to swear from DeMartin—and so he swore with an accent then.

"You, Mr. Bowie, and you, Mr. Whiteman, you get off of my land. I'm going to fish no matter what you say. Get off of my land, and don't ever come back."

One way to stop us from fishing was to try to tell us we weren't Indians. Another was in 1934, when recreational fishermen got the state of California to ban all commercial and subsistence fishing on the Klamath River. We weren't supposed to fish after that. As a result of that, my father never did fish.

But my brothers fished. I remember when I was little, they fished a lot. In fact, the game warden knew our family and told my dad to make sure my brothers pulled their nets out of the water every time he came by in the boat so he wouldn't catch them. One time, my brothers were fishing and heard a boat coming up the river. They didn't want to take their nets out. I remember hiding under a blanket with some of the other small kids. It turned out not to be the warden, but we were scared anyway.

Things got very scary during the Fish Wars here, around 1978 and 1979. People you never thought would be ugly turned ugly. But we believed in our right to fish, and we had to fight for it.

At that time, lots of Indian people defied the game wardens and fished. We have several traditional fishing holes in our family—one down here at the mouth of the Klamath and one upriver at the cabin. My brothers were fishing at night up at the mouth, and they weren't alone. Other men were with them. They all had smaller nets. When the game wardens came, the other men took their nets out of the water. They didn't want to go to jail. But my brothers agreed that they wanted to fight for their rights, and so they didn't cooperate. They went to jail to test the law used to confiscate their nets.

It went all the way to the Supreme Court, and they won in a case called *Mattz vs. Arnett* (1973). The court said that Yurok people, as Indians, did have rights, and that our tribe had never been disbanded. But even after that, we still had to fight many battles when the government tried to regulate us out of fishing.

These were the Fish Wars. Federal officers closed off fishing for the whole river, but our people defied them again and kept fishing. Susan, my daughter, came down to take part. My whole family, really.

Those federal officers were big, intimidating men. One was a black man. The Indians gave him a very hard time, calling him names, telling him they'd wish the white folks had gotten him in Selma. He didn't last long. They shipped him out, poor man. They must have made him feel pretty bad. They didn't need to say those things, but at the time I laughed and thought it was a good thing to say.

I laughed, you know, but we were very scared about what might happen to us and to our family. The federal officers were very rough. They had clubs, and they'd hit people with them. They held people under water. So many mean things. The worse part was, we never knew what they were going to do next.

My brother and his wife and kids went down to the mouth to fish a lot back then. We'd often go with them. My daughter Diane and this lady who lived up the way, Molly, never missed a night. We had a line with no net on it, and she put her bloomers on it and put it in the water so they could pull it up. So we had our own ways of rebelling.

One night, the federal officers and all the cops from Del Norte came together—so many—forest service people. I wasn't down there that night, but Diane was. She said boats came into the mouth. Flashlights shone on everyone from shore. Officers crossed our land. My mama told them not to. They didn't listen. Her dog was barking up a storm, and they told her to put it inside or they were going to shoot it.

They took all the men to jail, including my daddy, who was seventy-four at the time. He had a bad heart, so the girls went up to bail him out.

The whole community was divided. The white people were just horrible to us. They had signs that said, "Save a Salmon, Can an Indian." They dug a big hole and held a sort of ceremony to "burry Klamath." They got a casket. They played music. I can still see all the people standing around. We drove past that "funeral" in a convertible playing some jazzy Elvis music. I kept thinking, "Why would you want to bury your own town?"

I guess they believed that if we were allowed to fish in our traditional way, there wouldn't be enough for them. But I didn't ask them. I probably should have. I'm friends with a lot of them now. I should probably go and ask them.

Now things are totally different. White people are friendly and say hello. I was in the hospital getting some tests early this morning. A white lady saw that I was cold sitting in the waiting room, and she asked me if she could get me a blanket.

Just recently, I went to a meeting with lots of white women—and Indian women, too. It was a meeting to help get more women elected to office in our community. Those white women I met were so kind and caring. They were very interested in helping children, too. Smart, good, precious women. I thought to myself, if I'd have met white women like these growing up, things would have been much better for me.

I know there is still bullying in school, and it may even be worse than it used to be. Indian kids are still Indian kids. They're brown, and they still get picked on.

What makes it so sad is that some of them don't have mommies and daddies. Their parents are into drugs and alcohol, and they might not come to school clean, or they might not get enough to eat. A generation of Indian men went to booze. And maybe for the next generation, it was booze and drugs.

But then, a lot of poor white kids are in similar circumstances, and they're treated badly, too.

Think about it—all over the country where kids are bringing guns to school and shooting each other. You know those boys with the long, black coats and other kids like them? They're saying that kids like these were all bullied at school and abused. I believe it. We do have to get rid of the guns, but we also need to do something about bullying.

I've seen it. When I worked for a van driver for the United Indian Health Services, I transported kids in Klamath at Margaret Keating Elementary, down to the clinic in Trinidad. I used to walk into the school all the time. I saw teachers letting kids be bullied and abused.

I also witnessed police brutality at Margaret Keating. This was probably in the 1990s. One time, I went to the school to pick up somebody. I saw a girl running across a field, with somebody running after her. It turned out to be a police officer. Eventually he caught up to her, brought her into the school, and bent her over a desk and held her arms behind her back. She was just a little girl—maybe in sixth grade. He was being so rough with her, I had to say something.

I said, "What are you doing?"

The principal was right there, and teachers were watching, but nobody was saying anything.

The police officer said, "It's none of your business."

I said, "Well, it is my business."

He threatened to have me arrested if I didn't leave the school. Well, I didn't want to get arrested, so I left. I never did find out what that little girl did, but it can't have been so bad to get treated like that, could it?

Yes, it does seem like we're making things better. Or maybe I'm just in a place in my life where it seems like it's improved. I still know dark people who go through things like we did when we were little, though. I don't quite know how we can change things.

We do little things—help people here and there, individually. But we've got to do something to lift up all the kids, help them to be good people and act right. We live in a wonderful, beautiful county, and to be happy here is good.

*—April 13, 2018*

# Billy "Bebo" Reynolds

"There's many a night I would lay awake worrying about the next tree I was going to have to cut, how dangerous it was."

*Retired logger and avid outdoorsman Bebo Reynolds describes a life in Del Norte County lived mostly outside. Mixing straightforward narrative with humor and sharp-edged criticism, Bebo quips near the end of the interview, "I hope I haven't stepped on too many toes."*

I WAS BORN AT SEASIDE HOSPITAL in 1955. My father, who was a truck driver, will be 90 this year; my mother passed away at age 54. She was a stay at home mom and worked sometimes at Redwood Elementary School's library.

Dad drove a truck and later ran the truck shop out at Simonson Lumber Company. Dad was born in Texas. His family came up here during the depression. They were cotton farmers until the bank foreclosed on them. The bank took everything, including the cows, the chickens. All they had was the Model T and the clothes on their backs. It took them two years to work their way out here to Del Norte County, picking fruit. All of them. Grandma and Grandpa, the kids. When he got here, my grandfather bought 13 acres at $28 per acre. It was a lot of money back then.

I went to Redwood Elementary. Great school. It was more hands-on than the other schools. Teachers interacted with the kids. It's still a great school. My daughter Sara had her kids going to Smith River, but Smith River is mostly Hispanic, Spanish-speaking children, and that wasn't working out for our oldest grandson, so she enrolled the kids at Redwood.

This is a hard place to leave. We did move in 1964. Between the tidal wave and the flood, we moved down to Clear Lake for my mom's asthma. They said it would be better for her health, but the drier climate didn't really seem to help, and Dad struggled to find work, so we only lasted a year there. We moved back to Del Norte County.

I've always felt like I belonged here. It's God's Country. Everything that you want or need is right here. We've got the Smith River, one of the cleanest rivers in the United States. We've got the beach. I like to hunt deer, and I like to fish. So, yeah, this is where I want to be.

I felt like I fit in when I was a kid. It was a logging and fishing community, and that's what everybody did. I went fishing and hunting for fun a lot with my dad.

I wasn't the best athlete. I played flag football. We lived up in Mud Hen Village, and there were lots of kids to hang out with. We did lots of things. Caught garter snakes. Built our own go-karts. We didn't have these devices like kids today have. We had to make our own fun.

Yes, I graduated from Del Norte High—barely. I had to sign up for the draft, and then the year I was out, 1973, they abolished the draft, so I never did get my number. I wasn't really interested in high school. They passed me with Ds, and I skipped class a lot. My buddy had a motorcycle. We'd leave school and go cruise town. Hell yes, we partied.

The cops were different back then. You could legally blow a .10 then, and they would just say, "You go home now. I don't want to see you drinking and driving again." Now they'll put you in jail for that.

I could never live my youth again. Too many car wrecks. But it was fun. Wild and crazy.

I started working my senior year, before I graduated. Dad helped me get a job sweeping the floors in the truck shop at Simonson Lumber Company in Smith River. I would get home from school, go to work until midnight, come home, go to sleep, and go to school again. I got eight hours in every afternoon.

I wasn't tempted to go to college. I say I went to "Loggin' College of the Redwoods." I did all kinds of work in the industry. I joined a forestry crew, planting trees, thinning trees, and lots of slashing after they finished logging. I eventually made it to foreman. But I hired friends—never hire your friends when you're the boss. They just refused to work. So I asked my boss to get me out of that job, and I started setting chokers.

What does it mean to set chokers? I hooked cables to fallen, bucked redwood trees so Caterpillars could haul them out. I did that for a while, but eventually, I wanted to be a cat skinner—a Caterpillar operator. So I did that for $13.42 an hour. That was a good wage back then in 1980.

But gosh, I saw these timber cutters at the work site, driving new trucks. I saw that they left early, maybe worked a six or seven hour day. I wanted to do that. I worked around them, helped them out and learned a little that way. My plan was to do that next.

But when the recession came in the 1980's, I was still running cat. Everything stopped. Building stopped. Logging stopped. There was very little demand for lumber. Everyone was scared. We had just bought our house and property. Our daughter was not even two years old, and I had to find work because Simonson had nothing for me.

But I could get into the Simonson property and cut firewood. The wife and I, with the baby in the car seat, would go up together. Then, we went knocking door to door where we saw low wood piles. We sold firewood for $50 a cord just to get enough money to eat. I cut a lot of fence posts, too, and sold those to the farmers. We got through it.

Finally, I went to work on a rock crusher. I did that for about three years. Then, a friend of mine, Leonard Branton—he died later in a logging accident in Idaho—he asked me why I didn't buy a chainsaw and go cutting. He loaned me the money, and I bought one.

I cut all over the country. "Have saw, will travel." I learned a lot from that. When the recession was over, my dad's old timber friends started their own timber cutting company, and they hired me on as a cutter.

I'm retired now. Too many injuries. When you have a bone spur in your neck, and you can't look up to see which way a tree leans, you better quit. You know, timber cutting is very dangerous work. A cat has nine lives. I've had 999—I've been that close to death that many times. I lost some good friends out in the woods to accidents. There's many a night that I would lay awake worrying about the next tree I was going to have to cut, how dangerous it was.

I think the first major injury I got was when we were falling and bucking trees out in the old growth in Klamath. It was a steep slope. I was taping—measuring logs—and one of the logs took off and came rolling down at me. I made a thirty-foot jump down to where I saw a big redwood stump I thought would protect me. When I hit, I blew my right ankle up.

There we were, a thousand feet down from the pickup, but still 500 feet from the creek. The Simpson truck shop sent these fat boy mechanics up the creek with a stretcher to get me out of there. Fat boys? Some guys from the shop who don't get out much in the woods.

My partner, best friend, and "brother," Wade Gist, and I worked together for twenty-three years. We drove one to two hours one way to get our chainsaw and the timber. It seems like I spent more time with Wade than with my own wife. He knows me, and I know him.

Cutting timber is one of the most dangerous jobs. But hey, every day is a picnic when you don't have anybody looking over your shoulder telling you what to do. I don't like Walmart, and I don't like stoplights.

But as far as injuries go, they're going to happen. The chain on the saw is razor sharp. It goes through flesh faster than wood. I've helped Wade out of the woods and he's helped me out. "How many stitches this time?" we'd say.

Reaching down for my saw one day after the tree I just felled bent another over, I suddenly had a new elbow between my wrist and my elbow. The tree I bent over threw a piece of limb when it came back. I had to learn how to wipe left-handed for six weeks.

They say the little tree kills more cutters than the big one. Well, a little tree ended my career. It was only four inches in diameter and about twenty-five feet tall. I was cutting my way to a big tree, and I just kind of pushed it out of the way after I sawed it off. I thought, "That's kind of weird. Where did that little tree go?"

The tree I'd cut just before that one had bent a little oak tree over. It looked like an upside down U. The little tree caught the top of the U and the butt came down on my hardhat. That little tree probably weighed about two hundred pounds. I don't know how long I laid there, but when I woke up, I thought, "This is how a quadriplegic feels."

I could hear Wade's saw running in the distance. I was hoping he could hear my yell when he shut his saw off, but he never shuts his saw off unless he needs gas. Ten minutes later, I started to get feeling back in my toes. It worked up my legs, and finally to my arms.

Wade saw me staggering to the pickup and yelled at me, "It's not quittin' time yet!"

I waved him down, and he checked out the ostrich egg on my head. End of career. I can't turn my head to look up any more. And in this business, you have to be able to look up.

What do I do now that I'm retired? I hunt and fish. I'm at home as Mr. Mom and Grandpa. I have dishpan hands. I do lots of laundry. The only thing I'm not allowed to do is fold bras. My wife says it gives her wrinkled titties. She still works—she's a secretary for the Superior Court Judge. She could actually retire now and make the same amount of money she's making right now, but she loves the work.

My wife and I love the beach. We're agate-maggots. We go after agates at low tide when the sun's out. My buddy's a top-picker. He has knee pads, and he just goes along, picking them, picking them. I sit in one spot and sift the rocks, just looking and enjoying the sound of the ocean.

As far as what's fair and not fair, there's lots of things that I don't feel right about. I wish that Southern California and Northern California were divided because our vote comes from Southern California. There's people down there in the cities who have never seen this part of the country. But that's where the vote comes from.

We used to have a lot of deer around here. But they put a moratorium on hunting mountain lions. They said that there were only four breeding pairs in the state. There was more than four breeding pairs here in Del Norte. While working in the woods, I saw them all the time. That's an issue that still bothers me. The lions have decimated the deer, and now they eat people's dogs and cats. You could be next!

The study on the number of lions was an environmental farce. In my lifetime, I have counted fifty-four lions. I've recorded each one. Only 1 percent of the US population has ever seen a mountain lion in the wild. The lion is a beautiful animal, and so are the deer. I think the lions should be controlled to an acceptable number. Kill one lion, save 1,000 deer.

Several years ago, a man and his wife were out walking a trail by Orick, California. A lion came out of the brush and had the husband by the neck. All she had for a weapon was a ball point pen. She started stabbing the lion in the eyes, and it let go and ran off. She saved his life.

Now, there's the thing that gets me. Twenty or so years ago, they gave park rangers guns to protect us. But you can't pack your own gun in the park to protect yourself. You could go to jail or prison for having a gun in the park—or at least get a hefty fine.* Several years ago, a park ranger was walking his dog off leash on South Beach, and a lion came down to the beach and threatened his dog. He found a stick and fended that cat off. Now, if it was you or me, he would have wrote us a ticket for not having our dog on a leash,

---

* As of February 22, 2010, federal law allows people who can legally possess firearms under applicable federal, state, and local laws, to legally possess firearms in National Park Service-administered lands within Redwood National and State Parks.

but Mr. Ranger could be ten miles away when the lion is attached to my neck.

Now they put the sea lion on the endangered species list. There's hundreds of sea lions lying on the river banks up here. They go in the water, they get as much fish as they want. When they're full, they'll still bite the belly out of a fish even if they don't eat it. The fishing isn't anything like it was twenty years ago. It's getting worse every year. Like I said, we didn't vote to put the sea lion on the endangered species list.

In Washington and Oregon, I think they're going to do something about the problem. But here in California, I don't think we ever will.

The sea lion, like the mountain lion, is a beautiful animal. But, you know, it's kinda like when they killed all the wolves in Yellowstone. When they did that, the elk overpopulated, ran out of food, and starved. Man intervened in that ecosystem, poisoning the wolves, and it had a negative effect.

Environmental regulations did make things more difficult for us in the logging industry, too. When I first started driving Cat, we just drove the thing right down to the river. Now, they say doing that kills fish, and they made us stop doing it. But you know, we had more fish in that river then in those logging years than we do now. Like I said, I don't think people who make the rules really understand what it's like up here.

As far as cultural differences, the Native American didn't have much of a chance when the "white man" came to God's land. The white man had advanced weapons and numbers. We massacred them, and they massacred us. It's not my fault for what our ancestors did. Their ancestors, too. I just think they should be proud to be Americans. Nobody really owns this earth. It's God's gift to mankind. All wars are fought over property, religion, and politics. I have known a lot of Native Americans who went and fought for this country we call the USA. I can't wait until the white man is a minority, so I can get some white man money. The Jews should get German money. What do you think? I have a lot of Native American friends, and we've discussed this. I hope I haven't stepped on too many toes.

As far as Mexicans, I have a few good friends who are Mexican, but growing up, there weren't a lot here yet. And through my senior year, there was only one black kid in our high school, Anthony Sanders.

You asked about the Hmong refugees who came here in the 1980s. You know, a lot of people were curious about the Hmong. You would see them up there in the mountains deer hunting. The does aren't legal, but you see them cutting one up on a paved road. The entire family would be involved in skinning out a female deer. I mean, they'll be fifteen in one Toyota van. They've got to eat, too, but they don't always follow the rules. When it comes to the Hmong, the game wardens gave them time to learn the state rules and regulations. The warden would give them a slap on the wrist, but if it was me, they'd cuff me and stuff me. They've harvested these beautiful sea anemones down at the beach. You don't see those anymore.

What are some ways our community has changed that aren't so good? I wasn't really happy when the prison moved in. Again, nobody voted that in. It was stuffed down our throats. It brought traffic and an increase in population. And a lot of the new folks moved to our small town. The Correctional Officers (COs), families of the inmates, and more. It took time to adjust to all of this. They built the prison in our back yard, you know?

I was tempted to apply for a job, like a lot of people in the timber industry, when the prison came in. I started to fill out the application, but when I came to that page about "Have you ever been arrested," I thought, "I'm gonna be out of paper writing all this down. I don't think they want me." Pot was taboo, and they could fire me.

No, I don't feel my family had any advantages over other families. We worked for what we have, and we worked hard. For my kids, I just want them to be happy and successful. Both went to college—one to beauty school and another went to Butte Community

College and is still finishing up. It's taking a while. It's expensive. I know all about that.

Would I ever move? We've got everything we could ever want right here. And when it gets too foggy here, just head up 199 and hit the river. We love it. This is where I want it to be.

*—April 17, 2018*

# Shellie Babich

"In the medical profession, it's not really good to have your patients be your friends or your family. But here we don't have that option. I mean, if you refuse to see people you know, you're not going to see anybody, really."

*You might imagine a medical professional and home-grown local like Shellie Babich would feel like an insider here. But as you can see from her interview, that is not always the case.*

I WAS BORN AND RAISED HERE in Del Norte County and left right after high school to go to college. I came back about ten years later, and I've been here ever since.

My dad was a logger, and my mom was a stay-at-home mom when I was young, and then when I was older, she worked at the post office. My dad didn't want me to go to college. He said girls were supposed to stay home and raise families. He was very traditional. The reason my mom didn't work was because he didn't want her to. But from when I was small, I knew that being a stay-at-home-mom was not going to be my choice. I was a rebellious kid and always had my own ideas.

First grade through ninth grade, I went to the Seventh-Day Adventist School. I remember they had a big gym with a carpet. We would skate around in there, pulling each other on ropes, playing horses. It was a very small school. We were all very close. I do remember sometimes a new kid would come, and it was hard for them because the rest of us had been together for so long.

I went to Del Norte High next. I liked it fine. I liked my teachers. I think teachers can make a big difference in kids' lives. I remember several teachers who were really good to me, encouraging, and kind. Mr. Van Meter was one. My AP English teacher, Doris Whalen, was another. She influenced half the people in the school.

I was always a really good student, but I remember when I was a senior, I started partying a little bit—I got drunk the night before my SATs. I wrote about it in my journal in one class. I really heard it from that teacher!

So I went to UC Davis first. I lived off campus in an apartment rather than in the dorm, and I was lonely. I ended up coming back and taking some classes at College of the Redwoods. I moved to Santa Barbara, and took classes there in nuclear medicine, and then worked in that field. I needed to do this to get the required experience to go to school to be a Physician Assistant. I went to P. A. school in Chico. Luckily for me, there was a branch of Western University in Chico at that time. It was a very circuitous route, but I got there.

How did I find myself back in Del Norte County? In 2001, I was married and living in Paradise, California, which I really liked. But I found out my husband was cheating on me, and I was devastated. That's what brought me home to Del Norte. I told him he could come with me, but he didn't.

Here, I worked as a PA for Dr. Hawthorne. He was a wonderful, wonderful man, very loved in this community. He died in a kayaking accident about a year after I joined his practice. So, I worked for Dr. Morrow, and then Dr. Tynes, and then eventually Dr. Sund and Dr. Caldwell. I've been with them for about thirteen years now.

The number one thing that keeps me here is my family. Most of my relatives live here. And I like the beauty of this place. I like outdoor things. I love the ocean where I can go to the beach and see hardly anybody there. I love to hike, and mountain bike, and ride horses. I can ride a horse from the redwoods right down to the beach.

What's hard about living here? Well, I've wanted a pair of black leather boots for two years now, and I still can't find them! I've ordered a few on Amazon which never worked out. So one drawback is that it's hard if you have something specific that you want or need.

Another hard thing for me is the size of the community. You can't go anywhere without seeing people you know, and that's kind of a double-edged sword. I really liked living in Paradise. I could go to Chico and not see anyone I knew. You can't do that here. You can't be anonymous. I see my patients everywhere.

In the medical profession, it's not really good to have your patients be your friends or your family. But here, were don't have that option. I mean, if you refuse to see people you know, you're not going to see anybody, really. You can't really help anybody if you insist on seeing strangers.

But overall, it's better to be somewhere where you know a lot of people. Those people will help you if you need it. I found that out the hard way. I don't know if you knew this, but my sister Hollie was the post office supervisor who was caught stealing opiates out of the mail. This was in the newspaper about a year ago. That's when I found out how good it was to be able to ask friends for help. And people helped me. That was a wonderful thing.

But there is one negative thing about living here I also learned during that time. If you don't know *them*, if you're not in with *them*—certain people in the criminal justice system—things can be harder for you. If you're not part of these little cliques, then you're going to get treated differently. I'd heard that was true about living here, but this was the first and only time it personally affected me.

Judges are supposed to rule similarly in the same jurisdiction. There shouldn't be a big difference between sentences for similar crimes. Well, a woman who did something similar to what Hollie did was put on probation by one judge here. My sister Hollie was sentenced to six years in prison. Judge McElfresh gave her the maximum sentence, even though the substance abuse counselor said she was an ideal candidate for rehabilitation.

I'm not really sure what happened—why the sentence was so different. But I do know the judge did everything he could to prevent Hollie from being evaluated by the people who could have assisted in her defense; He repeatedly denied requests for Hollie to be evaluated by a forensic psychologist and delayed the evaluation by the substance abuse expert to the point that the expert had just hours rather than weeks to write her report.

How hard is it to get help for drug addiction here in Del Norte County? Well, my sister was incredibly stubborn. We saw the problem in advance. We begged her to get treatment. So in her case, if she had wanted help, we would have bent over backwards to get her help, even if we had to fly her somewhere. And we did help, when she finally did ask, though it was a bit late. The horrible thing about drugs is that they make people someone they're not. My sister's addiction came from an injury. She needed more and more and more in order to cope with the pain.

But she wasn't the first family member to battle addiction. My cousin died from a methamphetamine addiction. He'd been a wonderful person. He did meth so long, he was hearing these voices in his head telling him to kill himself. We knew about it when it was happening. We all pooled our money and sent him down to some great rehab in Southern California. He got clean—and then he went right back to his old friends here. And eventually, he listened to those voices and killed himself. So he was another example of someone who had help, but just didn't follow through.

I do hear success stories. The son of the lady who does my nails got clean, and he's doing wonderfully. But he committed to a year. And he didn't return to his old friends.

What are some ways we could do better at treating addiction? One thing I hear from my patients who are in NA or AA is that here, people get ordered to go to NA or AA. They get assigned by the court to attend, and it changes the whole atmosphere. When you're forced to do something versus when you want to do something—well, it's a world of difference.

But there is a wonderful thing going on in our community

called "Oxford Houses." They're a kind of group home run entirely by recovering addicts. Those actually work. Oxford Houses are made up of people who want to be clean and want to live in a supportive environment. They want their life to be different, and they get support from each other, like a family.

I actually own one of the houses. I rent to a group of Oxford men, and that's how I know about them. They have two houses for men and one for women. They've been super-successful at staying clean. There's a waiting list for people who want to get in because we don't have enough houses.

And for people who have used drugs as a way of life…I don't know what works.

As a health care provider, I would guess that Del Norte has a higher level of drug use than other counties, but I don't know why. Weather? The culture here? You should probably interview a health care provider from the public health clinic. The type of patients we see aren't usually struggling with addiction.

I did have one patient who became a meth addict. She ended up living in the woods. Her teeth were all rotted out. She had a baby while on meth. I suspect she became an addict through work. I suspect her colleagues got her into it. It was part of the work culture.

What are some ways my values differ from the values of those around me? A lot of the people I'm around here are hunters and like killing animals. I don't like that. And I'm more pro-environment, too. A lot of people around here are more like, "Chop down every tree and make money off it!" I don't fit in with a lot of the people here in that respect.

But it's okay. They're people I love and get along with. I just don't bring up how I feel about things like that because I'm not going to change any minds. I've learned to keep my mouth shut. I guess it might be fun to live somewhere I would have people who felt the same way as I do about some things. There's a city somewhere. [Interviewer: "Around Eugene, Oregon?" Interviewee laughs.]

I still do feel part of this community. One thing that helps is that

I volunteer for things, like doing football physicals. I do things like the Wild Rivers Run. If there are people who feel like outsiders, they might consider participating in some community activities. For people who don't have a lot of hobbies or interests, that might be harder, but I think if they just try, they might find themselves connecting in ways they never imagined.

As far as cultural differences, I do notice—usually in Walmart— that there are some people here who don't really seem to care about their kids. It seem like there are folks—I don't know how to say it—who don't want to work and don't want to better themselves and just want to live off entitlements. It seems like there is a large group of people like that. It's not something that falls along racial or ethnic lines. It's actually a white person thing here.

The value in my family is hard work, but I see more people now than ever who don't want to put out effort and expect a lot of things given to them. If they're great parents, I can let it pass. But if they're crappy parents, it's really upsetting. Because the children of these people are just doomed from day one, and it just breaks my heart. I wish there was something we could do for them—to make it even from the start.

As far as my kids, I think that they'll be just fine growing up in Del Norte. If I can find ways for them to get involved in school and activities, they'll be fine. I'm not expecting them to be senators. But if they wanted to, I would certainly try to help them. I do sometimes have concerns. I do sometimes think about moving, but...I don't think I will.

*—March 26, 2018*

# Taysha Robinson

"People think they know you, and their assumptions are
not necessarily founded in reality. But in a small community,
rumors get passed on. Assumptions become a kind
of reality we impose on each other."

*Like a growing number of Del Norters, Taysha Robinson is raising her family
on a homestead with animals and a big garden. She and her husband try to live
sustainably. But she faces many challenges, not the least of which is the association people make when they hear her maiden name.*

BOTH MY PARENTS WERE BORN AND RAISED HERE. My mom
is a Yurok Native. She had me when she just turned 18. My dad was
about 21 when I was born. He was a logger, and a fisherman, and
a chainsaw artist. He passed away. My mom is still here. She works
for the school system.

Growing up here, I hated it. I just wanted to get out as soon as I
could. And I did. When I was in eighth grade, I applied to Gonzaga
Preparatory School in Spokane, Washington, and I went there for
high school.

A lot of my discomfort about living here was just being a teenager—thinking there wasn't anything for me in this small town. I
wanted to be in a big city where I imagined there would be more—
I don't know what—excitement?

Looking back now, I think it was "the grass is always greener"
syndrome. I felt like I was way cooler than this town—way more
"diverse." I didn't fit in with the hicks, the cheerleaders, the jocks,

or the popular kids. I was listening to punk rock music, and I was weird. I was poor, too, and while I did have a few friends, our only connecting factor was that we felt disenfranchised. We didn't really have common interests—other than getting out of town.

I also had the unfortunate situation of a recognizable last name—"Mode"—not the name I have today. Some of my relatives have been in trouble with the law. One of them was on *America's Most Wanted* when I was growing up. They had a big man hunt for him.

People treat you differently when they know things about your family. Between that and growing up in poverty—it was isolating.

I really enjoyed escaping small-town life and going to Gonzaga Prep. I felt like the kids there were way less cliquish. A lot of them were privileged and had money, but they didn't seem as self-conscious as kids here. They didn't bother making other people feel bad about themselves. Everyone was already so confident and self-assured. They didn't have to establish a weird pecking order.

I also enjoyed the education there—especially the class discussions. Teachers and students were open to talking about real issues like abortion and gay marriage—all these things that we don't talk about in schools here because teachers are not focused on critical thinking. Well, with a private education, you can talk about subjects off the curriculum. The teachers there really cared about opening up your mind. I got a lot out of that experience.

Even though I was at a prep school, I had to work all through high school. My mom couldn't afford things for me or any of my siblings. I was used to hard work, so after I graduated, I stayed in Spokane and worked both a full-time and a part-time job. I was a telemarketer for this shady, low budget company, and I was a piercer and tattoo artist's apprentice. My boss at the tattoo shop got caught up in some kind of sex crime. He was involved with an escort service. I think he was trying to be a pimp or something. I don't really know. But he got himself in some trouble, and his shop was getting shut down.

That was the summer my dad died. So I took some time off to

come home to Del Norte County to be with my family. I was here about two months. Work kept calling me, but I didn't have much interest anymore.

I decided "I'm done working. I don't want to do this anymore." So I hit the road. I did a lot of traveling with a band of other young kids. I hopped a couple trains. I hitchhiked. I went all over the northwest for a couple years. I drank a lot—there was a lot of drinking.

Eventually, I ended up in Portland. I'd only planned on being there a couple months. I rented a room in a house called the Orphanage where they played grunge music and had house shows. That's where I met Steven, who would become my husband. We had a daughter together while we lived there.

Then, back in Crescent City, my brother passed away unexpectedly in his sleep. It was just a few months after my daughter was born. Steven thought we ought to come back here so that I could be near my family. He knew what I didn't know: it was going to be hard to deal with his death, and he was worried I was getting postpartum depression. So we came back here and moved into my brother's room, in a house on Wendell Street.

It wasn't the best housing situation, so eventually we started thinking about my father's property near Fort Dick. We knew it wasn't in good shape. The neighbors called it "the tweaker property." The grass wasn't mowed, there was trash everywhere, and it was covered in abandoned trailers.

My grandmother was the custodian of the property. She didn't live on it—she lived down the street—and she was getting frequent tickets for blight. I was the only sibling that had much interest in the place, so Steven and I decided to clean it up.

It took us *years*. We had to remove trash and old trailers, clear the land—but we've made it really nice and we live out here now. We raise chickens and dairy goats and have a garden and an orchard. We don't have a lot of money, but we do a lot of salvaging and upcycling.

The big motivator for me to stay in the area? Having kids made me feel differently about safety. When you live in a small town, you take for granted the feeling you get when you see familiar faces. One time, in Portland, shortly after my first daughter was born, someone knocked on the door of my apartment, and I wasn't expecting it. I had a panic attack. I ran to the back room and hid.

Taking risks as a teen—hitchhiking, jumping trains, living rough is one thing. But when you have to worry about your child, things look different.

I reflect on that now, and I think there's really a benefit to knowing the people in your community. You go to Safeway and see people you know. You bump into your old grade school teacher who admires your baby. I don't feel that weird anxiety here I've felt other places. And now that I have more kids, living here seems like the right thing for us.

Working on this property and chronicling the story on Facebook of how we transformed it—we got so much support from people. For example, we needed to weld the tongue onto the front of our mobile home to move it out of here, and we posted something about it. An old ex-in-law relative from way back saw the post and pitched in to help. Getting that kind of support, all these people coming together who wanted to see us succeed out here, it made me feel really good about this place—this community.

I don't want to tell on my family, but some of my relatives had drug problems when I was growing up. We always had money issues. We rarely had electricity. Power bills were chronically unpaid. In fact, when Steven and I tried to get the power hooked up here when we first moved in, we found the power company had ripped out the power box—taken it right down to the ground, lines and all. Same thing with the water line. They would not let me put anything back in until I produced that relative's death certificate and a notarized statement stating that he was not and would not be living here.

That was my upbringing. A lot of poverty, and a lot of missed school. I often didn't get to school on time—or even at all. I was consistently late and always felt ashamed of it.

But I did have some advantages. My grandma Vlayn McCovey had a very big influence on me. She was an old school hippie and did a lot of youth organizing. She was a leader in the Yurok Tribe and helped draft their Constitution. Growing up, I didn't feel very connected to the tribe, though, because I have such light skin and blue eyes. I didn't look like everyone else. Both my brothers had the dark eyes and skin, but not me. Also, I'm freakishly tall at five feet eleven inches, which is unusual in a Yurok person. That made me a target for a lot of bullying and subsequent feelings of estrangement.

But I was putting it out there, too. I felt like I didn't belong, so I thought it was natural that other people wouldn't accept me.

But my grandma, a four-foot-eleven firecracker, wouldn't let me be the shy and quiet girl. She made me get out there and stand up for what's right. She took me to protests, like one to insist Caltrans fix the road in Weitchpec, and another to protest the fish kill. She helped me participate in cultural events, too. I did brush dances and even a white deer skin dance. She built me up. I don't know who I'd be if I had not spent those years with her.

Growing up, it took me a while to learn to stick up for myself. I had really low self-esteem and I remember getting picked on a lot. I was frequently called an ogre—the Shrek movie had come out—and I was tall, even when I was young. I never told the teachers or my mom about the bullying. I was worried telling them would make it worse. I didn't want to be called a tattle-tale, and I knew my mom would overreact, so I just suffered quietly. In fact, I told my mom lies about all the friends I had.

I remember the moment it changed. There was this girl named Cindy. This teeny-tiny-little cheerleader girl who was super rude to me all the time. She shoulder-checked me into this locker. And I remembered this thing my grandmother had said to me, and I thought, why am I letting this tiny person push me around?" So I turned and shoved her back. And I saw the terror in her face, like "Oh no!" I realized I had to stand up for myself—that I could stand up for myself.

I think economics played a big part in being bullied, but I knew poor kids who didn't have the same problem, and I knew kids who weren't poor who got bullied. I think being insecure, feeling powerless, that's what gets you bullied.

One of the things that disempowers people here is small town prejudice. My maiden name marked me early on, as I mentioned before. But it *still* does. For example, when I gave birth to my second daughter here in Crescent City, the nurses and hospital staff were rude to me. They treated me like a drug addict and tested my child's cord blood for drugs. I thought about why they might do that—and I realized one of my relatives recently had a drug addicted baby born there: Then it made sense. Of course the nurses thought I was just another one of *those* people. Changing my last name helped me escape that prejudice, but not everyone is so lucky.

I think about my younger brother. He's done some bad things, but he's going to get the book thrown at him. The systems sees him as coming from a notorious family of criminals. But he's so young, and most of what he did was because he's a drug addict, and there's no support for recovery here in this community.

My grandmother—the one who made such a positive impact on my life—struggled with addiction in her younger days. She was able to overcome it and live clean for almost twenty years, but it left lasting damage. She died of complications from Hepatitis C.

This isn't just a family problem. It's a community problem. People who can't get better on their own just get worse and continue to make bad decisions. They're stuck in what they know, and people are stuck in the pattern of seeing them in a negative light, which doesn't help. We can't really expect people to act in any way other than what they've been shown and what's expected of them. My generation included. The poverty, isolation, low self-esteem, missed school—life could have been different for me if people in my life had gotten help sooner.

Small towns encourage small-mindedness. Here's an example: a friend of mine witnessed a terrible crime. She saw her boyfriend shoot and kill another young woman. My friend was drunk—very drunk—and they threw out her testimony in court. But the community perceives it as her sticking up for her boyfriend—that she didn't do her part to convict him. She's been bullied as an adult for that perception.

People think they know you, but their assumptions are not necessarily founded in reality. But in a small community, rumors get passed on. Assumptions become a kind of reality we impose on each other. It's one of the most challenging things about living in a small town.

But despite these challenges, Steven and I have chosen to live here. This is our base. Our roots are here. And we like being isolated.

We're not big shoppers. We're not into name brand stuff. We've got a good thing going, raising animals and kids and dreaming about the future. I'd like to go back to school and become a teacher. We'd like to travel, maybe live in Germany for a while. Steven has family there. But this is our home. Our roots go deep down. This is where we're meant to be.

*—November 11, 2017*

*Postscript*
*This story, used by permission, is from the author's social media page, and was posted a few weeks after our interview:*

Last night's shenanigans left me carless, spending the night in jail, with a little road rash on my face. What did I do, you ask? I gave my little brother a ride to town to meet up with his lady friend in my fully registered, insured, and legal vehicle. We got pulled over for a tail light, though I call bullshit on that one. I check those lights pretty often to avoid this kind of shit. I think the police dude was bored.

I thought I had left my wallet at home, considering that it wasn't in the normal spots when I left the house. So I tell the officer my name, birthdate, license number, social, all that jazz to hopefully get myself identified. He's incredibly suspicious, condescending, and downright rude about it. For a minute, he even forgets that married vs. maiden names are a thing. Seriously, he snapped at me when I told him my name was Taysha Robinson, not Mode, like he was trying to enter into his little record thing.

"Oh, so you're a Mode?"

"Uh, no sir. Robinson. I was a Mode, but now I'm a Robinson.

He still looks confused, "So, Mode-Robinson? What are you *legally*?"

"Robinson, sir. Taysha Robinson." I've said it about seven effing times now.

He then asks me to write my brother's name down. I accidentally started to write down my other brother's name, and since there was an inconsistency between Mykah's and I's scripted name, we were asked to step out of the vehicle and put our arms behind our backs.

This is where it all went bad for me, I suppose. Sidenote: please tell me I'm not the only one out there who *consistently* calls their siblings, children, etc. by the wrong name? Good God, especially if they look alike? And my baby brothers all look alike, ok?

So I had a brain fart under stress, I'm all sleep-deprived from a teething baby, and it's midnight on a school night. The MomLife doesn't lend itself to crystal clear memory or focus. Hell, I even effed up telling him how old I was. "Twenty eight? Twenty-nine?"

This cop calls all his cop buddies for back up. This is the real deal guys, what they train so hard for! People who miss court dates and call their siblings the wrong name! Get out of the car, hands up! This shit's about to get real!

Since my brother felt guilty about the situation (he had a warrant for missing a sentencing a few months back which is what prompted this whole ordeal), he starts jogging toward me while I'm getting cuffed, yelling "HEY! Leave her out of this, she didn't do anything! Just leave her the fuck alone! This is all my fault."

Well, the cops took that as resisting and put his ass on the ground. I'm absolutely fucking horrified at this point. I begged them to call my husband and let him know so he wouldn't be worried, so he could wake the kids up for school in a few short hours and make them breakfast.

Nah, these guys were *much* too busy patting each other on the back to extend much simple human decency. Well, there was one officer who let me lean up against the squad car for heat, but I was told I had to keep my fingers visible so there was no warming those lil' icicles up.

So there I leaned, hands cuffed behind my back, no bra on. I was just running him into town real quick to drop him off! I'm trying to ask these "peace officers" what I was being charged with, how long I was going to be out in the bitter cold, what my brother was in trouble for, and when I could call my husband to let him know I'm alright and that he needs to wake up earlier to get his *and* my chores done before school in the morning. No way, bruh. This is cop bro time. You get no answers. Instead, you get asked if you're high on meth with a flashlight shining directly in your eyeball every time they speak to you.

Oh, and they say it so surely and confidently. It's not a question. It's a direct accusation. I actually started wondering if somehow, I *was* high on meth, and that's why none of this entire routine traffic stop made any effing sense! After all, I have a clean record, I'm licensed, insured, and my car is registered through next year. Do any of *you* do background checks on family members before you give them rides to insure they don't have some silly warrant that could have you pulled out of your car and sent to jail?

At this point, I'm sobbing softly to myself at the thought of the career I've worked so hard for going right down the drain in front of me. I have a degree in Early Childhood Education, and I am pursuing an additional teaching credential. These are not exactly fields in which you can have a prior arrest record. As I sit there, watching these men rip apart my car, tossing car seats to the side, probably ripping the interior up (I still haven't picked my car up because I don't have the $430 to get it out of hock just yet, so we'll see. I'm pretty sure I heard ripping, though).

An officer comes back with a smirk on his face, shines his flashlight in my eyeball and says "Ah! You DID have your wallet! Why are you lying to me? What else am I going to find in that car? METH?" He shines flashlight in my eyeball even closer for dramatic effect.

At this point, it has become evident that I have moved from "being detained in handcuffs for questioning" to "Bitch, you goin' to JAAAAAAIL tonight."

The ride was a blur. Not sure if it was all that meth-light-show action my poor pupils took, or the sinking feeling of my dreams and hard work dying in between two dude bros who looked like they graduated high school last month.

We get to the cold, dismal, cement compound known as the local jail, and I'm told to take half my clothes off and go sit in this completely cement and metal room, where I can freeze my ass off further while staring at my shoes and jacket just on the other side of the glass. The word "torture" came to mind. Just then, I see my brother coming through and he blurts out "I'm sorry, Sissy!" The look in his eye. It was literally the saddest moment of my night.

From there, I was handed off to some cute lil' lady cops who did their best to answer my questions and get me out of there as quickly as possible. It still took over four hours, at the end of which, I realized, I don't have my fucking car, or money, or people's phone numbers because I got a new phone. That's when I started texting some of my night owl friends, begging them to come rescue me. I'm pretty sure I would not have made it from Crescent City to my house in Fort Dick with how chilly that air was coming off the ocean if I'd had to walk home.

Oh, and speaking of ocean, it was eerie coming out of that jail, seeing the streets covered in fog with no cars anywhere. Turns out there was a tsunami warning in effect, so I was literally the only one in the area. I found this out because the one car that did pass me pulled over, and the lady driving it started yelling at me to get somewhere safe, that she can't give me a ride because she had to be somewhere, but that there's a tsunami coming and I needed to get off the streets. I thought to myself "At this point, let it take me."

[The tsunami warning was lifeted shortly after it was issued and the interviewee did get her car back, though she wrote the following the next day in a tongue-and cheek post.]

"Got our car out of impound and, big shocker, tail light is working *just fine*. It only took two trips to CHP, two trips to the towing company, a trip to DMV, a trip to our lawyer's office, and an emotional meltdown, but we got it and now get to spend the next week and a half on $12 bucks. So if anyone needs me, I will be down on the corner with my cardboard sign, s'panging up money for gas and goat feed. Robinson, over and out."

# Johnny Jones

"They say when you have an addiction, you experience
either jails, institutions or death. I experienced all those things.
I don't feel like I have another do-over."

*A father, husband, and student at College of the Redwoods, Johnny Jones has
experienced more of life's hardships than most people can imagine. But he's
pulling his life together and holding on tight, as his interview reveals.*

I WAS BORN AT SEASIDE HOSPITAL on July 18, 1974 and
raised in Crescent City. A lot of my early childhood I kind of block
out. I don't remember much. It's starting to come back to me more
and more as an adult.

It was pretty troubled. My parents were addicts—alcohol, marijuana, and meth—although I didn't figure that out for a while. I remember the rain. That's what I remember most. It started raining,
and it never stopped for months. I also remember that we lived
lots of different places. We moved from house to house. I stayed
away from home as much as I could. It wasn't that I ran away, I just
remember they had to come find me a lot.

When I was twelve years old, my three brothers and I went to
live with my grandparents. My parents checked themselves into
a substance abuse rehabilitation center. We boys were supposed
to stay with my grandparents for just 90 days, but we ended up
staying there permanently. My parents sometimes stayed with us
there, but my grandparents had custody of us.

My grandmother was Delma Nix Jones, and my grandfather

was Clifford Jones. My grandfather had been an old growth logger—nothing but the biggest trees. But he lost his right arm in 1979 in a logging accident while he was training a new guy. He was very well known around town. He couldn't go anywhere without being stopped by people all over the community. They would talk and share stories. But other than that, I don't remember him talking very much. I don't know if the communication was verbal, because I don't remember him talking to me—but I remember how dedicated he was to raising us right. He always made sure we were up, he always made sure we made it to school. He got us into sports and made sure we got to practices.

He had us playing sports year round. I played baseball, basketball, soccer, football, and wrestling. I never got into track, but all the other sports, that's what we did. He was like Mr. Miyagi from the *Karate Kid*. He's had us doing work all the time. He would take us out to Pecker's Nob, and take that trail all the way down to the beach. We'd walk the beach until we got to the rocks, and we'd harvest mussels there. I never knew until I graduated high school that you could drive up to these places to collect mussels! He had us doing all this strenuous work, but it basically trained us to work hard, and it made us all superstars at sports. For two of my brothers, it was basketball. My youngest brother and I were really good at football.

My grandfather raised eight of his own kids, and then the four of us grandkids.

My grandma was a strong woman. It was alarming the stuff that came out of her mouth sometimes. She had no filter. She could be very vulgar at times. I remember being embarrassed by the way she talked on occasion. But it was funny—so funny—the way she put things. I couldn't be mad at her. I couldn't ask her to stop. She wouldn't. She was also really hard working and worked so long in the lily fields that she was able to collect retirement.

When I was growing up, that's where I got my first job. It was hard labor. I worked with a lot of Mexicans, and a lot of Indians, too. It was hard for the two groups to communicate, and sometimes that caused a lot of friction. I ended up getting into some fights with them, too. It was the Mexicans against the Indians, both Yurok and Tolowa. I'm both. My dad is Yurok, and my mom is Tolowa.

Was there friction between the two tribes? When I was younger, there was really no separation. Even though people had their own tribal identity, everyone was on the Yurok rolls. What changed that was the Jessie Short case being settled. It was a 1963 case over the distribution of timber sale money, and it took until the mid-1990s to settle it (and actually, longer). The Yurok Tribe won about $90 million which they had to decide how to distribute. Well, a bunch of Tolowa folks got kicked off the roles at that time. So things changed a little between us then, but mostly in the fields in Smith River, where my ancestors have been living and working for thousands of years, it was the Indians against the Mexicans, who were newcomers there, who sometimes made remarks about "taking over" the land. The irony is that it's owned by the Westbrooks, and the Crockets, and the Stanhursts—white folks.

So we fought over a lot of that land out there. At that time, there were a lot of drugs coming in from Mexico, including meth, and field workers were taking them, sometimes just to get through the day. I had a real problem with that—my younger cousins were getting strung out on that. They would take meth to work, to get boosts of energy. But if they took it for long, they would need more and more. And soon, you'd see them only until pay day, and then you wouldn't see them again for a while. They'd do whatever they did and then come back later.

The owners had a hard time finding laborers, so they kind of allowed this, letting people come and go as they pleased. I didn't like that. I also didn't like picking up the slack for other people. It created some resentment. So did the drug sales going on at the reservation. Also, some of the older Mexican guys—in their twenties and thirties—were hitting on underage girls on the reservation—my younger cousins.

So I got into some altercations, and at sixteen, I ended up getting felony charges for being in a pretty big fight out there. It was over the weekend. A bunch of us went out there. A white guy who was also having some problems with Mexicans stopped by our house and rounded up me and my brothers, and we went out there and started a fight. There was a lot of testosterone in the air.

I got put on probation. My probation officer, Allan Morris, was my football coach and my wrestling coach, and I was a pretty good player—an All-County player—so I never had any problems with getting violations for my probation, even though I never officially checked in with him other than showing up to practice.

I was one of the popular kids. I liked to drink. I liked to throw huge parties out on the river bar—a different place each time. I would get four or five kegs and a garbage can full of whiskey, and I'd sell drinks. I made a lot of money, and I'd use the money to finance the next party.

I think my probation officer knew what I was doing. That's why, eventually, he would send me to treatment. But he didn't know all that I was doing.

I got into selling meth, even though I wasn't using it at the time. I was basically selling drugs to all my friends' parents. The kids weren't really using it, although a few were experimenting. It was adults. I'm not sure why they started. When I came into the picture, they were already addicted.

I'd see the signs in the parents, and I'd approach them. They became my customers. It did affect my relationships with my so-called friends. I wasn't doing them any favors. I knew the effect it had on families. I'd lived it. But hustling—that was the lifestyle I knew.

We never had a lot of money growing up, and my grandfather had taught me to work hard, so selling alcohol and drugs was sort of an extension of that. It was illegal, but it felt right because it was *work*.

Growing up, I'd always had to work some job or some hustle. As kids, we used to peel chinna bark, dry it, and sell it in Brookings. When I was thirteen, I started commercial fishing, all season. I got addicted to money. I had to buy my own things, but I always had the nicest pair of shoes and new clothes for school.

I think my probation officer wanted to help me with this addiction—not just to drugs, but to money. He wanted to find out what I had missed—what I needed to learn to change my behavior—and that's why I was sentenced to seven years. But there might have been a little bit of jealousy there, too. My probation officer had twin boys my age. We were friends. And by the time I turned eighteen, I had thousands of dollars saved—and a settlement from the tribe for over $40,000. I was one rich eighteen year old.

I went a little bit crazy. This is when I moved to Hoopa. I wanted to explore. I moved to Hoopa. With cash, I bought a '55 Chevy, fully restored. Three or four of my uncles had owned that specific make and model. It felt like a family thing.

I drove down to Southern California and all the way up to Canada. When I was growing up, I never got to travel. I never went to Disneyland. So I took myself to Disneyland. Six Flags. I also went to Indian reservations. I was curious about how other Indians lived, and I wanted to hang out. I knew the language—I call it "Res Ebonics"—and most of the time I was welcomed and had a place to stay. Sometimes I got into fights. That's kind of how it can be at first. You get put to a test. You have to show that you're strong.

Like me, a lot of them were looking for opportunities—opportunities about what I had, what they could take, what they could be a part of. I know that's a lot of why I put people to the test. I used to do that a lot—find out what they had. Most of the time, it was about what we could do together, although sometimes they could be malicious. I met a lot of cool people. I met a lot of real people.

Coming from Humboldt County, I always had a good weed connection. So I would buy pounds and pounds of weed before I left and sell it at concerts and fairs. All these places were new to me. It was an adventure.

Up north, I stayed with a friend of mine in Puyallup, Washington. We sold fireworks for a time and made pretty good money. It was just one hustle to another—some legal and some not.

But when I graduated, turned 18, and took off to Hoopa, I got all these probation violations. I had to go in to court to fight them. The judge wanted to know why, after almost four years on probation, I had never checked in or signed any paperwork the whole time. When I tried to explain to him that my probation officer had never asked me to check in before because he'd been my coach, he didn't like that excuse. Yes, I should have done the probation like everybody else. I knew I was getting special treatment. But I didn't realize it would stop so soon, when I was no longer of any value to my coach.

So, they sent me to a juvenile rehabilitation center and told me that if I could complete the rehab, I would be off probation. But I got kicked out and sent to the California Juvenile Authority (for offenders under twenty-five) where I was told I'd need to serve seven years.

So, I left Crescent City thinking I would be gone for seven years.

At first, since I was a drug addict, I went to the part of the California Youth Authority for addicts. Then, when I was a little older, I moved to a different facility. I was shuffled around frequently. I did 2 ½ years, and was released back to Crescent City.

It was very hard to stay out of trouble. When the cops saw me, they always pulled me over. Always. They had a right to, because, as a parolee, I had a search and seizure clause. But it didn't matter if I was driving or just riding in a car, I was getting pulled over, and I was getting questioned.

I got a job as a roofer at McMurry and Sons. We had an all-Indian crew. It was just me and some guys from school that I played sports with. But even with having a job and going to work, I still got harassed by the police. And I kind of pushed back.

Well, I really pushed back. I'd always had a problem with authority. Growing up, I remember police officers always coming to houses we lived in. Del Norte County sheriffs were rough on my dad and his brothers and Indians in general. I never had a good experience with cops. I witnessed a lot of racism from them, too. I was raised to resent them and everything they were about.

But I soon had another reason to be angry at police officers. In 1996, my dad—technically my uncle and stepdad, but the only father I ever knew—was beaten to death by Shasta County police.

They were watching him because they thought he was a drug dealer. He'd just gotten a lump sum from the Jessie Short case, and he was driving a new car and partying and drinking. I don't know if he was dealing. He might have been. He was well within those circles.

But when you ask about injustice—what's fair or isn't fair around here—I can't help but think of what happened. They put him in handcuffs, and then they roughed him up. Actually, they beat him so bad, he had to go to the hospital.

In the hospital, they had him handcuffed to the bed. That's where they said he went for one of their weapons. An officer hit him with a billy club to the throat and crushed his windpipe. He died right there in the hospital.

At first, I was so angry, I was going to go to war with them. I loaded up my truck with every gun that I had and started driving over the hill. I was going to shoot it out with them until they shot me. But the clutch in my truck went out, and I had to come back. That was the only thing that stopped me.

You know, when I think about it now, it's possible that cop didn't mean to kill him. I know that a lot of police are racist. I've seen it. I've felt it. But maybe my dad did reach for one of their weapons. I don't know. The only thing I do know is that my clutch going out is the only reason I'm still here now.

A friend of mine called me and called a friend of mine in Washington. I stayed up there for about six months. I walked away from my job. I walked away from my probation officer. I wasn't supposed to leave the state. But at the time, it was probably one of the best decisions I made. I don't know how I could have stayed after that. It kept me from doing something really stupid.

Another time, I flew out to Texas and visited a cousin of mine out there. I drove all over Texas and the southwest and had another adventure. I went to Indian reservations there, too, and attended this big powwow in Albuquerque, New Mexico, the Gathering of Nations. I almost ran out of money out there, but I asked my cousin to send me $200, and I took it to a casino and won enough to get me on the road again.

Up in Washington, I'd been in a knife fight. I cut someone from his ear down to his collar bone, and I got cut across the throat. They had me strapped down in an ambulance on the way to the hospital. I guess the police were going to meet us there. But when we were going down the freeway, I unhooked myself and made the ambulance driver pull over. I jumped out and I ran. They never did catch up to me.

When I finally made it home to Crescent City, I was here only a couple of days until I got arrested and sent back to the California Youth Authority. But by then, I was tired of running. I was looking for a reason to stop.

What changed it all for me? When I was twenty-six, I met this girl. It was kind of a fling. She got pregnant and had my son. I wanted to be a father so badly—I always did, even when I was younger. My dad had been killed, and my grandfather ended up having a stroke and passing away that same year. I just wanted connections to people so bad, and this was my chance. We had our son, and then two years after that, a daughter. That was 2002. We eventually split up, but we stayed friends.

I gave up the fighting and the violence then. That was my first step. The only thing I couldn't stop so easily was the drugs and the drinking. What drugs? At first it was marijuana, then coke, meth, and ultimately, heroin, which I was introduced to in prison.

As an adult, I got charged in Del Norte County a lot. I had a drug problem. I needed a couple hundred dollars a day just to stay normal. I never broke into anyone's house or anything, but I was definitely bending the law. I was involved in petty crime.

On the other hand, I got charged a lot for things I didn't do. I was a frequent target of harassment by the police. I ended up in court a lot. I beat thirty-four separate charges against me. It was a real hassle.

Something dramatic happened to me that finally got me off
drugs. I died. Twice. The first time, I was in the California Rehabilitation Center, the CRC. I was there as a "civil addict." It's basically
a lockdown for drug users. Ironically, the place is full of drugs—by
the bucketful. And the drugs are *better*. You can buy them with
Reload-It cards from the commissary. I overdosed on heroin there.
And I died.

They brought me back to life. I managed to stay clean after that
for a long time, and I stayed in there nine months. But when I got
out and came home, so many people in my family who had been
using meth were now on heroin, and it was hard to stay away from
it. It was in the house.

I overdosed a second time when I was commercial fishing down
in Klamath. This was about four years ago. I was using heroin to
treat the pain of an injury and also just to be able to function. I
died then, too.

They hauled me in to Crescent City by ambulance. They had
to breathe for me all the way. That was it. I couldn't do drugs anymore. I never did them again.

They say when you have an addiction, you experience either
jails, institutions, or death. I experienced all those things. I don't
feel like I have another do-over.

I started thinking about how I grew up, how I didn't have a dad
or a stepdad. I wanted it to be different for my kids. I wanted to
be there for them. It was easy to give up everything at that point. I
don't know why. I go to the Community Health Center and I take
Suboxone. It takes away the cravings and the desire to do heroin. I
participate in the group therapy.

I just had to have hip surgery, and they prescribed me opiates.
What was going to happen really worried me. But the pain before
the surgery was so great that I had to go through with it. I'm working with the doctors, and they're monitoring me carefully to make
sure I don't get too much.

I really do have hope for my future and my role in the future
of this community. Even though racism is not over, it is certainly

headed in this direction. I do not believe this world, or this community needs to continue to grow in hate, bitterness, and resentment. We all have a very real part to play. We all have choices to make. It boils down to what hope and desire we have for our children's future. I would prefer very much for them to live in a community surrounded by the challenging work and feelings of connectedness that can make something great. I watched the movie *Peter Rabbit* today, and in it, Peter Rabbit says, "We do not inherit the earth, we borrow it from our children." With this in mind I believe I have a lot of work to do.

*—March, 21 2018*

# Richard Griffin

"Just yesterday, I dealt with a parent who is losing
custody of their kids. All they had to do was get sober
and pass classes. But they can't make that choice yet.
That's the saddest thing in this world."

*Richard Griffin is a Deputy and Patrol Supervisor for the Del Norte County
Sheriff's Office. As an expert in drug enforcement, he has a lot to say about the
challenges our community faces when it comes to controlled substances. But he
also has a lot to say about other, more personal challenges, like finding work/
life balance in a place where he feels like he is always on duty.*

I was born and raised in Medford, Oregon. I went
to Southern Oregon University. I played football for them and
lived in a dorm with a lot of other athletes. It was kind of like the
study hall dorm. My resident dorm advisor was Clinton Schaad,
and he kind of laid down the law for us, making sure we weren't
drinking, or smoking, or making too much noise in the evenings.
Clinton and I became lifelong friends.

At SOU, I got my Bachelor Degree in marketing, with a minor
in criminology. Through Clinton, I met his cousin, Seth Wilson,
and we ended up going to Alaska after we graduated, working and
playing, and just trying to find our way. I lived in Juneau and did
carpentry work—learned it, actually.

But I knew I wanted to try law enforcement. As a kid, I'd
watched the *Lethal Weapon* series, and I thought the job would be
constant action and stuff, so I really wanted to do it. Clinton called
me one day and said there was a job open. He thought he could get

me into it. He was working as the fiscal manager for the Sheriff's Office at the time. I said, "Okay, why not?"

I started working in the jail as a Correctional Technician for about $7 an hour, and I just worked my way up after that. I'm currently a Deputy Sheriff and Patrol Supervisor. My first interview was with Tony Luis. Just that interview with him ushered me into my first experience with Del Norte people and how real they are. He was the Jail Commander at the time, but he'd worked at the mill and was really well-known and respected by the other families in town.

I think everybody knows there's a few Del Norte families, like the Wakefields and the Schaads, they're kind of like the prominent, well-liked people. They do a lot for everybody. Once you get into the sports—that's huge around here—then you just get to know everybody. Mr. Luis was one of those people. He would go to the ends of the earth for you. He gave me my chance.

The way I look at it, Del Norte is God's Country. Thousands and thousands of people visit us every year. It's a little unfortunate for locals because we sometimes get numb to the idea that we live in such a beautiful place in the world. There's a reason people come here—the beauty is what Del Norte County is all about. The town is a little older—it could be remodeled a bit—but you go five minutes in either direction, and you're in the most beautiful place in the world.

I have a wife and kids, and one of the best things about living here is the family support we get. There's a strong bond with family. My wife's mother is a Hartwick. Them living here, it makes it so great. It's a small-town atmosphere. If you know a few people, you're going to know everybody. That can go both ways. It can be bad, because everybody's going to know what's going on with you. But then it can be good, because everybody knows what's going on with you, so they can help you when you need it.

Also, access to the outdoors is really special. Just the other day, we went down to South Beach and then drove up to Pebble Beach and had so much fun. I grew up camping, hunting, and fishing in

Oregon, and my kids get to experience similar things here. Everyone here can, as long as they're not letting themselves get tied to their electronic devices.

Drawbacks here? Things I wish were different? One of the biggest challenges we have is health care. My son just had to go to the Emergency Room. We were lucky that he and my wife were in Medford, Oregon at the time. The cost of care here is so high, and the quality isn't as good. Everyone has a story about health care here. My wife had complications with both her pregnancies and had to be flown out of the county each time. We didn't have the care we needed here—no NICU for premature babies. It's not that folks at Sutter Coast don't care, it's just that we are so isolated and don't have the necessary technology.

The economy isn't that good here, either. I kind of wish I lived here when the logging industry was booming and it was a bustling, growing town. But it seems like we're making some steps to improve here, and that's good.

What about drugs? Yes, I can say drug use is a serious problem here, and I do know a lot about it. For many years, my work was out of the Drug Interdiction Grant. My job was to go out and locate meth users and then work up the food chain to locate suppliers and go after them. That's all I did. My main focus was drugs.

Ask any officer here, that kind of work made the job fun for us. There was a lot to do, and we were busy every night. I worked with all the agencies, and I became a drug expert—testified hundreds of times in court—so I can say that drug abuse is one of the bigger challenges that people in the county face.

We have a lot of end users here, not a lot of suppliers. Most of the suppliers are in Mexico or the southwest. In major communities, you have people dealing with pounds, quarter pounds, not ounces. I have a friend who works down south. They're taking out twenty pounds in a bust. The most we ever took was two pounds. The suppliers drive it up here in cars.

Meth looks like shattered glass or ice, like in the series *Breaking Bad*. That series is actually pretty true to life in terms of what users do. They warm it up—get it into a liquid. Most of the time they pull it in a syringe through a ball of cotton in the hope of purifying it. But then they still save the cotton to put in their mouth later to chew on if they can't get another fix. In the meantime, they inject it, smoke it, or snort it.

It's actually rare to find people making their own meth here. I've only busted a few—one was a kid who didn't know what he was doing. When people report meth labs, it's usually just people smoking it.

Most of the labs we have in Del Norte are hash labs. We have a huge marijuana culture here. Mostly we have butane hash labs where people use butane to extract the THC trichomes—the molecules—off the plants to make a much stronger high. You fill a tube with marijuana and drain the butane through it. A mixture drips out into a pan. The butane mixed with the THC will eventually evaporate, but some people don't want to wait for that, so they heat it, and if they're not careful, it goes BOOM. So not only is the hash a problem, but making it poses a danger to people.

I've served several hundred search warrants to shut down drugs here, but most of that work has ended. The money we had to fight drug use is mostly gone now because of changes in the drug laws. We used to proactively go after marijuana users, but we don't do that anymore, except to go after growers on public land. We do go after them.

But the laws have changed for other drugs, too. For example, use of methamphetamine used to be a felony. Now, it's a misdemeanor, or sometimes an infraction. We don't get funding to go after users anymore. We're very strapped in terms of manpower in our department. We're not even supposed to arrest people if we find them with meth. We're supposed to cite and release. That's where we're at with that. This is a statewide policy. And as local law enforcement, we don't have the authority to enforce federal law.

What about heroin and opioids? We do see heroin here. It's crazy in Humboldt County, but less of a problem here. I think we'll see more opioid users soon, what with the increased use of marijuana. We're already seeing over prescribing of prescription drugs by doctors, including to kids. That's kind of a way to solve bigger problems in our society now, instead of getting people to put down their electronic devices and go outside or something.

I had an issue, myself, when I had an injury. I broke my leg in a bunch of places—shattered it. Well, I'd done my research, so when they asked me, in the hospital, what I wanted for the pain. I told them I didn't want anything. Opioids block your body's understanding of pain. It stops telling you that you have an injury. So your body's not going to repair itself at a fast pace. I didn't take any pain killers, and my body adapted. In three weeks, I was back to work, full duty.

Unfortunately, time after time, I have to tell addicts, "The best thing for you is to get out of this town, and go to a town with good services. Go to San Francisco or something."

It's not just that we don't have drug treatment facilities here. The other benefit to leaving town is they get away from their friends and family who are enabling them. People living with addicts need to provide tough love (and that comes from having personal experience of addicts in my family). But here, often, families don't set those boundaries. They're often doing drugs, too, or dealing. If an addict is looking, it's not hard to find someone to sell them.

Everybody knows each other. For someone in law enforcement, that's another drawback of living here. I run into people all the time who I just busted. And I'm very recognizable. There's no privacy. No separation.

How do I cope with that, having a family? Well, my kids are still young, but as a parent, when they start to socialize and make their own friends, I'm just going to take it on a case by case basis. I'm not going to prejudge people. Just because I've arrested you six or seven times in the past, that doesn't mean that is who you are today. I know people change. Years after, people will come up to me and thank me for busting them and saving their lives. They've turned their lives around, they've gotten a family, and they're totally people I'd trust my kids with now.

But it's hard to get there—to beat addiction. Just yesterday, I dealt with a parent who is losing custody of their kids. All they had to do was get sober and pass classes. But they can't make that choice yet. That's the saddest thing in this world. I think it's a rock bottom issue—they haven't hit it yet. They're not ready. I experienced that with my own family—hoping a loved one was ready to change. It's rough. You don't want that person to go there—to rock bottom—but they've got to do it if they're going to find the willpower to beat their addiction.

Another time, I was serving a drug warrant to a parent. Child Welfare Service was there because they had kids.

The parent said, "Don't take my paycheck."

My brain didn't process it. I said, "What are you talking about? I'm not taking your paycheck." I didn't get what they were saying.

They said, "Yes you are. You're here with CPS. You're taking my paycheck!"

It hit me like a ton of bricks. They meant that because their kids were being taken away, they wouldn't get the money they normally got to help provide for them.

I had trouble sleeping that night, just thinking that anyone would say that about their children—right in front of them, too. They didn't care about the kids. They cared about the money. Their addiction had made them that selfish.

You know, I would die for my kids. But I have learned something about being selfish, too. I had an incident last year where I almost died of stress. It acted on me kind of like an allergic reaction, and I ended up in the hospital. It had been building and building for years, with all the hard work I put in, and then several incidents that were really hard to get through.

The first thing I did when I got out of there was get a life insurance policy to make sure my kids were provided for. That is my main job—to care for my family. It's not about what I can achieve in life or how I can succeed.

I go home every day and hug my kids. I've learned to work less—and that's hard because I made a name for myself as a hard worker, the guy who was always there. You call me, I answer. That made work fun for me. I wouldn't take it back those years. But after I had a family, I realized I was sacrificing my time with them for my job. I had to sit back and focus on what needed to come first. I wanted a relationship with my son and my daughter and my wife, and so I'm forcing myself to find that balance. I'm also taking time for myself and getting exercise in the gym.

What feels unfair here? I looked at that question, and I don't know what my answer would be. Things seem fair to me. I came here with nothing. I started at the very bottom of the department and worked my way up. All I did was work. And now I'm at one of the top positions, I have a house and a couple of cars. I can't say anything was unfair.

But I guess I could say that there are those people who—if they know the right people—they get a leg up. There is favoritism here that I see. But I don't think that's unique to Del Norte County. I think it's the same anywhere. I just come from the mindset that if you work hard, if you stay in that grind, things will happen. And they completely have for me.

My experience in Del Norte County is that we're the real Northern California. We're unique, we're cut off, but we're hard-working, good people. We're good families. I was given nothing but support. It seemed like I was considered a local the first day. I still have more years living in Oregon than I do in Del Norte, but I really do consider this place my home.

*—March 28, 2018*

# William Follett

"I often wonder how history is going to judge how we
performed during this law-and-order phase, with the three-strikes
law locking people up for life, putting people in prison for
drug use, and keeping others in SHU indefinitely.
I'm not sure history's judgment will be kind."

*William Follett has lived in Del Norte County for most of his professional life.
Here he tells the story of how he and his wife came to live in Crescent City. He
also provides a candid look at the drug culture in our community and discusses
ways the judicial system—a system he knows well as a Superior Court judge—
has changed in response to shifting values about drug addiction.*

I WASN'T BORN HERE. I grew up in Lemoore, California in the
San Joaquin Valley. My family had been in Lemoore since shortly
after the Civil War. I moved to Fresno for college where I got a
degree in journalism, and then worked in the Virgin Islands for
nearly four years, first as a VISTA Volunteer. I helped set up high
school newspapers on the islands. It's also where I met my wife,
Maureen, who was a teacher in VISTA. When we got out of VIS-
TA, we stayed for a while. I worked as the public information officer for the island school system and then as the editor for a daily
newspaper.

I went to law school in Sacramento. At first, I wanted a law degree. I intended to write about legal and governmental affairs for a
major paper. In the Virgin Islands, when I had covered the courts
for the paper, I'd watch lawyers and think, "I can do better than
these guys." By the time I got through law school, I decided since

I'd worked this hard, I was going to practice as a lawyer.

I came to Del Norte right out of law school and worked for Shafer and Cochran. With three attorneys, we had the largest law firm in the county. But it almost didn't happen. My wife was born and raised in Pennsylvania, and she wanted to move back east after law school. I really didn't want to do that, so we made a deal. We would stay on the west coast if we found a place on the ocean.

In law school, I had a friend who always talked about how great it was on the north coast. I'd never been up here, so during Easter break of my second year of law school, Maureen and I drove up to see Eureka. The whole time we were there, we noticed an unpleasant smell in the air coming from the mills. I heard later that locals referred to it as "the smell of money." After a couple nights, we hated that smell so much, we decided to drive north to Crescent City.

When we first got to town, I had a lot of work to do and holed up in the motel room while Maureen went out exploring. When she came back, she said, "You've got to see this place!"

She'd found this road—Pebble Beach Drive—and the view was just stunning. Most of the homes there were modest, one-story houses. We thought we might just be able to afford to live on the ocean here. Plus, I wouldn't have to go east to Pennsylvania.

About a year and a half later, when I finished law school, I got an interview in Crescent City. It's kind of a funny story. Another friend of mine was offered the job before I had heard about it. He accepted, and he and his wife drove up here the weekend before he was to start work. They arrived during a huge storm, with the rain blowing sideways. His wife refused to live here. He called up Monday morning and said, "I won't be taking the job after all."

So the position opened up again, and I ended up getting it. What sealed the deal was that Maureen was offered a special education job with the school district at the same time. There were only two severely handicapped teaching positions in the entire county and one of them happened to open up in the middle of the school year because the teacher who had been doing it was pregnant. So when we were both offered jobs at the same time, it seemed like fate.

We absolutely loved the place. Still do. The beauty blows me away. Living on Pebble Beach Drive lets us enjoy the ocean in all its different moods. I like to ride my bicycle along the ocean, and my wife was down on the beach just last night celebrating a friend's birthday with a bonfire. The remoteness is challenging, and it's hard to maintain family connections and old friendships because it takes so much effort to visit, but the friends we've made over the years are like family. For me, the natural beauty and the people are what make it worthwhile.

I'm on the board of the Wild Rivers Community Foundation, and I hear people from other communities, like Curry County, say how impressed they are with how involved in the community people are in Del Norte.

There's a generally collegial legal community here. It's smaller. That's part of it. I've seen how cutthroat law is often practiced in LA. Every time you got into some kind of minor dispute, someone would threaten "sanctions," which are civil fines a judge can impose on an attorney for various rules transgressions. As a judge here, I can think of very few times when I've had to issue sanctions. Attorneys have to deal with each other tomorrow—next week— next month. You may need an accommodation or a continuance the next time you work with that attorney, so you can't afford to make enemies over little things.

Moving to a small town, I knew I would be in general practice. I used to joke that I "specialized" in anything that walked through the door. I intentionally did very little family law—I only did five divorce cases my whole career, and two of them were for a family member. My partners in the practice handled the family law cases. Over my twenty year career I did a lot of real estate and criminal law, and by the end of my practice, my concentration was representing local government agencies such as the harbor district, solid waste authority, and several community services districts.

As an attorney, I always thought I'd like to be a judge. But openings for judgeships don't come along very often. When an opening did occur, I put my foot forward. I was elected in March 2000, but my term wouldn't begin until the following January. After the election, Judge Shafer retired early, and the Governor appointed me to fill the position until my full term began.

You asked about ways I identify with or share values with different cultural groups here. I didn't join the local Rotary Club right away. Rotary International had been accused of being discriminatory, but when it changed its policy to allow women in, I joined. It's been great for me. I've made so many friends and professional connections. It's really enriched my life.

My wife was a teacher, so I've spent a lot of time with educators, too. I feel a real connection with the education community. I served on the school board for a short term as well. Both of our daughters received good educations in the public schools here and both went on to become teachers.

I believe the Native American culture deeply enriches our community. I can't claim to have a deep understanding about it, but I've made some connections over the years. I got to know a lot of people and learn quite a bit when I was on the first Gaming Commission for the Elk Valley Rancheria. I've had the great pleasure of working with Judge Abby Abinatti who is the Chief Judge for the Yurok Tribal Court. It has been enlightening to see how a legal system with so many differences from the one I'm familiar with can work effectively.

Another culture I've learned a lot about from the outside is the local drug culture. Substance abuse and drug addiction are certainly challenges for people in our community. I run a drug court, and it's been truly rewarding to work with people trying to escape their addictions. It's difficult for people in that culture to break out. I've seen a lot of tears, but a lot of cheers, too.

If you're in the drug culture, your addiction has probably changed the way you behave. You've lied to your friends, you've lied to your family, and you've lied to your employer. If you're really into it, you've probably lost your job if you ever had one. You make excuses for everything. It is a really, really tough place to be.

Some people assume that those abusing drugs are just lawless and out to party. Many don't realize that addicts often get into drugs because of some kind of mental illness or trauma. Researchers have identified four traits that put people at risk for addiction. One is impulsiveness. Someone offers you a drug at a party, and you're more likely to try it. You may not even think about it. Another trait is anxiety. People with anxiety often have a tendency to take drugs to self-medicate. Someone offers them an opioid, and it makes them feel better at first, it helps the anxiety. Another trait is hopelessness. People get terribly depressed. Methamphetamine can make them feel good temporarily. The fourth trait is sensation-seeking. This may include the partier-type person. Most of the people I see are people who are depressed and are self-medicating. By the time I see them, they may have lost their kids or the kids resent or don't respect them because of what they've done. You get a mother who's trying to get her life together, and she has to cope with her thirteen-year-old kid who says, "Who are you to tell me what to do?" That kid's been with grandma or in foster care, and the relationship with the parent is seriously damaged.

The drug culture is all over the United States, but what makes matters worse in Del Norte is that we have fewer programs and services here. We don't have residential rehabilitation, needle exchanges, or a detox center. A lot of our "detox" consists of putting people in jail for a while. When we send someone to rehab, we have to send them to a different community. You temporarily separate them from their real life problems like their dysfunctional family, lack of housing and transportation, and drug-culture friends. They might do great in rehab. They get clean, but as soon as they come home, they run into their old buddies and the problems that they had before. And they start using again. Treating people with drug addiction in the community where they live is a better solution. They can get help with the specific triggers that fuel their addiction.

The drug court program holds people accountable. Participants must work recovery every day, going to classes and 12-step meetings, providing drug tests, meeting with their probation officer, and coming to court. Recently, we've put more emphasis on aftercare to help graduates continue with a lifetime commitment to sobriety.

I think what the community is now doing is better than what we used to do. We have three Oxford Houses—residential clean and sober houses organized by the recovering addicts themselves. Oxford came here in the last few years, and they've provided supportive living environments for people to get fresh starts. Humboldt Addiction Services Programs (HASP) has been successful, too. We also have more mental health services available. We have Jack Breazeal who oversees treatment for people who weren't treated before.

We have also started the Integrated Treatment Court (ITC) for people suffering mental illness. A typical participant might have started a small fire, forcefully resisted arrest, or led officers in a high speed chase. In each case their crimes are related to their mental illness. ITC is an attempt to treat the mentally ill in a more humane way and also to save taxpayers money. It's incredibly expensive to lock people up, and putting mentally ill people in jail doesn't help them get better or serve society in the long run. ITC won't cure people of mental illness, but we aim for harm reduction by providing services to manage their illness by ensuring, for instance, that they keep their doctor appointments and take their meds.

The impetus for ITC came one day in the courtroom when I sentenced a man to prison. His mother was there, crying and insisting that what he really needed was mental health treatment. I don't know if that was really the whole story for this young man, but I vowed to work on the problem of lack of coordinated mental health care for people in the court system. I was amazed when I started talking with the local officials how enthusiastic they were. They recognized the problem and said, "Yeah, let's do this!"

A bunch of us, the heads of the county Mental Health and Health and Human Services, the DA, Sheriff, Chief Probation Officer, a public defender, started meeting and then visited other counties that had working programs. We observed the courts, talked with judges and team members, got lots of good ideas, and then wrote our own protocols.

Because it's so resource-intensive, we've had to limit the number of people in ITC. There is probably a need to serve five times the number of people we do now, but we'd need more resources such as additional case managers. We've made the decision to start small and not apply for grants yet. We'll make do with the resources we have now, make our mistakes, better identify what works and what doesn't, what we need and what we don't need, and then seek grants to expand the program when we're ready.

Another thing we really haven't talked about is the economic disparity here. I struggle sometimes with how to deal with a teenager who violates his probation by not going to school, but he's living in a car and coping with the myriad of issues that come with homelessness. Our economy makes it hard to be fair, because people don't start out with an equal share. I don't recall there being a visible homeless problem in Del Norte thirty years ago, but now it's visible and widespread, and it creates all kinds of challenges.

We try hard to treat people fairly here in the court system. Everyone gets an attorney if they're facing even the possibility of jail time. Right now we don't have overzealous prosecutors, but we have in the past. We went through periods of time where prosecutors were trying to send people to prison for even a small amount of drugs. Some of the changes to the way we prosecute drug crimes has come with the changes in the law and with the recognition that sending people to prison for drug use didn't really work. That's been positive.

This is a law and order community like most rural areas. It's a red community in a blue state. It's more conservative than most of California. Here, our attitude has often been that if you commit a crime, you ought to be punished for it and put away. People running for office have often felt they needed to be tough on crime. But with mandated reduction in California prison population, we've been forced to rethink how we deal with some societal problems previously dealt with—not always effectively—with criminal laws.

There's probably a larger percentage of people here who are

rugged individualists than in urban areas. Also, I know I'm generalizing, but having Pelican Bay State Prison here has probably entrenched our community's values about law and order. But overall, I think having built the prison has been more positive than negative for the community. Back in the 1980s, we had unemployment in the mid-20% range. Property values were so low people were having a hard time selling their houses. Young people who had grown up here had to leave because there were few jobs. The tax base was down. I think building the prison really did help bring back middle class salaries that were lost when the mills shut down, and it brought in people making good wages. It has been a tremendous change, and overall, I think it's been good for our community, but it did influence community values.

I've been working for the legal system for almost forty years, and I see that how the law deals with crime over the years is cyclical. A shift is happening now. People are once again seeing that there's a benefit to rehabilitation and treatment. For much of my career, the emphasis has been on punishment and getting the bad guys off the streets. Changes in the law mean now we can't send people to prison for simply using meth. It forces us to do things more effectively—and save money. It costs a lot to send an addict to prison. That can be a terrible waste of resources if it doesn't help them recover from addiction, and they just keep coming back to the community and continue using.

With Prop 47, crimes that used to be felonies aren't felonies anymore. And there has been a sea change in marijuana laws. The first time I had to order the sheriff to return someone's seized marijuana—well, I'll never forget how strange that felt.

Early in my career on the bench, I spent an awful lot of time with Pelican Bay cases. I would get dozens and dozens of petitions for writ of habeas corpus from Security Housing Unit (SHU) inmates complaining about conditions. Conditions were very harsh in the SHU. Inmates were locked down nearly twenty-three hours a day supposedly until they paroled, debriefed, or died. That was how the state planned to break the dangerous hold that gangs had on state prison yards. The gangs were even running organized crime outside the prisons. Many of the inmates in SHU were extremely violent and dangerous. The Legislature and prison officials had to make difficult decisions about how to manage the problem, and they came up with the solution of building the Pelican Bay SHU in our county.

So much of that harsh treatment is going away now. It is part of this cycle I referred to earlier. I often wonder how history is going to judge how we performed during this law-and-order phase, with the three-strikes law locking people up for life, putting people in prison for drug use, and keeping others in SHU indefinitely. I'm not sure history's judgment will be kind.

Drug abuse is horrible for society, there's no doubt about that. To combat it we enacted laws to send offenders to prison. We thought that would scare people into not using. Experience has shown us that has not been very effective. When our country was founded we didn't have heroin or methamphetamine problems. We had alcoholics, but we didn't lock them up for any length of time. As the drug problems grew worse, society decided we would treat drug offenders as felons, lock them up, and take away their voting rights. We've created a long list of crimes classified as felonies and disenfranchised huge numbers of people. We're getting away from that now, and people in the future will probably look back and conclude we were too harsh. Drug abuse is an intractable problem, and to deal with it effectively we need a more nuanced approach than simply locking people up.

You've said that you had a few interviews where people have been critical of law enforcement. I've seen some bad cops in my time here. There's no question about it. There was a highway patrolman some time back who frequently physically abused people. My clients would tell me about it, and while I was skeptical at first, after I heard the same story over and over from different clients about the same officer, I began to believe it. We had a guy on the city police force decades ago who burglarized stores on his night beat. It's shameful and very unfortunate when something like that happens because these people make everyone else look bad, including the officer who is doing an impeccable job. I don't see the problem here as any worse than elsewhere. For every bad apple, there are probably fifty or a hundred honest cops doing a good, professional job under difficult and often dangerous conditions.

It's very easy to accuse people who are in public service even if they are doing a good job. It's particularly easy to say horrible things and damage reputations now on the Internet. But that's a price we pay for free speech. As I said before, I think most people in public service are acting honorably and trying to do a good job. We can legitimately disagree but too often in the Internet age, our public discourse turns into scurrilous attacks on public servants.* One of the things I love about the American courtroom is that attorneys can heatedly argue over significant ideas, issues and honestly held opposing views, but it is done transparently and usually without personal animus.

I plan to retire at the end of my term. Maureen and I will stay here in Del Norte. We do want to travel. We have one daughter in Spain and another who is planning to move to New York. One problem for older Del Norters is they sometimes have to leave the community to get specialized health care. That's a reality of being in such a remote place. We're a long ways from a big hospital. My wife and I both have had cancer. We have lots of stairs in our house. As long as we stay healthy and can climb those stairs, we'll probably stay here.

Del Norte has been really good for me. It's a beautiful place. I have friends who are Obama supporters, and I have friends who are Trump supporters, but I appreciate them all. Moving from here would mean leaving the friends we've made over decades.

Living here, I've been blessed.

*—May 7, 2018*

---

* William Follett, like many judges, was a target of a social media attack over his ruling in a prominent rape case in 2017.

# Katrina Groves

"Connection was one of the things I was most afraid of
coming from the big city, and yet it's turned out to be one of
the greatest things about being a doctor here."

*Katrina Groves provides a physician's perspective on living and working in Del
Norte County, including challenges faced by her patients at Open Door Clinic.*

I CAME TO DEL NORTE COUNTY in August 1992 at the age
of 31. Working at Open Door Community Health Center was my
very first job as a family physician. What brought me here? Two
words: *loan repayment*. I had twelve years of education debts from
college, graduate school, and medical school. There was an opportunity for a loan repayment through the National Health Services
Corp for those willing to work in an underserved area. So, to be
honest, that's what drew me to Del Norte.

In my residency program in San Bernardino, I met my future
husband, Warren, who is also a physician. Warren actually wanted us to look for job opportunities more north, up into Oregon,
Washington or even Alaska, which was his dream. He's from Minnesota and not afraid of weather. But I'm from sunny, southern
California. So we argued about it and I eventually refused to go
past the state line!

Little did I know that Northern California is like a whole different state.

I interviewed with Herrmann Spetzler, the patriarch of the
Open Door. He and his wife Cheyenne helped start the first clinic
in Humboldt County and then added the Del Norte Community

Health Center on A Street in 1991, near the old Sutter Coast Hospital. Herrmann saw an opportunity to get two doctors—myself and Warren—to a medical shortage area, so he hired us on.

Herrmann just recently passed away and we all mourn his loss. Over the years, he and his wife Cheyenne have worked tirelessly to build many more Open Door Community Health Centers serving the North Coast. I'm very proud to be a part of this legacy. But, to be honest, when we came to this small rural town, we had no idea we would still be here twenty-six years later.

I was forty by the time I was able to pay off my loans. Yes, we'd been thinking of moving elsewhere. But by that time, we had children, and we all saw the advantages of staying in the area. Living near these amazing redwood trees, the clean air and water, the swimming and kayaking, the hiking, the ocean, the fishing. It was just paradise—a safe and healthy environment compared to Los Angeles where I was raised.

But it took us a while to really believe we could stay here. It was hard for me at first without the malls and the culture. Growing up in L.A., I was able to go to see plays like *Phantom of the Opera* and go to symphony orchestras with my mom. We saw movies like *2001: A Space Odyssey* at the gigantic Cinerama Dome. We saw Baryshnikov and went to many ballets. Even driving the freeways was exciting for me. We had so much access to so many activities.

When I first came here and heard on the radio "There's a little red bike lost around 9th street. Please call KPOD if anyone has seen it," I thought to myself, "What kind place is this?" The fog and the cold got to me. I would bundle up with extra layers even inside the office. I had to have space heaters at work in the summer! It was both a cultural and environmental shock.

Early on, Warren and I would talk. I would say, "Okay, we'll only be here for a few years, and then we'll leave because I'm sure the schools aren't very good." But once we had our two boys, we found the schools were actually great. The preschool teacher was kind and patient. All the teachers at Mary Peacock from K-6 seemed excellent. As a parent volunteer, I got to know the faculty and saw how hard they worked and how much they cared for all their students. You have to understand, Del Norte schools were not like the schools I went to when I was growing up. I was moved around a lot due my dad's work. We ultimately landed in L.A. where classrooms were huge and kids were sort of invisible. But here we found a close knit community with people who cared for each other and helped each other through crises.

We thought about moving again when the kids were in middle school and then "for sure" before high school, but by then we were hooked. It's just amazing how much there is for kids to do here if you get them involved: jujitsu classes, music lessons with Sybil Wakefield, the GATE program, the Madrigal Choir events and the Steel Drum Band led by Dan Sedgwick. He recently was proclaimed Teacher of the Year by the Northern California Band Directors and Choral Directors Association! Everywhere we looked to move, we just couldn't help comparing it to here. All the other places were just lacking.

But before kids, before all that, it took a while to adjust to the culture shock. The first few years I was in hiding. I did not want to get to know my neighbors or make friends. In my world, that just wasn't done, and I thought we would be moving soon, anyway. So we'd drive down to Eureka and go to Costco or over to Ashland to the Oregon Shakespeare Festival, or go have Indian food in Medford. We'd drive anywhere to get to a bigger city with more things to do and more variety.

But once we had our boys we stayed home more and found ourselves going to community events instead. Our best friends were our anchors then. They still are. Athena Csutoras is this amazing "earth mother" who can grow a huge garden, feed any number of people who just happen to drop by, make a picnic table from scratch, and fix pretty much anything that breaks. My boys and I were lucky enough to be included into her family, and we learned so much from her. Her husband Jimmy was a fisherman, so we learned to live more off the land. This reminded me of growing up with my dad, who was a country boy and used to take my sister and me on camping trips and other family adventures. So living in Del Norte County was like going back to what is really important—family, friends and nature. I got used to it again, and after a while, we hardly ever left town at all.

Now my perspective has changed. I hate the "long" ninety minute drive down to Eureka. I don't miss the malls. I don't like those big city freeways anymore. This place became my home.

I miss a little of the cultural events available in an urban setting, but we have found our own culture here. My husband and I enjoy singing in the North Coast Chorale. Christie Lynn Rust is the most energetic and fun director! With her passion for travel we have been able to visit Europe twice and sing in incredible cathedrals in Poland, France and Germany. I never even knew I could sing before! I also took viola lessons while my kids were learning violin, and I even got to play with the local orchestra in Lighthouse Repertory Theatre's rendition of *Oklahoma*. I have such special memories of my dad and mom who came to watch these performances. I could never have played in an orchestra in a big city.

Coming to a small town helped me get out of my preconceived notions of who I was. I thought I was a city person, but once I allowed myself to be at home here, things started to feel right. In Los Angeles, you don't know your neighbors. You don't want to know your neighbors. You don't want to know the person you're driving next to. But here in Del Norte County, I'll be riding with a friend, and I'm shocked as she's driving down the highway and saying "Oh, there's so-and-so" going by in their car or walking down the street. And everybody waves! Well, now I wave too.

As far as the medical care here, when Warren and I looked at other places to move, we kept comparing other jobs with the clinic in Crescent City. We did not see anything better than where we already were, except perhaps an increase in salary. I love the mission of the clinic—to compassionately care for all people, regardless of their ability to pay, regardless of their race, language, sexual orientation or religion. People tend to stereotype our patients at the clinic. Many people think that our clinic is "just for people on

Medi-Cal." But we have many people who have good insurance and can go anywhere and they choose, but they come to us because we provide excellent care. Some of our patients often do have difficult life challenges and conditions which are hard to treat. But I love providing care for these folks, even if the clinic can't compensate me as much as other places might.

For me, it's not about money or status. I don't want to work in some boutique practice where they're just about giving Botox or something. I don't want a mink coat or a Jaguar. I'd much rather be able to practice medicine one person at a time than worry about the business end of things. I have a roof over my head and live in a beautiful place. My kids have gone to college and are doing well. My life is about my connection to people—people who every day share intimate details of their lives with me and trust me to help them through tough health care problems.

You ask about what contributes to poor health outcomes here. Poverty, mental illness, drug use—yes. Just like many small towns across America. Unfortunately, people are being stigmatized and judged for these problems. In our county, and all across the country, there is a pervasive attitude that people on Medi-Cal or people who are homeless must somehow want to be like that, and they are "weak or lazy." I have found just the opposite. Many people have had traumatic childhoods and haven't had all the blessings in their lives that we have had. The stigma—the judgmental attitude of others, though, makes it hard for people to get the health care they need. Having to go out of town to see specialists and having no way to get there, for example, is a serious challenge. I think as a community, we are only as healthy as our least healthy resident. If we all try to have more compassion and empathy, we can help lift people out of poverty and homelessness. Homelessness won't go away by ignoring it or covering it up or shipping people off somewhere else.

One of the most rewarding parts of my practice has become treatment of addiction. The opioid crisis has been sweeping the United States, and it's in our little corner of the world, too. In the late 1990's, physicians like myself were taught that pain was the "5th vital sign" and that prescribing even high doses of narcotics to prevent pain was the right and humane thing to do. But now the pendulum has swung the other way, as some of those people treated with opioids got addicted, and many were still having pain despite their pills.

I felt that if I helped create the problem, I should try to help fix it. So we started the Suboxone recovery treatment program at the clinic in 2009. It began with just six people and it has grown to over one hundred.

There are a lot of misunderstanding and judgmental about addiction. The old-school thinking is that if you punish people enough (like sending them to jail or prison), they're going to learn to stop using drugs. But we have seen over and over again that punishment just doesn't work. We need to switch that mindset. Drug addiction is a brain disease. It's not a character flaw or a weakness.

In order to get better, people with addiction need compassionate treatment, medication, and behavioral skill and life skill training, just like patients living with any other chronic disease. These folks have PTSD, depression, anxiety and other problems, and they often come from terrible backgrounds. They are often traumatized. They're covering up their pain and their emotions with drugs.

Yes, they need to do their jail time for things they did while under the influence, but then if you can get them into a treatment program, over time you can help them heal and show them how to change their behavior. Otherwise the majority will be right back to the streets and the vicious cycle continues.

We need to remember that when somebody's addicted, they have an illness. We should treat them as such. If a diabetic eats a whole chocolate cake, are you going to kick them out of your practice because their blood sugar levels are too high? If we as physicians could see the people who are addicted in our community *as people with a disease* and work to help them help themselves, we could really make some headway.

There is a great quote I've seen about people who suffer from addiction: "We are not bad people trying to be good, we are sick people trying to get well."

I see people every day who have turned their lives around and are going back to school, getting jobs and taking care of their families—engaging in a full life—and that is the most rewarding part for me.

How does the methamphetamine problem compare with the opioid problem here? Well, meth is a serious issue as well. And to compound the problem, some addicts use heroin and meth together. In my practice, we focus on opioid addiction because we can do something about that with medications like Suboxone. But to date, there's no antidote or "drug blocker" for meth, though I hope and pray there is one soon. Research is ongoing. Sometimes we have seen people be able to get off meth as well as opioids when they get into a recovery program.

Many crimes are directly related to drug use, and so if we can get these people in treatment, the crime rate will go down and our community will be safer for all of us. But sometimes law enforcement officers see things differently. They look down on addicts because they see them at their worst—committing crimes and injuring others. They just want to think of them as "bad guys."

But other law enforcement officers are beginning to see that we need to work together for the good of the community. Our local Sheriff, Eric Apperson and our local Superior Court Judge, William Follett, have been very open and willing to look at ways they can help break the cycle of drug addiction and crime. They see that we need to offer these people treatment.

Open Door Community Health Clinic is also working with the local Opioid Coalition, along with the Public Health Department, other community physicians, a local pharmacist, mental health care providers, and law enforcement. We're doing some really important work, helping to spread the word that treatment is available for addiction. We're also trying to get the narcotics off the street by prescribing them less often and in lower quantities. We're also trying to get more Narcan out in the community, which can save lives when someone has overdosed.

I think it is terrific how a small town can really get things done when people work together for a common goal. We're making inroads into looking at systems and policy change locally, but we still have a long way to go. It's hard to change preconceived beliefs about drug use.

Stigma also makes helping homeless people more difficult. Moving them out of the county is not the answer. We need a homeless shelter *here*. Most of the homeless population suffers from mental health issues, and often from drug addiction. Ironically, in a lot of communities, being homeless disqualifies you for drug treatment. The outcomes for recovery are so poor when you don't have a home. So it's a terrible cycle that just perpetuates itself.

I have been impressed by acts of kindness that have had big payoffs here. Del Norte County Mental Health Department went into a homeless area recently and brought a person into a recovery house, and then into our drug treatment program. That person is now getting needed medical care for the first time in forty years. *They went in to get him.* Sometimes, to help people, it has to happen one person at a time.

Do I plan to stay in Del Norte County? I wish I could. My mother died about a year and a half ago, and so my sister and I have been taking turns looking after my dad. But it's been a challenge doing that and working.

After twenty-six years, I've had to tell my patients that I'm leaving. This has been one of the hardest things I've ever had to do. Lots of tears. Leaving the clinic staff feels like leaving my family.

I knew I was going to be sad, but I can't believe how sad I really feel. I can't believe how upset my patients are, too. Not only have I helped them over the years with their health problems, I've also cheered them on through their successes. They watched me go through my pregnancies and were so understanding during my own ups and downs in life. Of course there are professional boundaries, but I felt it was okay for me to be human, too, sometimes. I learned that here. Connection was one of the things I was most afraid of coming from the big city, and yet it's turned out to be one of the greatest thing about being a doctor here.

I love these people, and I'm having to leave them. Sometimes I feel like a traitor. But my husband and my patients tell me that I am doing what I need to do to be a good daughter, and I do believe that. I know that doctors will come to replace me. But no matter where I go, I will always have a special place in my heart for this place and these people.

The closer I get to leaving, the more I find there is to do. So many things to wrap up. That's part of the reason I wanted to do this interview, so people can understand what it has meant to me to be a doctor in this town for so long.

We've lost of medical providers at the clinic many times. They join us, and then they leave for various reasons, often because of the isolation. We've had to just pick up the pieces and be there for the patients. Now, I guess other people will have to pick up the pieces for me.

But my heart will always be here. And who knows. I may come back.

*—May 3, 2018*

# Marisol*

> "She told me, 'You dream too big,'
> 'You're not going to make it,' and
> 'You don't have the money.'"

*Marisol, like many youth in our community, is undocumented. Her legal status has added to her suffering in many ways. As you will see, her experience provides a unique perspective on justice in Del Norte County.*

I LIVED IN JALISCO, MEXICO until I was nine. In late 2004, my parents made the decision to bring our family to California.

My father went first to raise money for our crossing. Then me, my mom, my younger brother, and my younger sister traveled by bus to Tijuana. We stayed for a few months with one of my dad's cousins.

When we were finally ready, we took a bus from Tijuana to Mexicali. We went to this hotel—a high-rise—and went up to some floor where there were other Mexicans who were waiting to get crossed over.

I got crossed over first, without my family. I crossed by car with a lady who went by the name of "Lala." She had red hair—she was beautiful. Since I was so tiny, she hid me in this little space between the trunk and the backseat. She pulled over a few times to let me get out and breathe, but when we got to the border, I had to be very still and quiet. I was so scared. The cops checked the trunk. They even banged on the space I was in. I could feel them hitting it. But

---

* Some names have been changed to protect the contributor's anonymity.

78

they didn't find me.

After we were across, she let me sit in front. Then we got to her boss's house, which was this mansion. The boss lady was nice to me. I remember there were a lot of cats, and she let me play with them. She got a hold of my family in Los Angeles—we had cousins there—and they brought her the rest of the money my family owed in exchange for smuggling me over.

I stayed with my cousins for about three months waiting for the rest of my family to come over. It was hard, waiting so long.

My brother was next. The same lady used her son's passport to bring him over by car, so he didn't even need to hide in the car. He just had to remember what to say to the border guards, to remember what his name was supposed to be and who his parents were. Things like that.

The crossing was more difficult for my sister. They tried to cross her over several times, first with the same lady, and then with another lady who was going to take her across with her own daughters. But my sister didn't want to be out of my mom's sight, and she ended up biting the second lady who was supposed to take her across. Eventually, they gave her some NyQuil or something so that she slept the whole way.

My mom, who was pregnant, actually crossed on foot. She crossed with four or five other women and fifteen or twenty men. A couple of the women got raped on the way. It would have happened to my mom, but some of the men defended her. Unfortunately, their group got caught, and she was deported.

She made it across the second time, but she arrived in bad shape. She was very skinny. I remember her legs were so thin. Her feet were in terrible shape, too.

From LA, one of my aunts came down from Crescent City with a van and brought us all up together. We arrived in Del Norte County around Thanksgiving. My baby brother was born a couple of months later.

I've been here thirteen years—versus nine in Mexico. Now this place feels like home, but it didn't in the beginning. I hated this area when we first came. It was rainy and cold, and I didn't know any English except for a few simple words, like "hello" and "baby." But I started school right away. I went to Joe Hamilton.

My teacher assigned two students who spoke Spanish, a girl and a boy, to help me. The girl just kind of blew it off. The boy was rude to me—but he did help. But then one day I heard him making fun of me in the hallway—calling me "dumb." Kids don't understand that it takes time to learn a new language.

But most people in Del Norte County were good to us. When I first arrived, I met an amazing couple who I now consider family. I started to make friends with kids my age, too. I had my cousin, Carlos, and we became very close. He knew a little Spanish, and I knew a little English, and so we taught each other. I met Elena, who also spoke Spanish, and we became very close, too. It was nice to hang out with them.

I did well in school. I wasn't "dumb" after all. I learned English in a year. I asked a lot of questions and probably annoyed a lot of people, but I did it. I had a hard time being interested in some subjects in school. For a long time, I didn't like studying history. I didn't feel like an American, so I got bored with all the emphasis on America. The only time I really liked it was when they were talking about Mexico. So that wasn't my best subject.

I didn't have much of a social life, though. I always had to be around for my younger siblings. I had to drive them to school and pick them up, and I had to translate for my parents any time they needed it. My senior year, I had to beg my mom to let me join a sport. I actually told her it was a requirement. That's how I got her to agree. I wish I could have done more.

I knew I wanted to go to college. I got several awards at the high school scholarship banquet, but I didn't get as many as some kids because I couldn't do sports or other after school activities. My mom wanted me to stay local and go to the community college. When I got accepted to a CSU, she was really negative about it. She told me, "You dream too big," "You're not going to make it," and "You don't have the money." But I did have support from other people, like the couple who became like family to me, and two teachers I became close to. They all helped me financially, but also, just by believing in me.

I ended up withdrawing from school and coming back home because of something that happened before I left Del Norte. I got raped. Just before I left for orientation at college, I went to my first house party here in Del Norte. I'd never been to a party where there was drinking before, but I brought my cousin with me, so I thought I'd be okay. The guy throwing the party kept checking up on me, trying to get me to drink. He seemed like he was just being friendly, but I think he was working with this other guy, who was trying to get my cousin to go to bed.

I think I must have been drugged. I woke up in a closet. My phone was gone. And my clothes were on wrong, inside out and backwards. I was in a lot of pain. I could barely walk, and I was really out of it. I'd had a tampon in, and it wasn't there when I woke up, so I knew something had happened. I figured they took it out before they raped me.

I didn't report the rape here, at least not at first. I was too shocked. And I didn't think anyone could help me. And I'm undocumented. But when I went to my college, after a few weeks, I started having health problems. So I went to the student health center. There was a tampon still inside me. When it came out, I just started crying. I could have died from toxic shock. I could have died from the rape.

When I finally worked up the courage to tell me parents, my mom blamed it on me for being there, at a party where there was drinking. She blamed me for being raped.

I went to counseling all that year at school, and I joined a group for girls who had also been sexually assaulted. It helped a lot having people to talk to. But I really missed that parental support. My parents would call, but not to encourage me. They called when they had a bill to pay. No, not a bill for college. They didn't help me with that. They called when they needed a favor.

Even though I got help for my depression, I was just overwhelmed by sophomore year. I was taking sixteen units and felt like I was drowning. I wasn't eating, I was constantly crying, I was staying in bed and not going anywhere. So I dropped out. I came back to Del Norte and got work. I lived with my family at first, but then I moved out and lived with friends. I've found a good support network. And I plan to get my Associate Degree here at College of the Redwoods and then go back to my old college someday.

Even now, I do try to help my parents. They never got a good education. My mom never finished grade school. My dad went to high school for a short time. But I try to say "no" more often. I try to worry about myself first.

Right now, though, my future is uncertain. I'm a Dreamer, a "DACA." DACA stands for Deferred Action of Childhood Arrivals, and that program—DACA—has given me hope for the last five years. Established by the Obama administration in June of 2012, it allows people like me, who were brought to the U.S. illegally as children, to legally work, drive and go to college. I have to renew my DACA status every two years—and it's an extensive process. If it expires, I could be sent back to Mexico—a place I barely know.

In the meantime, I am working now with a local non-profit. I feel like I'm really giving back to the community. People tell me I'm doing a good job, and that makes me proud.

Yes, I'm afraid. But I don't mind people knowing now. It feels good to speak out, to say how I feel. I agree that my parents should have done it the legal way, but I'm not to blame for that. And so here I am. I hope that Congress comes together and creates a pathway to citizenship for the 800,000 of us enrolled in DACA. I hope people will be able to put themselves in our shoes.

*—September 22, 2017*

# Walker True

"You can't teach someone to respect school by kicking them out—especially not someone who is like five or six years old. Being away from school for five days does not make a kindergartener respect the value of education."

*Walker True reflects on his struggle to get help for his disability in the school system, as well as his recent work as an advocate for better mental health care for youth.*

I WAS TWO when my mom and I moved here. It was just us. We lived in the apartment just across from Jack-In-The-Box, the one with the big bush around it. We lived with my aunt and three other families. We slept in the kitchen.

For me, the quintessential Del Norte experience is the Smith River. It's everything for me. After swimming in the river, I come home exhausted. And my hair feels clean but like…river hair. You know how when you're in the ocean, you get ocean hair? Well, for me, it's river hair. I absolutely hated taking showers after a swim.

But I didn't get to go to the river very much this summer. I was working with the Youth Training Academy (YTA). I don't know if that's a typical Del Norte experience, but that's what I want Del Norte to be. We had *community*. And there aren't times outside of that when I've had the experience of coming together, really coming together, except maybe the Fair and the 4th of July. In the YTA, we really came together as a community this summer.

There's a massive separation between people in power and regular people—especially in schools. Teachers and staff—people who make decisions about students' lives—aren't really engaged with us. A lot of us feel like we don't have positive role models. There's a really big opportunity for teachers to do that for us, but there are hardly ever any conversations going on outside of class. There's hardly ever any give and take. It's no different than if you walk into a classroom and you have just a screen with a teacher on it.

It's the same at Del Norte County Mental Health. In the Mental Health building, to get your diagnosis, the doctor comes in through Skype. So it's not the people diagnosing you, legally speaking, who are giving you your medication. You miss saying important things when you're talking over a screen. You miss asking questions. You don't feel comfortable having a real conversation. How are you supposed to tell your deepest, darkest feelings to a screen?

But it's not fully a fault of teachers. It's the fault of the system itself that puts forty kids into a classroom. Learning will only happen with kids who are motivated by something else—something inside themselves. Some kids really have an advantage because their parents help to motivate them. And parents also help motivate the teachers and administration, like my mom. I wouldn't have gotten through school if it hadn't been for her. There was no help or support from the school for my mental health needs until she intervened for me. They didn't want to acknowledge the problem. I have ADHD, and it affects people differently. For me, I get anxiety and depression. So, inside of school, it's really hard to handle a lot of assignments.

Kindergarten through third grade, I went to St. Joseph's. I barely went to recess, I was in trouble so much. Looking back on that, I can't see suspending anyone. Ever. You can't teach someone to respect school by kicking them out—especially not someone who is like five or six years old. Being away from school for five days does not make a kindergartner respect the value of education.

Eventually, I went to Redwood, and I continued to get detention and to be suspended until sixth grade. I was consistently bullied throughout this time, and I was an anxious mess. Then I moved to Unchartered Shores, and then after that, Klamath River Early College of the Redwoods (KRECR). KRECR had a beautiful curriculum design, but it should have just started with younger kids. It didn't work to have kids in the middle grades coming out of traditional public schools without the independence necessary for the work. So when I was there, I just kind of sat around and didn't do much. I can say that KRECR helped me develop myself as a person more than any other school, though. I became more confident. I could talk to people about things. I developed opinions about things. I do remember a lot of sitting in the upper cohort with—for lack of a better word—stoners. But it felt like more of a community than any other place I ever went. I remember "community meetings," where, every Friday, we would come together. It wasn't like in a classroom where just the teachers talk from the front. Anybody could talk.

After KRECR, I went to Castle Rock Charter School and Del Norte High School. At Del Norte High, there were teachers who were personable and created a positive atmosphere, but they were rare. The teaching is archaic. There are not discussions, at least not in "normal" level classes. Sometimes in the Advanced Placement classes, the teaching methods are better. They're more Socratic. But everyone should have access to good discussions with deeper responses. Classes at Del Norte High never form the shape of a circle, you know? You've got just a teacher at the front and students looking at the teacher. Students are not encouraged to treat each other as equals. There's a hierarchy, because when you're in the back, or on the side, you can't quite see the board, and you're marginalized. We're literally depriving students of access to education. And negative classroom experiences create anxiety, which makes for even worse classroom experiences. That sets you up for failure. And the "good" students, the ones who are motivated already, lucky enough to have parents who pushed them forward, are going to sit in the front. But someone then has to sit in the back. So it's not fair.

Another big issue today is that our school system doesn't recognize disabilities early. It doesn't intervene. At Redwood, I would break down and cry in the middle of class, and my mom never knew about it. She was never told about any of these incidents. It was only through my talking to her that I got help—and with my mom's help—going through like five psychologists and psychiatrists until I found the one who could help.

I know many other kids with similar circumstances right now who have experienced this kind of thing—and their behavior is considered the problem rather than a symptom of an illness. We just don't have any solid mental health resources in our school system. I don't think anyone has ever been referred to a mental health counselor.

Part of what needs to happen is a mind-shift towards restorative justice, so that we stop punishing kids who just haven't learned good communication skills and instead help them work out their feelings and learn to empathize with others. Detention, suspension and expulsion just set kids up for more punishment. They don't teach them the skills that they need to change their behavior and develop their understanding of other people's needs and feelings.

You've probably heard of the "school to prison pipeline." Well, here in Del Norte it's the school to unemployment pipeline. We live in a town originally built on logging and fishing—and you didn't need college for those. And that's still ingrained in our society. So the system of punishing kids used to work, in a way, for everyone's benefit. It meant that kids who didn't do well in school could drop out and get a job. They might not get to go to college, but they could still make a living, and then the schools were left with just the smart kids. Well, that system for school is still in place, but the economy isn't the same. The kids who get pushed out have nowhere to go and nothing to do.

The school district is trying to make a move towards restorative justice. Tony Fabricus is doing great things at Sunset High School on restorative justice. Youth leaders like myself, Manny Saavedra, and Sam Bradshaw are getting administrators like him to listen to youth voice in their decision-making processes. We're in a group that calls itself LYON (Local Youth Organizing Network). I think we're making progress. It's difficult to work on this while going to college—all of us involved in the work are enrolled in the community college, but we're trying.

One of the things we're finding—myself and the folks involved in LYON—is that looking at the suspension and expulsion rates at Crescent Elk, the Middle School—you're more likely to be suspended or expelled if you're a person of color—African American, Native American or Latino. White kids tend to get lesser punishments for similar behaviors. So in addition to harming everyone, suspensions and expulsions are disproportionally harming students of color.

My involvement in the Youth Training Academy and in LYON have really helped me change my attitude. Until recently, I didn't feel Del Norte was the place for me. But I'm becoming proud of Del Norte. Not because it's great now, but because there are a lot of youth trying to make it a better place.

*—September 7, 2017*

# Manuel Vidal

"Growing up here, friends would ask me
why I moved here. I had a list of answers
I used to deflect from the truth."

*Living in a prison town takes on a whole new meaning when your family members are incarcerated just down the road. Manuel Vidal shares his experience trying to fit in here and his political awakening as an advocate for "collective liberation."*

I'M A FIRST GENERATION US CITIZEN. It's weird when I say that because my family is indigenous to this continent. I don't think indigenous people can ever be "illegal." They should be free to travel and not be stopped or arrested as outsiders, but they aren't. I recognize the privilege that comes with my US birth certificate that isn't afforded to others like me.

I was born in San Diego County. My family moved here to be nearer to my stepfather and other family members who are incarcerated in Pelican Bay State Prison. Most of the men in my family are in prison. When I was younger, my family would have to travel the whole state, every month, so that we could visit them. But when I was about 15, we moved here to make it easier and safer for us. I'm 18 now.

When I first got here, I thought Del Norte County was like Forks in the movie *Twilight.* A lot of trees and forests and cold. I was an inner city kid, so seeing what a redwood looked like was amazing. And it *is* cold for me all the time, even in the summer when it's sunny. When I first moved here, I was freezing. The air was so moist. I thought I was going to die of hypothermia, and all these folks were running around in short-shorts and flip-flops playing disc golf. It was crazy!

I've been here about three years, and I'm just starting to feel like I belong. It's very white and conservative, so being a person of color, I didn't think of it as home. When I first got here, I worried about how people might treat us. I worried that some redneck would run over my family. I would get dirty looks a lot, and I felt scared. I still worry sometimes.

This is a prison town. Most of the COs who keep my family members incarcerated are also my neighbors. When I was younger, I would go into a convenience store and see a CO, and I would immediately tense up. Because I knew what they could do—what they could do to my family—to my father and other relatives who are incarcerated at Pelican Bay just a few miles away.

I know who the COs are and the COs know who I am. They've known me for a long time. They saw me grow up, coming to the prison every month even before we lived here. My experiences with COs have not been very positive. When I was younger and we were still driving up from San Diego, they could make our lives hell if they wanted to. And they often did. During visitor hours, after we'd come so far, they would often make us drive back to our hotel and change our clothes and make us put on kh2akis. They could be very strict with the dress code if they wanted to. Sometimes we felt like we drove sixteen hours just to be harassed.

During my time in high school here, there would be moments when a friend I'd made would get picked up by his dad out in front of the school—and then we would never be friends again. His dad knew me from the prison, knew I was related to an inmate, and must have told his child not to hang out with me anymore.

Most of these friends were white. The COs are mostly white men. The inmates are mostly men of color. And—for them—I was just a person destined to repeat the cycle and become an inmate myself. This just added to the stigma I experienced.

Most people still don't know I have family members who are incarcerated. This isn't something I've talked about a lot, even in my organizing work. Growing up here, friends would ask me why I moved here. I had a list of answers I used to deflect from the truth. I would sometimes just say, "The prison." Then they would say, "Oh, snap! My dad works at the prison, too!" They didn't realize their dad oversaw my dad in this prison-industrial complex.

I never said, "Oh, snap! Your dad is making tons of money off black and brown bodies—my relatives!" But I could have. It would have been true.

I hate to admit it, but I had all these excuses I would use for why we moved here so that I didn't have to explain it to people. I caught myself self-censoring for my own protection, and later, to comfort people. People don't want to know a guy who works at College of the Redwoods has incarcerated family members. I don't usually talk about it.

Even in the youth leadership activities I participated in, even in the Youth Training Academy, I didn't want anyone to know. I rationalized that I had all these cool opportunities I was being exposed to, and I didn't want to blow it. There were kids whose parents were CO's, and our groups got involved in these deep discussions about racism and safety and inequity, and I had to share space with them. It was uncomfortable. They would make comments about people who had been incarcerated—and I think sometimes they *knew* about my family—but I couldn't just lash out and be the stereotype they expected me to be: the crazy and angry and reactive person of color. I was silenced before I opened my mouth to share my experience.

The way people talk here about inmates is very hurtful and disturbing. They call them "bad guys" and "monsters," and that's not even the worst of it. I've heard them say things like, "Man, if it wasn't for my job, I would just put a bullet in every last one of them." Really? You're talking about mass murder and your job is to protect the safety of the men incarcerated? I want to say, "That's my stepdad you're talking about!" But I don't.

It's ironic, because a lot of these COs are bullies. They bully each other and they bully the inmates. But in high school, their kids get bullied. I *protected* their kids from being bullied. I *protected* their kids despite the fact that they weren't providing basic protection for my family.

You asked me when I started to understand the prison-industrial complex and the school to prison pipeline. You know that I studied the subject here at the college and in the Youth Training Academy. But I understood it long before moving here simply by seeing the cycle so many of my family members went through. *Every single man in my family has been in prison.* And I knew so many people in inner city San Diego where it was like, "Wow, your family member is in prison, too?" It's scary how common it is for people of color. It's an untold truth that we're caught up in a huge system of injustice, and it makes me feel so hopeless sometimes. Fighting to change this system—to dismantle this system—it's a big job.

I still don't feel fully connected to this place. But through my community organizing work, I realize that I need to claim the space, to say "This is my Del Norte." And I don't just think of this place as my training ground anymore.

One of my favorite mentors is Gracia Rojas from True North Organizing Network. She's this bad-ass woman of color. I learned so much from her. I would think I understood racism, and then she would blow my mind. She reminded me that, as a man of color organizing against racism, I have to combat the patriarchy as well. It's not just one issue. All of these issues intersect.

Sitting with my friends, Gracia and Jacob Patterson, I'm starting to get it more. This revolution will be all-inclusive, will be wheelchair accessible. It will love its trans community, will be welcoming to all undocumented communities, will be led by indigenous people.

With this current administration, it's scary. It feels like a lot of the work has been in vain. We've gone back so much. It sucks, but deep down, I'm not too surprised. I know the injustice this country is capable of. The well-meaning liberals were surprised when Trump won. But I knew.

It's like this: the rule for me has always been, don't drive in a car with a lot of other brown people, right? And my white friend is along for the ride. And we're pulled over, and my white friend is surprised. And he starts arguing with the cop, and he's upset. But we're all like, "Dude. We were expecting this." He's getting a taste of what it's like. So Trump? We were expecting this.

Looking at the prison system, we're trying to fix a wheel that's already broken. We're trying to fix a shitty wheel. Law enforcement isn't used to *help* people. It is used to *enforce policies and rules and regulations* to protect its own system. At one point, it was plain old slave patrol. So trying to fix an agency rooted in racism sounds crazy. In my eyes, that's not going to work. It's an inherently racist system. There are no good cops. The positions make shitty, racist people when they're in it for long enough. Police officers and correctional officers, those are positions that maintain the status quo. And the status quo is harmful to communities of color.

I think that's what most people don't understand—we have these people advocating that "blue lives matter." There is no such thing as a blue life, a blue person. They're talking about an occupation. Having a particular occupation doesn't make you more deserving of life than Philando Castile, or Sandra Bland, or Trayvon Martin. And the list goes on and on and on.

Law enforcement today is the new Klu Klux Klan. I mean, there may be that well-meaning good-old-boy from Kansas who goes into law enforcement because he wants to help people, but being in the training and in those tense situations just feeds into the shoot-first-and-ask-questions-later thinking that hurts communities of color.

One of the experiences I had that helped me understand what we're up against was when I went with a group of friends to the Dakota Access Pipeline protests. It was overwhelming and traumatic. The camp was amazingly structured, probably because there were so many community organizers involved. Lots of people came to offer up skills and trainings, like how to be peaceful, how to respect native space, how not to appropriate native culture, and how to be on the front lines of the protest. We were even trained on what to do if you get pepper sprayed.

The first night was one of the most violent nights there. At Backwater Bridge, we came face to face with paid mercenaries representing the corporation, and we heard they were advancing and going to take over the bridge. So we went out there to stop them, to be a blockade. They met us with brute force. We were pepper sprayed, shot with really big rubber bullets, and exposed to flash grenades. We were sprayed with ice cold water, too. Seeing my friends in danger was terrifying. It was a night filled with violence. Again, I wasn't surprised that law enforcement was doing this to a group mostly made up of people of color, but it was terrifying to have my fears reaffirmed.

Being an organizer, I'm part of a long lineage of ancestors who were bad asses. We've done it before, and we'll keep on doing it. I was afraid, but I tried to be mindful that I shouldn't be. The fear is just part of a colonial mindset. After all, I had nothing to be afraid of. I was not the one building a pipeline across sacred ground. Even though we were being painted by Fox News as crazy protesters who wanted to see the world burn, the truth was that we were there to protect the same clean water that law enforcement officers needed, too.

One of the many takeaways from that one night was not worrying about being afraid. I reminded myself that Malcom X, Richard Aoki, Caesar Chavez, Angela Davis and others were probably afraid, but they didn't let it stop them. I wasn't going to let it stop me, either.

But coming back from Standing Rock was strange. When I was there, I was in a war zone. Helicopters were flying over the camp 24/7. We couldn't sleep properly. We weren't eating. We were at a constantly high level of anxiety and stress. Coming back home from that trauma was hard because my friends all dealt with it differently. I would hear a little sound in my room, and I would wake up thinking police were coming to get me. It was heavy. Being here, it's so white and I felt so out of place. I remember a law enforcement officer here asking me if I was okay, and I just broke down in tears. I thought, "You are capable of doing so many bad things, Mr. Police Officer." I still have a lot of things to deal with, coming back. I still have nightmares about being on that bridge.

I want people to understand the collective liberation of our communities depends on our being intersectional with what matters. We can't get to the place we want to be unless we acknowledge our biases and unpack them. And I think that's where I get stuck the most.

Being in white spaces does not help at all. Here in the organizing work, most of the people are white. At the college where I work, most of the people are white. A lot of the people around me are white. I can't escape it. Yesterday, I was having a mini-panic attack. I couldn't get away from it. Take a look at our city council, our local officials, our school system. This isn't to say that every single white person is bad, but every single white person who has power doesn't realize their privilege. How do you dismantle these systems that are so embedded in Del Norte County? How do we get all communities to see this—to come to understand that, yes, we all have our privileges? That's the work.

*—September 15, 2017*

*Numerous contributors discuss Del Norte County's timber industry, which thrived for decades—and the local economy along with it. The reduction of available old growth, increased regulation, and the Spotted Owl are variously blamed for the industry's decline.*

# PART II:
# RESOURCES

*Where do we feel abundance?*
*Where do we sense scarcity?*

# Jack Owen

"Well, I know on private land they logged quite a lot of the
redwoods. But that shouldn't have shut all the mills down.
My God, there's hundreds of acres of fir timber in this country
on US Forest Service land. They should have had plenty left."

*Long-time Del Norte resident Jack Owen of Hiouchi reflects on his life in the
trucking industry during the area's timber boom—and beyond.*

I WAS BORN IN THE ILLINOIS VALLEY in 1929. My folks
lived in the Page Creek Ranger Station, about four miles south of
Takilma. My grandparents' homestead was about six miles upriver.
They built it themselves with homemade shakes. People didn't have
money back then, you know. But it was a comfortable old place. I
remember when I went to visit, I slept in a room where, instead of
wallpaper, the walls were covered with old newspapers.

I came to Del Norte County in 1962. I'd been driving a truck for
Grants Pass Plywood, but they closed down. They would reopen
later, but at the time, I was out of a job, and I couldn't find anything
in Grants Pass. It's a shame, because my wife Marcheta and I had
just bought a brand new house there, a real nice one. She had to
stay behind until we could sell it. Meanwhile, five of us came from
Grants Pass Plywood with a guy named Rocky McCormick. He
leased his trucks to NorCal Plywood, and we were his drivers.

I kind of liked Crescent City. I don't care for huge towns. I'd
been hauling plywood into some pretty big places like San Diego
and Los Angeles, but they seemed pretty crowded to a country boy

like me. But my job was hauling—so I didn't spend a lot of time here in those days. I was away from home a lot.

The time I did spend here—well, I couldn't get over the natural beauty. I still can't. Back then, I had small boys. We loved the Smith River. I'd take them swimming in the summer on my days off. I don't swim now. It's a cold river. It never does get warm. But we used to swim a lot, years ago.

You know, I waited a long time to get baptized. I was nearly 80 years old when I finally did, and I got baptized in the Smith. Believe it or not, when I came out of the water, I thought to myself, "Jesus must be alive, because I don't feel the cold!" Everyone else was freezing, and they didn't even go in the water.

I love the river, but I never was a fisherman. My dad liked to take me fishing, but when I tried, I never caught anything. So I didn't care much for it.

When I think about the beauty of this area, I think of Young's Valley. We camped there a lot, me and the boys. They've closed the road now. The only way to get in is to hike. I could do it in my 70s, but not anymore. Anyway, I've never seen anything more beautiful than Young's Valley.

Yes, I was here for the tsunami in 1964. I came into town early that morning for a cup of coffee. I noticed how strange the town looked. Well, a third of it was destroyed. I could tell something terrible had happened, but I didn't know what it was at the time. I would learn later that day about the tidal wave.

I was here for the Christmas flood later that year, too. I came through town with a truckload of plywood in the morning. It was really storming. The wind was blowing, and there were so many small trees down on the road. There wasn't a freeway then. As you went toward Klamath, and further south, you went through the area that is now the park, you know.

I made it through Klamath that morning. I had to jump out of the truck four or five times to wind a piece of chain around those downed trees to pull them out of the way. I was maybe halfway from the county line to where the town of Orick begins when I came to a huge redwood blocking the road. Well, I couldn't even begin to do anything about that. The wind was howling. The rain was coming down in sheets. I just parked the truck.

It was scary, being in that storm surrounded by giant redwoods twisting and moving in the wind. The cab of my truck was thin. A falling twig could have come through it! For a while, I kinda knelt down in front of a tire—a set of duals, you know. Finally, in the middle of the night, in the dark, here comes Caltrans, some of the bravest guys in the world. They came up there with a big power saw and cut right through that redwood so that traffic could pass. They figured, "That's my job. I'll do it." I've got a lot of respect for them.

The bridge in Klamath had been there when I went over it. By the time I got to the reload in Arcata—they still had the railroad working back then, and that's where I was supposed to drop off my load—it was late, and I was so wore out, I just jumped into the sleeper and fell asleep.

Next morning, Bill, the guy who owned the place, came out and talked to me.

"Jack," he said, "You don't have to be in a hurry to un-tarp that plywood. The bridge went out last night."

Well, Bill invited me back to his house. There was no way to get in and out of where I was. It stormed so bad, they couldn't get a plane in and out of Del Norte, and all the bridges going south were out, too, except for the bridge going in and out of Ferndale.

I ended up staying a week with Bill and his family, over Christmas. They were great to me. His wife took care of me like I was their kid. Washed my clothes. Fed me. Actually, they had a kid who was about eighteen. I was in my thirties, but me and that kid, we buddied up. I bunked with him.

Finally, they put barges across the Klamath River, but even that kinda shook me up, too. Every time the bargeman pulled out of the dock, he would point the barge out like he was going out to the ocean. But he'd gradually put the power on, and we'd get there to the other side. It was a little rough during the landing, too, but that's how we had to do it for quite some time until they rebuilt the bridge.

The community was really impacted by the flood, and not just south of Crescent City. All these little bridges went out between Gasquet and Idyllwild, too. The Army engineers started working right away to fix the roads and put in temporary bridges.

Other big changes I saw here? Well, when they came in and established the Redwood National Park it was a big deal. Eventually, the big sawmills got weeded out. Gosh, there were a lot of jobs before then. Big plywood mills running, two or three of them. Simonson had a huge sawmill up in Smith River. McNamara and Peepe had two sawmills: one here and one in Blue Lake. I worked for them for many years.

What was the cause of the end of the logging industry here? Well, I know on private land they logged quite a lot of the redwoods. But that shouldn't have shut all the mills down. My God, there's hundreds of acres of fir timber in this country on US Forest Service land. They should have had plenty left. I probably have a different view of it than other people around here, but it seems like a waste just to let that timber grow old. About 80% of our land here is public land, government land. There's not much private land left to log. I know that's one of the concerns.

I'm old now and retired, and I don't have to look for a job. But back when I was young, you could find a job. There's very little industry here now, and that's a problem.

Yes, I did survive economically, even during the tough times. At one point, McNamara and Peepe went union, and they were deciding to go on strike for higher wages. About the second meeting, I got back from running a load down south, and I got up and talked against the strike. I said, "You guys are making a mistake. These people who own this company aren't as rich as you think. They're having a hard time."

And they were. It was around 1979.

They booed me at the meeting. I said, "You're making a mistake. Chances are, if you strike, this company is going out of business."

They did go out of business, you know. I was right. I was able to get a job right away with Dutra Trucking. But what makes this story interesting is about twenty years later, I met one of those sawmill workers who was at the meeting that night.

He said to me, "I've often wished I'd listened to you."

I was working for Dutra Trucking when Miller Redwood still had the sawmill. That was my last job, picking up at Miller and hauling redwood up to Merlin, Oregon, where they had a reload station. I retired before Miller-Rellim quit business here. I was 63, I think. I'd driven five million miles in a truck, lots of long hours. I was kind of tired.

Why did Miller-Rellim shut down? They got a new manager up in Forest Grove, Oregon, and he didn't like the mill down here in California. That's why they quit and moved the business out of here. I understand their main operations were up north.

I knew the manager of Miller-Rellim here real well. His name was Charles Howe. My wife Marcheta worked for him at Miller Redwood in the office there for twenty-five years or so. We went to his birthday party up in Portland a little while back. He just passed away, but he lived to be 100.

I don't think I'll make it that far. I'm still cutting my own wood, though. More slowly than I used to, but, you know, I like the feel of wood heat better than kerosene. I'm old fashioned that way, I guess.

What other changes have I noticed? Well, we live out here in Hiouchi, which is not very far away from town, but it's isolated. I think I'm happier here than I would be living in town. I'm not blasting the town, but it seems Hiouchi is more peaceful. There's not as many problems as you have in town. I read in the paper all the little things that happen down there, robberies, and such.

I don't know what's happened to our country. It's changed, and not for the better. You see more people breaking the law. Where I was raised in the Illinois Valley, you pretty much knew everybody. You never heard of people breaking the law. Maybe it's because I hear more news now. There is a lot more information out there, but

I don't know. It seems like crime rates are going up. People don't feel as safe as they used to.

For example, my friends that still live in the Valley say they hate to leave their houses for fear of being robbed. In Cave Junction, there can be three or four businesses broken into each night. I guess the timber industry used to help finance law enforcement. But now it's like there's no law there, in Cave Junction, Selma, and Takilma.

That's why when I go over to mow my 15 acre field near Selma, I take my pistol with me. We've had our cabin there broken into two or three times, and they had to go through a locked gate to do it. The last time, they came up an old logging road and took everything that was worth something out of that cabin. They even took my favorite little Honda generator, which they had to carry out by hand. It weighed about 70 pounds. I wonder how many guys had to pack that out, more than a mile and a half out that road. I figure there had to be three or four of them at least.

I suppose I should be able to think of some positive changes in the community, but they don't come to mind. I guess that has something to do with my politics. If you look at it, about ten to fifteen years ago, California was the $7^{th}$ largest economy in the world. Now it's just about the worst economy in the US, and it is being run by liberals.

I realize we have to have both sides in our nation, but I love being a conservative, and I don't think liberalism has worked out in our state.

We have to have jobs for people. It doesn't help people to just give them a living. We have so many people on welfare here. There's some of them where we have to give them a living; they really do need help. But there's a lot of them who are just smart enough to fool the authorities. That's my opinion.

I'll tell you, I was a Democrat all my life until Jimmy Carter. He was a good man. Don't get me wrong. But he wasn't a good President, and he was a liberal. We had gas lines, high interest rates and inflation. So I voted for Ronald Reagan, and things got better.

He straightened out the oil companies, and we had gas again. The economy improved.

My folks were strong Democrats, and I do believe we had President Roosevelt when we needed him. Harry Truman, the little farm boy from the country, became a great President, too. He was honest. That's what we need today. Honesty.

But I changed to Republican after Carter. Not all our Republican politicians are great, but that's my political philosophy.

You asked about cross-cultural experiences with people from other ethnic groups? My son used to go with a Native American girl, beautiful girl, Bonnie Moorehead. They got along real good. But they broke up for some reason, and he moved back to Portland. Not long afterwards, Bonnie came and stayed with us for a week, and we really liked her. She was a lovely girl. We went to her funeral a little while back at the Shaker Church up there in Smith River. You know, she lived a quality life and went on to help a lot of people.

We had another real close native friend, Fawn Norris. She and her folks used to have Dad's Camp down on the Klamath. Fawn and her husband became good friends of ours. She would say, "Don't call me a Native American. Call me an Indian." She was like Barbara Bush, Grandma Bush, who just died a few days ago. Fawn liked to run things, too, and was a strong character. She was a leader in her tribe. In fact, at one time, her portrait was hanging up in the state capitol.

Yes, there was tension—a lot of tension—between Indians and white folks going back to the early settlement of this country. I've gotten along with Indians really well, but I can tell you there is still a lot of tension between white and brown people here. Some Indians resent the fact that our ancestors drove them off their land, which happened. There's no doubt about it. They have a right to be angry about that.

But they got even with us. They built a lot of casinos, and we give them our money—or at least some people do. I've never been a gambler. I've had to work too hard for my money.

What would I like to see happen here in the next fifty years to leave it in better shape? I don't have the answer to that. I'm sure the natural beauty will be here. I believe that. But if you ask me, it seems like we've got too many people in government. Mostly the federal government, but even in Del Norte County. I'll bet you two-thirds of them are working for the government and doing nothing. I think more of them should be in private enterprise.

I have qualms about education, too. Not in the lower grades. But in colleges. You're supposed to go to college to broaden your minds, but you see college students rioting in the streets these days. I'm just a little truck driver, but I didn't do that. I can't respect that kind of behavior. I think we need some changes in our colleges.

I do have two grandchildren who just graduated, though. Got great educations and good jobs. Little Rupa got a degree in business administration. She got a job right away. Now, her brother Joe didn't go to college. He went to work for TSA in the airport. My gosh, he's only been there three or four years, and he's got a management job already. I'm real proud of him, too.

In fact, I've got nine grandkids, and they're all doing well. That makes me happy. And if my own children are a success—and I think they are—it's all due to my wife, Marcheta. She raised our boys and did a good job. She reminds me of Mrs. Bush, too. Marcheta stayed at home until the kids were in school, and then she went back to work. We had a little old neighbor lady, a real fine woman, who came down to the house about the time the boys came off the bus, and she'd be with them until we got home. She was like a grandma to the kids. A lot of women here worked outside the home, like Marcheta. There were a lot of jobs they could get, too. There was work for almost anybody who was willing to do it.

What can I say? It was a different time. I don't know if things will get better any time soon, but I certainly hope they will.

*—April 18, 2018*

# Charles Schnacker

"Yes, it's hard to make money, and the money's never good
all the time. But it's quiet on the ocean…I like being alone,
or with just a few people. And I like the excitement of seeing
what we're going to pull up. It's a scavenger hunt."

*Charles Schnacker reveals an intense tenacity and love for fishing, one that goes
deeper than profit. But his essay also reveals hidden gems about scarcity and
abundance in Del Norte County.*

I WAS BORN IN NASHVILLE, TENNESSEE, and I grew up in
Idaho—Lewiston, Craigmount, Nez Perce. And then we moved
here in 1984, when I was in grade school. I enrolled in Crescent
Elk. Then I went to Del Norte High but transferred to Sunset High
School because they let me use math classes as my electives, and I
really liked math.

When we first moved out here my mom, my dad, me, my five
brothers, Grandma, three cousins, two aunts and two uncles lived
at Pacific Shores, near Kellogg Beach. We camped out on the dunes
for two months until my dad got a job at Las Palmas Trailer Park.
We lived there for a short time in one of the trailers until we bought
a house on Cooper in the 700 block. It was the first house I remember my family owning.

I liked it here. I grew up fishing. My dad started out beach fishing for smelt at night and for perch during the day. Then he bought
a boat and crabbed. I pretty much did the same thing.

I hated school. I always wanted to be doing something else,
anything. I dropped out in eleventh grade, got my GED, and went
to work at the Castle Rock Fish Plant, which was out on Elk Valley

Road. Now it's just storage buildings. I don't remember the pay—it was okay, I guess, for a young guy—but I knew I didn't want to go to school anymore, and my parents said I could either finish school or get a job. So I got a job.

I worked at the fish plant for about six months. Then my dad bought a boat, and I went to work for him as a deckhand on the *Wide Load*. My dad leased about a hundred crab pots, but I was able to get eleven of my own because at the end of the season, the guy we were leasing them from told us, "Cut the bridals off and toss them."

I asked to keep them, and I fixed them up. I had some pots that, once you set them on the floor, they would collapse. But once you put them in the water, the buoy attached to the pot would hold it up. So that's how I started building and repairing pots during the off season.

Then, in 1997, when I had the opportunity to buy a boat, I bought one. That was the *Smokey*. Business went up and down. Mine was one of the small boats. They always have it harder. They can't haul as much gear or as much product. And they can't stay out for more than a day, while the big boats can be out there a good while and set a thousand pots—and go out much farther. They can hold 80,000-100,000 pounds of crab. In the early 90's there was no pot limit, so they could run as much as they wanted.

To prevent overfishing, in the mid-1990s, the government did a buyout. They bought a lot of the boats that had drag permits. When you drag, you pick up a little bit of everything.

In the buyout, if you sold your boat to the federal government, the drag permit associated with your boat went away. Those boats could no longer fish again commercially. But some fishermen sold their boats to the government, and then turned around and bought another boat, which still had a permit. So they never really got out of the commercial fishing business. They just got better boats and money they didn't have to pay back. I think there's about four boats left in the harbor that still drag.

The *Smokey* was an old boat. It wasn't safe. I fished it for a few years and then took it apart. I cut it up. You can't just leave it in the harbor. Otherwise, you have to keep paying rent there.

My wife had been working at a hardware store called Square Deal. Around the same time, I cut up the *Smokey*, Square Deal went out of business. So we got the travel bug. We went to Michigan to see some of my wife's family. While we were there, I got bored. I got myself a roofing job with a company that works with a specialty shingle. Our team started on a barn, and before we finished it, I was the foreman. We did really well in Michigan—bought a house—but it just wasn't near enough to the ocean.

We came back here when my grandmother passed in 1997.

After we returned to Crescent City, I went back to being a deck hand. But I also found another boat to buy, a boat I renamed the *Smokey II*. It had a crab permit and, until the sale was final, I was able to crab on it for a short time. After the crab permit went back to the original owner to put on his new boat, I used the *Smokey II* to set crab pots for other people and bottom fish. I could haul a hundred pots. They would go with us and show us where they wanted us to put them, and we'd set the pots for them.

Typically, for setting the gear for other people, we charge them per pot. But when you own a boat, you get a percentage of the take. Sometimes you make next to nothing. Sometimes you make a thousand dollars. That's why I worked on a different boat, and my dad and brother ran the *Smokey II* at the same time.

The boat I was working on back then was the *Stormy*. It would be the next boat I bought. I ended up giving the *Smokey II* to the harbor because the dock fees were too high. It wasn't supporting itself, so the Harbor dismantled it.

Then I bought the *Stormy*. That was a crabbing vessel, and I was the skipper. But in 2011, when the tsunami warning came, I had a broken ankle. When everyone drove their boats out to sea to ride out the wave, I couldn't captain the *Stormy*. So I tied it up really well to the dock. Unfortunately, during the tsunami, the whole dock broke up. It sunk along with the dock.

I didn't have insurance. I couldn't afford it. We just weren't making enough as it was to spend the money on it. They pulled the *Stormy* out of the harbor. It was in the paper. Just a hull with wires and cables hanging out. There were a lot of people there to watch it come out of the water, including my son who had been learning to captain her during that season. Al Graves, one of the previous owners, was there to watch too. It was pretty emotional, and I left as they were putting her on the blacktop in the parking lot.

It's a high risk business, and you have to find ways to work in order to make ends meet. Most of the money I made fishing just went right back into whatever boat I owned—replacing the gear or something like that. Pretty much the whole time I was fishing, my wife was supporting most of the household expenses. She did housekeeping, staffed the front desk of a hotel, then got a job with the school district in special education, and then in afterschool care.

Yes, it's hard to make money, and the money's never good all the time. But it's quiet on the ocean. I like that. I like being alone, or with just a few people. And I like the excitement of seeing what we're going to pull up. It's a scavenger hunt. You don't know how it's going to be until you see the pot come out of the water.

Eventually, I bought another boat, the *Red Wing*, but I couldn't get the crab permit from the *Stormy* transferred over. So because I couldn't crab, I started hagfishing. Hagfish are slime eels. They are not nice to look at, and they slime up when they're caught. In fact, whatever eats a hagfish can die from the slime they create. And then the hagfish eats that creature from the inside out. They're nasty.

But you can make good money on them. They're popular in Asian markets. Hagfishing started out pretty good. The problem was getting the fish to market. I sold to a seafood place here in the old brewery building. They shipped them out of here, down to San Francisco, and then to Korea. The money was good. They were paying a good price—until they stopped paying altogether. They basically ripped the fishermen off who were supplying them with fish, and I was one of those fishermen. I trucked the fish for a while, but there wasn't enough money in that. It meant the day that I trucked them was a day I couldn't be out there on the boat. I had to pay rent in the harbor either way. The easiest way to make money is for someone to buy them here, but we just don't have anybody who seems to be able to do that.

I wanted to rent a boat that was bigger than the Red Wing, but I couldn't find one to rent—only to buy. So I bought my last boat, the *Frontier*. I got it for $1000. That's really cheap.

Some boats keep their value for a hundred years. My last boat, the *Frontier*, was 110 years old when I dismantled it. When I took down the mast, I found a silver dollar under it. I knew the guy who'd owned it. His name was Buzzy, an old guy, still around. He had the boat back in the 1930's, and he'd rebuilt it. No one had taken the mast down since him. So I found Buzzy and gave him back his silver dollar.

It is hard to find people who see a future for themselves in fishing. It's hard to get deck hands. Deck hands don't make much money, and after the first month of crabbing, the money dies down, and the work gets harder. The point is, you have to really love the ocean to do this work. And you can't just give up when things go wrong, because they always do.

What's fair and unfair in Del Norte County? I don't know. I don't worry about that stuff. I don't pay much attention to things like that. I don't keep up on the gossip. My wife Denise has that covered.

What keeps me here? Most of my family's here. Most of my brothers, except for two. My oldest brother is a janitor for the school district. Another owns a trucking company, Schnacker's General Hauling. One works at Walmart. The other works at the prison.

Do I plan to stay? Yeah. We bought a house. But I guess if we wanted to go, I could give that to the kids. And if my folks pass away, I'm sure my brothers might move away. We're really here for them. Family is important to us.

I'm pretty much retired now. Every now and then I repair a few pots for people, do an odd job. I weld. I do carpentry. I cut bay leaves for making wreaths. I send the leaves down south. I don't have much of a relationship with the river or the mountains, although I do like to go for drives. For the most part, I'm an ocean guy. And I'm the type of person who likes to be by myself, no matter what I'm doing. One or two people maybe.

That's one thing I like about the ocean. There's only one or two people with me. Yes, I think I could live away from the ocean, but I couldn't live or work in a crowded area. I could never work a factory job.

I'm also the type who never gives up. So if the right boat comes along, I would go back to fishing.

[Charles Schnacker's wife, Denise Doyle-Schnacker, who sat in on the interview, couldn't help chiming in here: "Between the two of us, he's always been the dreamer. No matter what, there's always the next boat."]

*—January 25, 2018*

# Nick Svolos

"For about a month after we moved here, I couldn't
get the theme from *Green Acres* out of my head."

*When Nick Svolos' job in the tech sector "went to India," he and his wife moved
up from Torrance and learned to embrace a whole new lifestyle. Here he describes the benefits—and the trade-offs—his family experienced from the relo-
cation.*

MY FAMILY CAME TO CRESCENT CITY from Torrance, a
suburb of Los Angeles. In January of 2015, my employer, DirecTV,
informed my department that our jobs were going to India. We
had three months to train our replacements and find new jobs
before being terminated on the first of May. The job market was
rough, and I never managed to find a place to land. The months
flew by and on the last Friday in April, I carried out my box of personal property into the parking lot and toward an uncertain future.

My wife and I always shared a common dream, not much more
than a fantasy. "Wouldn't it be nice to move somewhere out of the
way, a place where we could actually own our home free-and-clear,
somewhere green, beautiful and with a slower pace, somewhere
that we could just enjoy our lives?" But, it was just a dream, something we'd joke about over dinner on date night. We never thought
it would actually happen. Months passed, though, bringing nothing more than unemployment checks. We were doing alright for
the moment, but our savings wouldn't hold out forever.

Then, my wife ran across an advertisement for a job. She's a special education teacher, and the Del Norte Unified School District was in the market for someone like her. She filled out the application and sent in her resume. In July, they interviewed her over Skype. In August, they made her an offer. Before she accepted the job, we drove up to get a look at the town. It was a brutal drive, thirteen hours, but the last two made up for the previous eleven. Amazing. Trees. Mountains. Farms. And everything was green! Once you get past Eureka, the ocean joins the party, ladling on its own helping of awesome sauce.

At first glance, Crescent City doesn't look like much. It's a small town, after all, and not particularly wealthy. It isn't until you start meeting the people that you pick up on the differences. The girl working the drive-through window at the fast food joint is *nice*. She's not *pretending* to be nice. She actually is. The barber talks about fishing, not politics. The guys working at the post office are happy to be there. You can get in and out of the DMV without taking a sick day. Plus, it's smack dab in the middle of one of the most beautiful places on Earth.

After two days of getting a feel for the place, we made our decision. It wasn't going to be easy, but we were going to make this happen. My wife signed the employment papers.

I did a hitch in the Navy and travelled the world in my past jobs. I've seen a lot of extraordinary places, but this one takes the cake. It's hard to explain to people back in Los Angeles, or really anyone who's spent their life in an urban environment. There are endless wonders to be experienced out here. Picking wild blackberries as we walk along the country road where we live. Waking up to find elk in your yard. A country fair that's actually fun with a ton of people, and yet it doesn't feel crowded. I have giant coastal redwoods in my yard that might have been saplings when Christ walked the earth. On a clear night, there are more stars in the sky than I'd ever seen outside of the Griffith Park Observatory.

As a life-long urbanite, I had a lot to learn. The things that you become accustomed to aren't there anymore. There's no sewer, so you have to learn how a septic tank works. The water comes from a well, so a crash course in pump maintenance becomes a priority. The trash starts to pile up until you figure out what company comes to haul it away. We weren't getting any mail, and it took a while to find the big communal mailbox a quarter mile down the road. My front yard is over an acre, so I had to learn how to take care of it. A riding mower is a wonderful thing. For about a month, I couldn't get the theme from *Green Acres* out of my head to save my life.

I also learned how isolated we are out here. These mountains are beautiful, but they're also a barrier. While Brookings, Oregon is an easy and pleasant thirty-minute drive, if you need anything out of the ordinary, you have to drive to Medford. That's a two hour drive, the first thirty minutes of which takes place on a winding mountain road that feels like a driver's test crafted by Seal Team Six.

We're isolated in other ways, too. When the Chetco Bar fire hit during the summer of 2017, it burned 190,000 acres and threatened towns from Brookings to Cave Junction. You'd never know it by watching the national news. We don't matter to the rest of the world. That's not necessarily a bad thing, but it takes some getting used to. Here, if there's trouble, you have to deal with it. "Thoughts and prayers" don't put out fires or find homes for evacuees. That's on us. But during this crisis, I saw a community come together in a truly astonishing way. People took strangers into their homes. A local business opened their parking lot to trailers to provide temporary housing to evacuees. Everywhere you looked, people were putting together care packages for our suddenly homeless neighbors.

You can also see the isolation when seeking medical care. There's a severe shortage of doctors in the county. It took me six months to arrange primary care for the family, and I won't be able to see a neurologist until next year. Many people here buy insurance policies that include air ambulances.

My wife and sons are outgoing, gregarious people who fit in with almost any crowd. They haven't had any trouble finding things to get involved with. Me? Not so much. I'm kind of a hermit. I know a few of my neighbors and a few people in town, but most of the time you can find me out at my place, hammering away at a novel or some project around the house.

That's not to say I haven't found this place welcoming. As with anything else, you get out of it what you put in. I towed the Cub Scout float in the Fourth of July parade this summer, an amazing experience I'd have never have the opportunity to do in Torrance. This place loves its community events, and I got to be a part of it.

From a cultural perspective, there are differences. One thing we noticed right off is that "Del Norte Time" moves a lot slower. Sometimes that can be a problem. If you need a specialized service, like getting a lawnmower fixed or a septic tank checked out, it'll take longer than a city-dweller would expect. Even Amazon takes a day or two longer to get a shipment up here. Our eldest son recently joined us in Crescent City. He found a job at the local Taco Bell, but it took over a month to get the paperwork done so he could start working.

On the other hand, if you have a question about your property taxes or a zoning issue, you can get the right person on the phone far easier than anywhere else I've lived. Dealing with the local and county government is a snap. You may not get the answer you want, but at least you can get one.

Racially, Del Norte feels a lot more homogenous than I'm used to. According to the 2016 US Census, Del Norte County has about 28,000 people, and 63% of them are white. Latinos and Hispanics make up about twenty percent and the Tolowa and Yurok Native American nations account for another ten. Considering the lack of jobs around here, I would have thought that might lead to problems due to competition or what-not. So far, I haven't seen anything to indicate underlying friction between the groups. That doesn't mean much, of course. I'm about as white as you can get without vampirism, so maybe I'm just blind to it. That said, the only indication of racial tension I've run across was a piece of pro-antifa "agitprop" artwork on the bulletin board at the college. Even that was gone last time I dropped by.

Personally, I believe people are pretty much the same, regardless of where they are or whose genes they're carrying. When I first moved here, a young Yurok man lived in the house behind mine. He played his music too loud and too late, and had equally loud friends. In that regard, he was pretty indistinguishable from my twenty-six year old son, or for that matter, me when I was that age. He just had a cooler name.

The politics up here are quite different. California as a whole is a bastion of the left, but only because all of the voting power is in the big cities. Here, the script is flipped. While voter registration is almost even, 32% Democrat to 36% Republican, Del Norte County went for Donald Trump in 2016, approximately 54% to 36%. As a conservative libertarian who's lived most of his life in the dense coastal population centers, this will take some getting used to. I'm eager to see how an election year will look around here.

Up here, if there are any divisions, I think they're along economic lines. This is an inexpensive place to live. There are a lot of retirees up here, and they're set up pretty well. They have nice houses, plenty of land if they want it, and the lack of jobs doesn't affect them. For those still in their working years, the lower housing costs help their paychecks go farther. However, the median household income is around $40,000, and the census says 23% of us are under the poverty level. Officially, the unemployment rate in Del Norte is 5.8%, but in a county of 28,000 people, the state's estimation of our labor force is in the neighborhood of ten thousand workers. There are a lot of people who aren't being counted in the unemployment rate. People who have given up.

Jobs around here in Crescent City aren't exactly plentiful. Speaking as a guy who's still in his rookie year in these parts, this is what I see:

Pelican Bay State Prison is a major employer. It's the only "Supermax" facility in the state, and it houses the worst of the worst. It takes a special kind of person to stand up to that sort of stress. Definitely not for the faint at heart, but they always seem to be hiring.

Looking at the employment ads in the newspaper, there are a lot of jobs for people in medicine. From lab techs, physician assistants and elder care specialists up to the highest professional levels, it looks like there are no shortage of opportunities.

The retail, foodservice, and hospitality industries seem to be fully-staffed. Occasionally I'll see an ad, but the feeling I get is there are people lined up for those jobs when they open up.

There are a couple of casinos here, run by the Native American Nations, and they always have a help wanted ad in the paper. In addition to casino workers, they seem to be on the lookout for people with specific skills to assist their people. Social workers are frequently sought.

There is lots of work for skilled tradesmen, but breaking into those fields is a challenge. As with elsewhere, it helps to know somebody, although if a person has the entrepreneurial chops, the barrier to entry is low, and there's plenty of need. Often, the best way to get a job is to create your own.

There's a lot of poverty here, and the financial stability of the families here seems to differ from door to door. For instance, in one home you'll have a family living hand to mouth. Perhaps they only have their home due to an inheritance, but they don't have the means to maintain it. Driving by, you see a ramshackle house standing on unkempt land. Yet, the next house over you find a vacation home or a retiree with a nice house and beautiful lawn.

There's a real disadvantage to growing up poor, surrounded by people who made it in life. But without personal examples in your life of how to achieve success, you can lose hope, and that's a soul-killer. To keep that hope alive, people have to believe, no matter what, that they can improve their situation. They need ambition. For those who have it, the answer is to get out into the world, to get an education and find their job opportunities elsewhere. The secret of America's success is the mobility of its citizens, the ability to go where the jobs are, to follow their dreams wherever they may take them. I see too many kids here at the age where they should pull the trigger and go, but they don't. I don't know why. Far too many young people here succumb to a sense of hopelessness and fall into crime and drugs.

It's possible to make it here. My barber is a former soldier, a young man in his twenties who came out of the Army with the skills to operate heavy construction equipment. When he came home he couldn't find a job anywhere. Rather than surrender to despair, he went to school, got his barber license and started his own shop. But he's a rarity.

Some folks get trapped by their own sense of defeat, and the culture here doesn't do much to support a change in their thinking. For instance, I haven't seen much in the way of job mentorship or small business training programs since I've been up here. A Google search only shows one such organization and I wouldn't have even known it existed if I hadn't just looked it up. For kids in generational poverty, it seems programs like these could change their lives. For a community with so many retired people with experience to share, it's odd they aren't being utilized.

I haven't been impressed by the schools up here, although my experience is limited to the elementary school my youngest son attends. Torrance had such high performing schools, so I might be spoiled, but I've noticed a huge difference. In Torrance, our boy almost always had homework. I'm not seeing a lot of that here. He learned fractions the year before we moved up here, but they hadn't started fractions in his grade when we arrived. I know he'll be fine. His mother's a teacher, and we both value education. We'll homeschool him if we have to. But, there are kids here who aren't getting those skills, and that's the sort of thing that needs to start early. You can't allow them to get left behind in the early years and expect them to catch up later. It feels like we're a year behind in elementary education.

All of that being said, after experiencing the lows and the highs, my family is grateful for the chance to make this drastic change in our lives and become part of this community. Some friends from Long Beach drove up this summer to visit and check out the eclipse. Like us, they fell in love with this quiet, spectacular place.

I wouldn't be surprised to see them make the move up here in a few years. For our part, we're happy to be here and wonder why we didn't do it sooner.

We love it here, and we're not going anywhere.

*—October 12, 2017*

# Teresa Iribarne

"I don't know what it is like here, but you know, in Bakersfield,
you gotta keep your kids plugged into this stuff [organized activities].
Otherwise, they can be roaming the streets and joining gangs and
mixing up with people you don't want them to mix with."

*Although Teresa Iribarne appreciates the beauty and quite of Del Norte County,
she acknowledges that raising her grandchild here comes with serious challenges.*

I was born and raised in Bakersfield, California.
We moved to the coast, to Pismo, when I was a teenager. I got
married at 21, and between Bakersfield and Pismo, I was there for
about 23 years. Then my first husband walked away. I went to visit
my mom in Arkansas for a while, and then my cousins in Oklahoma. When I went back to Bakersfield, I fell in love with my childhood sweetheart, and we got married.

I knew then that I wanted out of Bakersfield, and I told my husband about a lovely little place called Crescent City which I'd visited several times when I was younger. The scenery—the forests
and the beaches—and the closeness to Oregon. It was quiet and
serene. My husband said, "Jump, Honey, let's go!" And we did. That
was 2014.

I'd gotten a job with the California Prison Industry Authority. I
trained inmates to clean the facilities to OSHA standards. I knew
it was just a term job for two years, but it was a foot in the door. I
liked it.

But I am a Jack of All Trades. So when my term was up, I moved on to different work. I now work for North Coast Children's Services (NCCS) doing childcare. In Bakersfield, I did something similar with special needs kids, so I had lots of experience. Here, I work as a substitute at several different locations.

I got the job when I was looking for childcare for my grandson. I have custody of him, and he's four. I was talking to a parent at the Fred Endert pool while our kids were swimming. She worked for NCCS, and she helped me get my grandson into the program, *and* she helped me get a job as a substitute.

Now I'm not just working as a sub there, I'm also taking classes at the College of the Redwoods towards an Early Childhood Education certificate. I'd been grandfathered in as a child care worker in Bakersfield, but here, even subs need to get their twelve units.

The financial aid helps a lot, and that's part of my motivation. Right before my husband and I got married, he was in a motorcycle accident and is now disabled. He had never been unemployed until that time, but after that, my income was the only support we had until he was officially deemed disabled.

You get a year of disability from the state, and then you have to go through a whole process to get federal support. The doctors have to deem you unable to work, and that took time. For my husband, it was hard. He'd worked two jobs for almost 15 years before we got together. He was not used to having somebody take care of him. It was a real adjustment.

And at my job at NCCS, for a while, I barely got 40 hours a *month* because it's a sub job. So the financial aid helps a lot. The more classes I take, the bigger stipend I get. And it means I don't have to work two or three jobs. So I'm not just taking credits towards an Early Childhood Education certificate. I'm going for my AA degree. Lately, I've been working steady the three free days I have where I don't have to be in school. That's been hard, but it will pay off in the end.

Despite having to work and go to school at the same time, our experience in Del Norte County has been quiet and serene. We like to go to the beach when we can. My husband is thinking about getting a fishing license and doing some fishing. We've been to Trees of Mystery—a place I'd gone as a girl—and Ocean World. Plus we've done a lot of traveling with the grandbaby. He loves trains, so we've gone to Garibaldi, Oregon for the train ride there, to Portland, Oregon and then Multnomah Falls, to the coast to the Sea Lion Caves, and to Seattle. We'd like to be able to do more, but with my schedule right now, it is hard. But we're hopeful.

I asked my husband if he was interested in going back to school, but the only thing he'd be interested in would be a chef's job or a counselor for sober living. In the meantime, he's kept busy with a lot of Honey-Do's. He's the project man around the house, and he's found all kinds of driftwood on the beach. He goes for a walk after dropping the baby off at preschool, and he brings this stuff back. He wants to start doing crafts with it. We were blessed recently with a little windfall, and he's been able to buy the tools that he needs. So he's thinking about that.

As far as feeling like we belong here, it's been hard. We feel comfortable; we feel at home in the area. But we don't know a lot of people still. We've made acquaintances from work and school, but not many. And we've had a hard time finding what we consider a family church. There's a lot of churches in the area, but not really what we're looking for: a family church is a place where people embrace you and who are there for you at a time of crisis. They greet you when you come in—not just on the first day but each time. They ask you out to lunch and offer to minister more to you. They invite you over to their house. I had a home church like that in Bakersfield.

Here, maybe it's just because it's a small community, but it's different. They will greet you the first day. The second time or the third time, only a few people greet you. The rest just go off and talk among themselves. I'm not saying that everyone should be inviting us over to dinner, but it doesn't seem as friendly. It's like everyone already has friends. They don't need more. I'm used to—"Oh, we're having an event tonight. Why don't you come with us? You have six kids? No problem! We've got room. Bring them along!"

Also, some of them—well, we're not used to that style of preaching. They seem like they're in love with themselves and they want to talk about their lives instead of the word of God. Some of them make it all about them instead of their flock. Even though Bakersfield was a huge place, it seemed homier. Here, it's like you're invisible. Anybody new isn't fully part of the family. They don't embrace new people enough.

You don't have the sense of abundance here, either. Bakersfield had over 500,000 people. There were Walmarts on each side of town and Taco Bells and McDonald's restaurants—everywhere. You only have one of each here. In Bakersfield, there's were so many choices for good restaurants, too. But not here. If we want something good to eat, we go to Oregon.

And for my grandson, finding children's activities is very difficult. I've learned about events too late, especially sign-ups for sports teams. When I call, they tell me they've already taken registration. They're full. They can't help me. That's all you get from them. And I don't listen to the radio station where they advertise. On Kings Valley Road, we don't get good reception anyway. So we missed out on soccer, T-ball, basketball. I did call in time for soccer to see if I could pay the fee a week late because I couldn't make the deadline for the fee. I left a message. They never returned my call.

It's sort of like at church. You don't get the sense that they really want you.

I don't read the newspaper, so I do miss out finding about things sometimes. But I think there's too much bad news in the paper, and I don't want to waste my money on bad news. I like my Christian K-LOVE or my CDs in the car. I'm also not on Facebook much, either. I'd rather spend time with my husband and my 4-year old than read about all that drama. The school sites actually tell you a lot about what's going on, and the Home Depot kids' corner every month—we've got that one licked. And now I know about the Family Resource Center, a place where you can take your kid to play. They have a lot of handouts, too.

Not knowing about kids' activities is partly my fault. But I am working and going to school while parenting my grandson, so I don't have a lot of free time to find out about things. And I also don't know what I'm supposed to be finding out about. It's a challenge. This place isn't made for newcomers. Give me just one resource building and one handout that tells me everything that's going on. Plain and simple.

But the other part is that there isn't a lot going on. Where is Little Tykes basketball? Where is Tiger Cubs? I don't see any of that here. I got Girl Scout Cookies when I was at the prison. I don't see them any time other than when they're selling. Now I did see a Boy Scout the other day, and I did support him. But I see more information for Relay for Life than I see for any activity for kids.

I don't know what it is like here, but you know, in Bakersfield, you gotta keep your kids plugged into this stuff. Otherwise, they can be roaming the streets and joining gangs and mixing up with people you don't want them to mix with.

If it wasn't for some of our personal views on Cub Scouts, I would have signed him up already. Boys need to learn how to be men, and girls need to learn how to be women. They need the basic fundamentals of their gender—to do those things together as a group. That isn't guaranteed anymore in Cub Scouts, and it makes me uncomfortable.

I made sure when my kids were growing up that they had all these experiences. I was a Girl Scout all the way up to Squaw. And my boys were Tiger Cubs and Cub Scouts and Boy Scouts. They went camping and made go carts and all that. I was a den mother. And they did all the sports. They started at four years old with YMCA flag football. They grew up doing it all. Soccer, baseball, basketball, track, football. I didn't just drop them off at practice, either. I was the mom who stayed and watched. And I was the one who went to pick up their trophies and helped with the end-of-the-year party.

I want to do all that for my grandson. I just don't see that opportunity here yet.

—*October 19, 2017*

# Kent Burrow

"People say there's not a lot of opportunity—
but that's not thinking outside the box."

*Kent Burrow ran a ranch for troubled boys until recently when the Del Norte County Board of Supervisors shut it down. In this piece, written less than six months after losing his job, he reflects on the rise and fall of local institutions and what it takes to be successful in a place where resources and opportunities come and go without warning.*

I WAS BORN IN MARTINEZ, CALIFORNIA, and I was raised in Concord. That's the East Bay area. I did a lot of bouncing around. After a stint in the Navy, I moved to Texas for a while. That's where I met and married my first wife, and we had our first child, Angela.

In Texas, I was a consultant for a moving company. Later, I was recruited to do sales for a company in San Jose, California. Because I had good friends in Del Norte County, we found ourselves coming up here a lot to visit.

In San Jose, we had Angela in a private school. The company, Nike, was coming in. Demographics were changing. It was all about keeping up with the Joneses. We started asking ourselves, "Do we really want to raise our kids in this place, or do we want to simplify?" We were young enough—we had a few bucks in the bank—so we took the risk and moved up here in 1987.

I worked in moving and storage for a while. It didn't go well. I came from a big company mindset, and I had—let's say—a different approach to business. Also, I was pretty vocal about it. My personality: well, I speak my mind. So we agreed to part ways.

That was a scary time for me and my small family. It was a real risk. But I found a way to make money. I had a pickup truck, and I started selling firewood. It's funny because before I moved up here, I didn't know how to split a log. But I learned.

I did lots of different work. I did maintenance at our church, the Methodist Church in Smith River. And I helped unload boats at the harbor—a lot of the Evanow boats. Through being familiar with operations at the harbor, I was offered a job on the fishing vessel *Willolla*. We caught deep water fish, cods, and shrimp—until the bottom fell out of the fishing market in 1990, 1991. I couldn't afford to fish after that.

But I loved fishing. And one of the things that endeared me to Del Norte County happened while I was working on a fishing boat. I was on wheel watch one night. My skipper, Buddy, asked me to wake him up when we got to the area where the boat always got hung up, so he could help me. I was using the plotter—basically a screen with little lines on it—and I wanted to see if I could get around that spot without hanging up. And I did it. I plotted around the place.

Buddy gets up a while later and asks me why I didn't wake him.

"We never got hung up," I say.

He can't believe it. Fishermen around here share information, you know, and Buddy tells me that no one has ever successfully plotted around that place before. And we had an amazing catch that next day—just spectacular. From then on, Buddy jokingly referred to the place I plotted around as the "Burrow Bypass." Fishermen call it that today. My bragging rights? I have thirteen miles of ocean floor named after me.

This is kind of a silly way to feel connected to our area, but I do. I really believe Del Norte County is an area where you have a lot at your disposal, but nobody's going to give it to you. If you want it, you have to go out there and grab it.

People say there's not a lot of opportunity—but that's not thinking outside the box. And that's one of my biggest complaints about this area, and especially our county politics. There was a comparison study done here to see what we as a community needed to do to improve our tourist economy. They studied Newport, Oregon, which has a similar climate and economic situation but has done so much to develop its economy. They have a boardwalk and lots of shops. It's a thriving tourist destination now.

I don't know if it's infighting or what, but nobody here says, "Let's just do this thing!"

In my experience, the county is always out of money according to the budget, and yet it has the lowest paid county employees in the entire state of California. There's something broken here, and I think the broken part is that we're too afraid to take chances to improve what we already have at our disposal. We're too afraid to have the vision to change the way we do things. To take risks. I have always felt this has not served the hard working and dedicated folks of Del Norte well. If it's broke, fix it.

Of course, this criticism is a big part of why we lost Bar-O-Boys Ranch, which I'll talk about in a minute.

First, I should explain that when the fishing industry tanked, I went back to firewood and maintenance. And just when my first wife and I were wondering if it was time to make a decision— should we stay in Del Norte County, or should we go—I was invited to apply for a job at Bar-O-Boys Ranch, the County's juvenile correction facility.

A friend from church had seen me working with youth at our church, and he encouraged me to apply at Bar-O. It took a while for them to bring me on, but I got hired in a part-time position first. Boy, I grabbed that chance! The way I cut my teeth was that I'd call the Director, Al Smith, whenever I wasn't scheduled. He let me come there to cut firewood, so I got a lot more hours that way and earned a reputation as a hard worker. Plus, it was good for the ranch. It was heated with wood and they had a lot of timber.

Eventually, when a full-time position came open, I got it. The rest is history. That was back in 1992. I became Director in 2009.

At Bar-O-Boys, we practiced that "thinking outside the box" I was talking about earlier. We taught kids valuable skills that gave them a sense of self. We did evidenced-based programming, including cognitive-based group work where kids could make real connections and do some real work to see where things went wrong in their lives. We did family unification where we wouldn't let the kids talk from a victim standpoint, but from a behavioral standpoint. We taught the baby steps to problem-solving.

Taking pride in work was a big part of what we taught at the ranch. The kids learned a sense of accomplishment by doing all kinds of different work and learning many different skills. But we had to think outside the box to get them there. For example, when I saw that the US Forest Service was putting on a fire-training academy at the College of the Redwoods, I saw an opportunity.

I asked the director at the time, "Can I take some boys to the college with me?"

We all got our Wildland Fire Behavior certifications. And eventually, we did the academy up at Bar-O twice a year. They got all these valuable skills. I'm proud of that.

Later on, I started getting involved with the Office of Emergency Services. Cindy Henderson was reluctant to partner at first, but we started small. I got the kids involved in CERT (Community Emergency Response Team). Well, that turned into First Responder classes and then, at the pool, lifeguard classes. One of my kids became an EMT through us. He's working as one now in Contra Costa County, where he came from. When he arrived, he never in his wildest dreams felt like he had anything to offer. But look at him now.

You asked what we had to offer at Bar-O? I still feel like I have much to offer. It's rough, I'll be honest. Its closure in 2017 by the County Board of Supervisors destroyed so much good work and closed a wonderful facility that was often referred to as Del-Norte County's "hidden gem."

A lot of factors were involved. The new leadership in the Probation Department didn't trust Bar-O-Boys' leadership. Changing sentences in marijuana laws meant most kids just got a slap on the wrist. We had fewer boys coming in from out of county—and we relied on them to be sustainable. And the closure—well, it was a hit job. Most of our boys—95% of them—came from out of county. And word got out that we might be closing, so we lost so many referrals due to this unnecessary message being out there, although the new leadership was cautioned to never show our hand. It was inexperience and lack of trust from the new leadership that ultimately was a major contributor to the closure of the ranch.

I wish more kids had been sent to us from Del Norte County because they really could have benefited. The judge here generally sent kids out of county or to Juvenile Hall, which was a warehouse for kids, whereas we had a real, therapeutic program. Bar-O truly made a positive difference in young men's lives.

My passion was one thing and one thing only: looking out for the ranch. So it got very ugly in the end, and I had limited power and resources to keep it alive. The reality is that the ranch was losing money—albeit for reasons that never should have happened—reasons that are connected to the way our community operates. They don't invest in the "outside the box" thinking. They don't have a big vision. They aren't willing to take risks.

I've retired five years before I should have. And I'm really grieving the loss of Bar-O-Boys Ranch like a death. It really is hard.

I still live at the ranch. I'm the caretaker. But it's gone. The sound of the dinner bell. The sound of kids. It's still and silent now.

When I witnessed the activity after the ranch closed, it felt as if it were looted. People came in from the department and just took what they wanted. And they left messes. That spoke volumes about how some people felt about the ranch. And I—who was once jokingly referred to as the Mayor of Bar-O—became voiceless.

But I'm working on all kinds of opportunities for myself. Like I said earlier, Del Norte County is a place full of opportunities. I have a lot of interest in Wildland Firefighting and the support services it requires. So I met with some shot-callers with the US Forest Service a little while ago. Had them over to dinner. Asked a lot of questions. And I'm planning on working in that field as a contractor, providing greywater disposal services.

The key to being successful in our community is having the energy and capacity to see what needs to be done. It means talking to people, asking a lot of questions, and taking some risks.

Why aren't more people successful here? Here's what my experience tells me: Today's workforce has changed dramatically. There's no sense of ownership or belonging—dedication—a desire to work for and contribute to a team. When I was working, I hated to take sick leave. I had a sense that I didn't want to let down my co-workers. I don't see that much anymore.

I noticed, hiring for Bar-O in the later years, I didn't get much when I asked applicants questions about their skills, about what they could bring to the boys. Did they play musical instruments? Could they fix an engine? Do carpentry? They would say that they understood computers. But not much else.

I don't know if this is because in schools, auto shops are turning into media centers, but something is missing.

People in the workforce seem to want gratification right now—they get frustrated if they're not getting it from their work the first few months. They start looking for something else. I found myself having to teach my new staff about work ethics while I was teaching my boys.

Our community also suffers from a lack of professional services, especially where our kids are concerned, including mental health services here. At Bar-O, I had to send kids to see psychiatrists using a program like Skype—they met their shrinks on the big screen. It was too sterile. There was no draw for them to fully participate, so it wasn't effective. The same was true for medical and dental services. Any major surgery had to be done out of town, in Medford, Oregon or in Eureka, California. These issues are true for all Del Norte's kids—and adults for that matter.

So what keeps me here? I love this area. I'm in love with the river. It holds a lot of great memories for me.

I love the culture here. I've learned a lot about Native Americans living here that changed some of my perceptions. We often had local native kids sent up to the ranch. And we had a dress code. Hair was supposed to be short. And then one kid came in with a court order to not have his hair cut.

"How in the world did you pull that off?" I asked.

I learned how hair is a connection to the earth, the mother. I don't know if I was absent that day in school, but I finally got it, working at the Ranch. And it was cool, to learn about native beliefs. This goes back to thinking outside the box, too, because the kids would tell me about how they would do sweats in a sweat lodge. So we built a sweat lodge at Bar-O. And the other kids who weren't native got to experience it, too.

So what keeps me here is the beauty, the culture, my wife Becky, and my family. I'm in love with my grandkids and my kids, and I'm fortunate to have many of them here with me in an area where I love to live—and the rest aren't far away.

*—January 24, 2018*

# Hanna Hoener

"We are embracing the fact that our traditional industries are
going away, and there seems to be a new hope of coming together,
pulling in the same direction: tourism and economic development.
Many people have been working in this direction for years,
like my dad, but now there seems to be a critical mass."

*On Highway 101, just north of Klamath, travelers are greeted by a huge statue
of Paul Bunyan towering nearly fifty feet in the air. Flanking him is an equally
imposing thirty-five foot blue ox. Heir apparent to this piece of Americanna,
Hanna Hoener describes her youth in Klamath, her return to the family business, and her hopes for the revitalization of her community.*

I WAS BORN IN HUMBOLDT COUNTY, at Mad River Hospi-
tal, in 1983, and I lived in Klamath until I was fourteen. My parents
divorced when I was seven years old. My mom was a teacher at
Margaret Keating, and Dad worked in the family business running
Trees of Mystery.

I went to Margaret Keating, and then Four Square, and then
Crescent Elk. I have really good memories of school. I especially
loved Crescent Elk, though it was a lot of waiting around at the
bus stop in Klamath. We took the high school bus very early in the
morning. I was always carsick as a child—I would even get it going
to the Glen—but eventually I got used to it.

I remember a couple fights at Crescent Elk, but it was usually
within the different cliques. We had an Asian group—they were
recent Hmong immigrants but also other folks, too. We had what
some of us called the "Mexican Mafia," but really, we could talk to

133

each other. It didn't feel segregated to me.

I have vivid memories of cultural events and sharing related to helping us get along. We did a lot of that in Language Arts. We had this mediation group which I was a part of. I remember we had an all-day training for that. So, there must have been something going on that school officials were trying to address. But I don't know if it was bullying—stronger kids picking on weaker ones. It seemed that the conflicts were more interpersonal: "You kissed my boyfriend" or "You stole my weed" so "I'm going to punch you now."

Yes, there was a drug culture. Lots of kids smoked weed. The boy who was my first French kiss was actually arrested for dealing later on. He and his friend smoked on the playground sometimes, but not all the time. It was pretty normal.

In 1997, I moved with my mom to Kentucky where she went to seminary. I lived there for seven years, graduated high school, and started my adult life in Lexington. After a few years, I decided I should go to college, and I wanted to come back home to be closer to my dad. I chose Southern Oregon University because I love Ashland and it's an easy college to get into (Go Raiders!).

I met Kylan, my future husband at SOU. Both of us came here during the summer to work at Trees of Mystery, which our family owns. I ran the cash register, and served food, and learned a lot of the on-the-ground work. I got to spend time with my dad, John Thompson, and grandma, Marylee Smith. I came to the conclusion that I would probably never live here full-time again. I was quite certain that this was not my future, but I enjoyed being with my family.

Kylan and I got married in 2010 in the Rogue Valley. Kylan was doing an MS program in optical physics that involved an internship in Vancouver, Washington, so we moved to Portland and started our life there. I went to work for Intel. I loved it. I had a successful career ahead of me.

Grandma passed away in 2015. It was sad but a beautiful thing. She was almost 94. We were all there, the whole family. Max, my first son, was born. It was a peaceful time, and a time to reflect on our family. We're all fairly spread out. In every family business you're spread out. There is distance because you're working together. You have to negotiate a professional life and personal life. So the passing of my Grandma was a healing time.

That December, our little family went to visit my dad and his wife, Debbie, in Florida, where they winter. On the way to the airport to leave, Dad, Kylan, and I had the first real conversation about the future of the business, which he owned.

A little history of the Trees of Mystery: In 1946, Grandma and Papa Ray Thompson moved here to Klamath. Papa Ray's parents helped to pay for the property, and they learned the business. They were here about twenty years before they divorced. They had three children—one of them was my dad, John. When they split up, Grandma was the owner. Of their three children, Dad, his older brother, and sister all worked here. Yes, Trees of Mystery was run by a single mother. She was one of a kind.

My grandmother was actually married three times. Her second husband was a lovely man. He passed away suddenly during a trip up the Oregon Coast. They'd only been married a year, and it was a difficult time for Grandma. They were very much in love.

Later in life, she met Earl Smith. He was a Southern gentleman. They got married and Grandma called him the love of her life. They traveled, and he was a part of the business until he passed away. She was a pioneer, involved in many organizations. She was part of the Redwood Empire, a group promoting tourism. She had vision. She knew Highway 101 was our community's lifeline. A lot of people don't know that our county used to be much more involved in a bigger vision for our state. That's why I believe in our county, too.

While she grew this business, the children left. Their lives took them different directions. Dad ended up coming back. Debbie, his wife, has a real passion for this business, too.

So, in the car on the way to the airport, I asked Dad what the plan was. We'd never really had that conversation. But this time he said that he really would like us to come and learn to run it.

Kylan and I spent several months talking about how this could possibly work. We loved Portland. I loved my work with Intel, and Kylan loved his job. It was a very hard decision. We knew it would be surreal. We'd be living in Grandma's house. We'd be surrounded by all this history. Plus, there are so many moving parts to the work, and very little infrastructure in the county to support us. The labor pool would be a challenge, as there are not many people here. The educational statistics were not good, either. I looked at the test scores for Margaret Keating, and I was concerned about where Max ought to learn. I had one boy at the time—we have another, now—and I knew I wouldn't want to homeschool. Bless those families that do, but that wasn't going to be something I would be good at. Plus, I'd have a business to run.

We had a support system in Portland. Many of our neighbors and friends were starting to have kids, too. And there was cultural diversity. Coming here would mean leaving all of that.

But then there's the ocean…and that's home, and there's the redwoods…and that's home, and there's this important fourth-generation business that could peter out or go corporate unless we said yes. Trees of Mystery is a really important piece of history: a piece of Americana that has stayed true to its roots and been able to step forward to the future. We touch so many families' lives. Most of our business is repeat families made up of parents, bringing their kids, pushing them onto Paul Bunyan's boot for a picture because they got a picture and their grandparents got a picture. We joke and say that we're the Disneyland of the Pacific Northwest, but we are an important part of the culture here.

Ultimately, we asked ourselves, "Are we really going to stay in Portland and, when we take the 101, drive past the Trees of Mystery and say, 'Oh, look, kids! Our family used to own that'?" How sad would that be? I didn't think I could do that. So, we decided to move here.

I am excited, and I have a lot of hope and expectation for this area. Some of my peers who grew up here are also coming back. They came back, like me, because they see the value of this place.

They see the love. They see the beauty and the potential. I hate saying "potential" because that makes it sound like Del Norte County is not worthy yet, but it's the next generation's job to look to the future. We must move forward. We must grow. I know that there's been a depression here; there was a recession in the entire country that hit Del Norte County a little later than other places in the nation. But I would say we're coming out of the fog and the grief. Although many of our industries are no longer here, that's been a long, long process coming to that understanding. The impact of timber going away and of subsidies going away has been hard. It was hard all over the northwest. But Del Norte County is at a pivotal place. Timber is gone. Fishing is going. This is the time when we need to look at sustainability. What do we want this place to look like in the future?

I am heartened people are getting the vision for tourism. There's definitely a divide in this community, where there are people who don't want a lot of vacation homes here and don't want a lot of people gawking at their beaches. I think that's a legitimate fear. As an example, Cannon Beach, Oregon went a route where they built a boardwalk, and an arcade, and a giant timeshare hotel right on the beach. Yes, that's one way to go. And you can compare that with other towns nearby, like Seaside, Oregon, which went another direction: less developed—less of the entertainment route—but still embracing places tourists enjoy, like breweries and restaurants.

There's something about this place.

We are embracing the fact that our traditional industries are going away, and there seems to be a new hope of coming together, pulling in the same direction: tourism and economic development. Many people have been working in this direction for years, like my dad, but now there seems to be a critical mass. I think there's definitely a forward motion in this community right now.

Because there are so few people here, and we are in a spread-out area with different communities trying to take care of themselves, we are not always looking to the larger community. That's the part that troubles me. The political infighting that's happening is so incredibly disruptive for moving forward. It really frustrates me, for example, when we bring national politics into our discussions. That has to be my number one trouble when I think of local politics.

An example of that is the Crescent City / Del Norte County Chamber of Commerce. There's only one other chamber in our county, and that is the Klamath Chamber of Commerce. Now that alone is very telling. Why does Klamath have a Chamber and not any of these other communities? And why does the Del Norte Chamber of Commerce focus on Crescent City? Now, Crescent City should be a major focal point, but this whole county is a tourism destination, and we have to start focusing on that. People need a reason to stay and explore the whole county.

This is such a small area. I could literally talk to every single person in this area. I just don't understand how this political polarization happens in such a small place, and why we can't more effectively build unity, but we also need to look at what we are doing right. That's the way I live my life. I am always wanting to improve. I am always a work in progress. Unity makes us more powerful, and we need more power, for several reasons. For example, we are completely surrounded by Redwood National and State Parks. So how does that affect us? The positive is that the land around us is preserved for future generations. The National Park has protected the redwoods since 1968. But they have not completely held up their part of the bargain. They haven't invested enough in the park to attract and retain visitors. One of the biggest complaints of tourists coming through is, "Where is the National Park?" There isn't excellent signage and there isn't a central location. That hurts us as a community because we end up drawing up maps to explain to people where the park is.

But I do completely believe in the National Park system. The heart of this family business has always been about the redwoods, a species of tree that has lasted millions of years. Protecting redwoods is what Trees of Mystery is all about. We offer a place where you can take your dog on the trail. Your grandmother can walk and not slip on our paths. We have an old-timey look that I think is fun and interesting, this whole 1930s Ripley's Believe-It-Or-Not style.

We've also done some new things, including an interpretive trail about the biology of redwoods. You know, redwoods grow again after you cut them down. I think redwoods are a good representation of our county, actually. This is a place where people have endured tragedy. We have native tribes who were living their lives and then Gold Fever came up the river. They were massacred by newcomers. Their land was taken. We've had fish wars, and water wars, and agricultural wars over people's right to survive. People died because of these struggles. You have people on all sides who fought, and settled, stayed, and made a life for themselves here for better or worse, and sometimes it was worse. We had a tsunami, and a flood, and the loss of the very industries that brought so many people here. Yet we are still here. We endure, like the redwoods. We're resilient. All of us. And we are going into a new chapter, and hopefully, we'll do it together, like a redwood that keeps growing from a stump.

*—February 6, 2018*

# Tara Dettmar

"I am actually one of those people who measures—scientifically—the Smith's visibility, its clarity—as data points. I'm one of the people who does describe what is indescribable."

*Tara Dettmar is a young fisheries biologist who fell in love with the Smith River. In this interview, she tries to put words to the beauty she sees everyday on the job. She also wonders how long her love affair with Del Norte can last. How can she afford to stay in a place where the work she does is seasonal and sporadic?*

I GREW UP IN NORTH FLORIDA along the Atlantic coast in a small town on a barrier island just next to the Georgia border. All while growing up, I knew I wouldn't be there forever.

I was "California dreaming" at an early age, but I hadn't quite worked out the details of how I might get here. I went to school in Asheville, North Carolina, and that was a welcome change, but after college I started exploring different career paths through seasonal jobs. I made my way through about ten states, inching west. I liked a lot of those places, but nothing stuck. Nothing felt like home.

In 2010, I made it to Happy Camp. Oddly enough, it was one of the first times I felt a sense of belonging to a place. Happy Camp was weird and small and rural, and I could have stayed forever.

I traveled all around the region when I lived there, and on a couple occasions came up from Greyback to camp and swim in the Smith River. I also came to the Smith when I participated in the "dive circuit," doing Watershed Steward snorkel surveys. Coming in on Highway 199, driving up South Fork Road, and getting to Rock Creek Ranch—it was mind-blowingly gorgeous. To this day, Rock Creek Ranch is one of the most beautiful places I've ever been.

While I was there, a friend of mine mentioned her supervisor in Arcata was hoping to have a fisheries monitoring project on the Smith someday. Without a second thought, I told her to let me know when that day came.

And that day did come. In 2011, I was living up in this canyon in Eastern Washington. There was no cell service, and I was an hour's drive from the nearest gas station. So one day when I ventured down the canyon to connect with the outside world, my phone got service and started dinging with voicemails and texts and e-mails—all from my friend. The job was announced, and I needed to apply. I moved in the fall of 2011 and the rest is history.

I've never seen a river that looks anything like the Smith. It is one of the most beautiful, crystal clear, clean rivers I've ever seen. To the south in Del Norte County, the Klamath is big, but it's not a river you want to spend a lot of time in. In the summer, it's hot and brown, sometimes it's not even safe to touch because of toxic algae blooms. It does have lots of beautiful tributaries that run off the other side of the South Fork, but even those tributaries don't give me the feeling of awe I get looking at the Smith.

To get to the Smith, you travel along the rugged Pacific Coast, with the mountains visible in the distance. You follow winding roads through ancient redwoods—it's pure magic. And because it's not the easiest place to get to, you know you're experiencing something that most people will never even know exists—never get the chance to experience.

For me, the beauty of Del Norte all comes back to the river. To be in it—snorkeling—to have a fish-eye view in crystal clear water, it's *indescribable*. But I am actually one of those people who measures—scientifically—the Smith's visibility, its clarity—as data points. I'm one of the people who *does* describe what is indescribable.

For this measurement, most protocols involve a Secchi disk, a little round disk about 8 inches in diameter with quadrants of alternating black and white. You lower the disk into the water and when you can no longer see it, that distance is your measurement. But in the Smith, we don't *use* the disk. It's pointless. For our datasheets we usually write a code that indicates we can see the disc at *any* distance. It rings true with almost every spot within the watershed. The water is just that clear.

I still can't believe people pay me to work here. But they may not do so for long. Fisheries work is the catalyst for my love of rivers, but funding has become scarce over the years. The Smith isn't as impaired as other rivers in the state, so we aren't necessarily a priority for money, and it's unfortunate. Some of the last healthy stocks of salmon in the state exist here, but we are not without problems, and populations are still dwindling. Because of this, I've recently had my first bout of indecision about living here—because I need to work for a living. If the work disappears, I'll have to go, too.

*—September 25, 2017*

# Deborah Ghirardo

"People talk about a zombie apocalypse,
but when all these people can no longer have their
pain medication, you're going to see zombies."

*One of many seniors struggling to make ends meet, Deborah Ghirardo describes the challenges of finding good health care on a fixed income. She worries about the cost of housing, her ability to remain independent, and the obstacles to finding good medical care.*

I WAS LIVING IN NORTH SAN JUAN, CALIFORNIA. One night I got a text from my father. He said, "I need you today, not tomorrow, today."

I'd always told my dad, "If you ever need me, I'll be there." So I quit my job down south, I closed my trailer, I left my family and my friends, and I went to Bend where he was living at the time. I spent four months packing up my dad's house where he lived for thirty years and helped him move to Shady Cove, Oregon.

After that, I went home again to San Juan. I have lupus and other medical conditions I need to take care of regularly, so I couldn't stay in Shady Cove. I have California medical benefits, so I can't really leave the state, which really makes it hard, you know?

On July 27 of 2000, I'm sitting on my front porch swing in North San Juan, burning one,* and I lifted up my arms and said to God, "It's me, your rebellious child over here. I know in my heart that I'm supposed to go back up there and take care of my dad, but

---

* Smoking maijuana

143

I don't want to." I said, "Do what you gotta do. Just don't hurt me."

The next morning at 8 o'clock, I'm in the shower, and a truck ran right into my mobile home. It was destroyed. The truck put most of my trailer into the lot next door and came close to the propane tanks, but I was unhurt. I was in the bathroom, which didn't get hit directly or carried away. I fell out of the tub onto the floor, but I only got a few scratches on my arms.

I walked out to the center of the park, I looked back at what was left of my home, and I said, "I guess I'm moving."

I went to Shady Cove, Oregon, where my dad was, but like I said, I needed to be in California to have my medical benefits. So I decided to live as close to him as I could, here in Del Norte County. I would split the time with him. Every two weeks I would drive over there to Oregon, stay two weeks, and then come back here.

I got a room at the Gardenia Motel. It was like $600 for a week. So I paid one week and my dad paid for another. Eventually, I went down to the front desk and talked them into letting me work for my room. So I worked the front desk for eight months while I found a more permanent place to live.

I've been here in the trailer park in Hiouchi almost fifteen years now. I found this place just driving around one night.

I know what I like. I've always lived in rural towns. This seemed right. I looked at a couple of trailer models before I chose this one. And this felt like home. The price was affordable to me.

One of my biggest challenges living here in Del Norte County is healthcare. Yes, I have coverage, but the quality of care is very, very bad. I have lupus and fibromyalgia, alopecia, and Renaud's syndrome. It's all linked together. The doctors here don't have a clue what these problems are about. It's very hard to get specialized care.

I had a problem with my ears a couple years ago. I kept telling the doctors, "I have problems, I have problems." They finally sent me to an ear doctor here who shined a flashlight in my ears and said, "I don't see anything." I made him clean them anyway and two big chunks of wax came out of my ear.

So then he sends me to Grants Pass to a specialist. It cost me $200 to get a driver and a room. I went to the ear doctor there. They didn't even know what I was there for. My doctor here had sent nothing through. I was there less than ten minutes. They found nothing. They said they didn't know what to do for me.

I had a similar experience with bad health care with a foot doctor here. He tells me I have plantar fasciitis, and I need these expensive inserts and special shoes to walk right. I get home that afternoon and on my computer, the very shoes and inserts that he has told me about were there. I bought them. They didn't help me at all. I start going to physical therapy. They start doing trigger pressure points. I don't have plantar fasciitis, they say. It's a whole different problem.

You know, I think our healthcare is hooked up with the pharmacies and the shoe stores. I believe that most of the doctors who come here, this is their last chance. They can't get good physicians here. And the doctors who do come, leave after a few years—after they get their loan forgiveness for working in a rural area.

I did go back to North San Juan a few years ago. I'd been saying for years, "I've got to go home. I want to go home." I thought I might finally move back. I only spent two months there. All that time, I never saw my kids. They never came to visit. I ended up in the hospital again. Nobody was there to help take care of me. And it was freakin' hot: 110 degrees! I couldn't breathe. You can't take your dog in a car. It's a 45 minute drive to anywhere. People are so rude, too.

So when I got back two months later, I realized this was my home. I've *made* this my home. Unless my health forces me to move, I won't go back. It would be like sending me to hell.

As far as treating my illnesses, I've had to be creative. I've smoked marijuana most of my life. It does help with pain, but nothing works as well as the cannabis tinctures. You can make tincture out of marijuana. You can make oils and body rubs. I want people to be aware of this because so many of us can't afford good health care, and we need alternatives to commercial pharmaceuticals.

I have alopecia—hair loss. A few years back, a friend made me a tincture, and I started rubbing it on my head. I thought, "What the heck. I might as well try it." And it helped! I actually got chicken fuzz there. It's since disappeared, but it worked for a while.

I've gotten off at least six medications, strong medications, with the use of the tincture. Instead of reaching for a pain pill, I'd go take a drop of tincture or eat a candy or a cookie. I can just nibble at one all day long. I'm still able to function. I can still drive. I can still balance my checkbook. I take care of my home, my yard, my dog. Nobody knows. I don't change at all. Well, one time I ate too many cookies. I walked out the front door. My neighbor said, "Have you been drinking?"

I said, "No. I just ate seven cookies. I ate one. It gave me the munchies. So I ate more."

I think people should be more open about marijuana. I love going to the dispensaries up in Brookings, Oregon, and seeing elderly people, older than me, with their walkers going in there to buy marijuana, medical marijuana. They have a CBD (a cannabinoid that they pull out of the marijuana) which you can take just for pain. You don't get high. There's no THC in it. There's no high you get out of it. You have to take it all day long, but it takes the pain away.

Cannabis tincture helped me get off Plaquenil, which is a very hard thing to get off of. I got off of Neurontin and Remeron. I dropped my steroids from 20 milligrams down to 15, but that was because the doctor made me.

With this new opioid thing that's going on, they're taking drugs away from people who need that medication. I told my doctor, "You know what a drug addict looks like when they walk in the door. You can tell by looking at how they act. Take the meds away from *them*. Don't take them away from sick people like me—especially not seniors."

I live alone. I take care of my house, my dog, and my yard all by myself. I cannot do it if I'm crippled. But my doctor's taken my steroids away from me. I've started to break out in lesions again.

He dropped me 2 milligrams overnight along with my pain pills. I only took four a day in a 24 hour period, and now I don't have any. Donald Trump does not know what he's doing with this opiate thing. Number one, the United States of America protects the poppy fields in Afghanistan. Our government controls the heroin in this country. People talk about a zombie apocalypse, but when all these people can no longer have their pain medication, you're going to see zombies. By taking the pain pills away from people who have been taking them for years—middle class people—it's going to be bad.

They seem to be picking on women a lot more than men when cutting back prescriptions. But I also know veterans who have been cut down to half, too. It's terrible.

I asked my doctor what was going on—I begged him not to do this to me. I said to my doctor, "You know I'm not an addict. I've dropped lots of medication. I'm not asking for more. Just don't take what I have."

I yelled at him like he was my wife, so I feel like he's trying to hurt me now. And I'm not the only one complaining about it. They told me at the pharmacy that a lot of others are speaking out.

Other challenges to living here? Our county leaders get busted for things like drunk driving and writing false prescriptions, and they get a little slap on the hand. Then some kid walks into Walmart, steals a pair of tennis shoes, and he gets eleven years. The justice system is biased towards those with money and power.

I got my first traffic ticket in my life in Crescent City, and when I went to court, all the people in the front with the orange suits were getting suspended sentences and lesser charges. I think, well, I'm going to be able to get out of this ticket, and it was wrong for them to give it to me anyway. I get up there and the judge said, "Well, thirty-eight years of perfect record? You know we make our money off revenue here." He sent me to Driver's School, which cost me and gave me a fine on top of that!

This town is so politically corrupt. I've seen it in every little town I've lived in. As a waitress, I've always worked in the town restaurants where the cops go, and you hear everything that goes on. It's the same everywhere, and I'm tired of it. I'm tired of the way we are being treated and how powerful people are allowed to get away with everything. I'm even mad at the rich football player who beat his wife up in the elevator and the men in places of power who sexually harass women. Our kids are looking at these people as leaders, as role models. These men are in positions of power, and they are misusing their power. When they get busted, they're like, "Oh, I'm sorry." They should be sent to prison.

All this hate is going on. We're almost in the Civil War. I've never seen our whole world in this much unrest. I see a lot of things on the computer. It's not that it's all just happening here. But it seems like no one is nice anymore. Cashiers are rude now. They don't look at you. If you try to engage in a conversation, they just ignore you.

I watched the movie *1984* last night. In the movie, they're not allowed to touch, or talk, or look at each other. It seems like that's starting to happen here. There's too much hate in this world. I walk on the beach, and nobody's smiling anymore. I see kids walking down the street side-by-side texting each other. They don't even look at each other.

There's new owners at our trailer park. They don't live here. It's some kind of corporation. They like complete control. Instead of dropping the rent off in the office, now we have a slot. They're trying to figure out how to do automated rent, so we just go swipe our card and give them our rent like that. It used to be we would go pay the rent in the rec room, and we got to talk to the manager and joke and socialize. It was a neighborhood thing. Well, that's all changed. It's impossible to contact them. They don't answer texts or phone calls.

When they came in three or four years ago, they made us all these promises of what they were going to fix. They haven't fixed a thing. For example, our sewer here is so bad. It is a health issue. Our septic overflows. It doesn't work right. Sometimes it reeks of sewage, and for some reason, the health department lets it go. I think the owners might want to use that as an excuse to shut this place down. I mean, it's in bad shape. They've just patched it. A couple of years ago, I took pictures where there was poop floating in my yard from the drainage being stopped up down the road.

I looked up the owners of this place on my computer, and they had a park like this down in San Bernardino, California. They went in, bought the park, and within three years, it was taken down. They turned it into a gated RV park. I wonder if that's their plan here, too. I think they might use the sewer as an excuse.

If I have to leave this place, and I probably will if my conditions get worse, I'll have to get a one-bedroom apartment in Crescent City. But I'm not an apartment person, and I'll miss my yard. And I'll have to come up with the application fees, which are sometimes up to $35. It's going to be hard, even with HUD.

—*December 8, 2017*

# Roger Gitlin

"We are a beautiful community.
We could really be something… I'd like to sit here
and tell you that things are improving,
but I'm not sure they are."

*Roger Gitlin has served on the Del Norte County Board of Supervisors since 2013. He describes himself as "a fiscal watchdog, a limited government conservative, and a patriot."*

I'VE ALWAYS BEEN ENAMORED with California and its rural lifestyle, and I've always wanted to live by the ocean. I'd been taking fishing trips into June Lake and Bishop and spending time outside Los Angeles proper and just fell in love with nature. So, when I retired, my wife Angela and I began to scour the coast looking for a place to live.

I'd been in media and business, and then a teacher in the juvenile court schools of LA County about 20 years, and I retired with the idea that I'd see that magnificent Pacific Ocean every morning. But I found it to be cost prohibitive. We were frustrated because we couldn't find a place with a price we could afford, and then on one of our many trips trying to find the perfect place, I just kind of pointed up north. "What's up there—above Eureka?" And that brought us, in 1998, to Crescent City. As we were coming down Crescent Hill—in those days the trees were at a lower level so you could see not one but two lighthouses on a clear day—I was greatly impressed with this charming town. We ended up on Pebble Beach

150

Drive. Prices were right. Ultimately, we ended up in front of Battery Point Lighthouse. And that's where we live today. Our neighbors on South A Street renamed it "Lighthouse Way."

And it was about that time that we began to see that this could be a special little place. Cities were rapidly becoming unlivable. It was always rush traffic to go from point A to point B, even short distances. We came up from Santa Clarita, prices of real estate were very high, and the quality of life in places like Los Angeles County were really deteriorating. People like me, those baby boomers, they could really come up here and have a quality of life.

One problem that really stood out for me was blight. In 2009, I became involved in trying to improve my community. I wrote about it in the newspaper. We would talk to people—visitors from other places—when we saw their license plates. And in our neighborhood we saw no shortage of folks looking for Battery Point Lighthouse. So my wife and I bought an old surfboard and hung it up on our garage. It read "50 yards to the Lighthouse."

Towns have to evolve or they die. I took a look around and saw—I'll affectionately call them the Good Old Boys—who said, "No, we don't want this to change." But I saw the changes going the wrong direction. A higher and stronger dependence on Sacramento and Washington DC. That's not how you build a community. A community needs more private enterprise and private sector jobs that pay a decent salary. There's a heavier and stronger presence of government. Being a conservative, I believe in a limited government. We should provide law enforcement and fire service. We shouldn't be devoting one out of every two tax dollars into social services offered through health and human services and social welfare.

I was raised by two parents, the middle of three children. My parents were fair, and honest, and provided good role models for me. They left me with the impression that if you wanted something, you had to work for it. You don't expect someone to hand you something. It's not free. It will come with a great price. So, I have a very strong work ethic. Lots of people, especially in poor communities, they don't have a nuclear family with a father and mother to balance that.

So, I was asked to run for the Board of Supervisors, back in 2012. And it's been an E ticket ride ever since. It's been challenging. I declared to my colleagues I was elected as an agent of change. All four of my fellow supervisors opposed any motion I offered. I perceived an arrogant level of disrespect, absolute intransigence that was embarrassing to those who expected the board to work together.

One such instance involved my motion to ban motorists from handing an item, like cash, through a car window to those who panhandled. I related how this proposed ordinance had been passed and implemented in neighboring Medford, Grants Pass, and Curry counties. All four of my colleagues mocked my motion. The item failed to garner a second. The level of scorn was thick in the air.

A similar item, consideration of a non-denominational prayer before our Board of Supervisors' meetings in April of 2013 (after the Supreme Court affirmed prayer was legal before all government meetings) was also met with scorn and ridicule.

But the one thing that has really defined me is the passion to clean up our community. And I started a program "Take a Bite out of Blight" (I didn't invent the title—it came from a town in Connecticut that brought in goats to eat weeds). We cleaned up the outside of homes and properties to make them look presentable. We've completed over twenty-seven projects.

You don't have to go very far to see ugliness in our community. Go behind any untrimmed tree or bush or into any vacant lot. You can see fecal matter, you see drug needles, you see trash, and all the effects of human tragedy. The first clean-up project we did had the strongest impression on me. It was just east of Wal-Mart. It was just loaded with trash. We organized about twenty volunteers to do this and we collected a couple of tons' worth of debris. And it was pristine afterwards. Then we posted "No Trespassing" signs.

And sometimes these places we've cleaned become re-fouled.

Sometimes, it feels like an exercise in futility. Blight is created by human beings. I tried to introduce an ordinance through the Board of Supervisors to prevent people from begging on our street corners, receiving objects, such as cash, through a moving vehicle. Or when someone carries a gas container and it's a ruse to get money for drugs or alcohol. The idea is to *not* attract people with little or no means to come to our community. We will give you help. We will give you services. But we will not give you money. Because the money is part of poison that keeps them going in this vicious cycle.

We didn't always have this problem with homelessness. But in the late 60s or 70s, then-Governor Regan elected to close down so many of these mental hospitals and send patients who couldn't take care of themselves home to their families. Their families should take care of them. And that lasted about ten minutes. That was the first generation of homeless people. And now we have millions.

This problem is divided into basically four groups of people: mentally ill, alcohol addicts, drug addicts, criminals, and legitimate people who have just fallen through the cracks. But the people who need help shouldn't just be walking the streets. We're asked to tolerate this, but it reduces the quality of our lives. That may come across as me not being compassionate. I have great compassion. But you shouldn't allow someone to continue to assault our laws, assault our property, or operate with impunity in how they behave. We must address the problem that way—by not allowing people to act in an irresponsible manner. We should be requiring that everyone have a home—that you cannot just go and live in the bushes. It's unhealthy, dangerous, and unsanitary, and it subjects you to all kinds of crime. What does that say about our society if we allow a person to stand on the corner of Washington Boulevard and Summer Way and beg? It should be illegal.

I tried to address this and was met with some resistance. Things were so bad at Safeway that my wife did not want to go into the shopping center and enter the store. She was being harassed for money by people standing at the front doors, following and intimidating her. The manager said there was nothing he could do about it. That upset me. I went to the police department and the City Council. I put the heat under the manager to do something about it. We would see people defecating and urinating outside of Red Nails.* We're tolerating this. I was the only elected official who wanted to touch this. And I was demonized by the newspaper. But the new ownership of the shopping center has since hired a security guard, and it's a different place today because of the things that we have done. You're not harassed. Did I take some heat? *Yes!* That's what happens when you step on someone's toes.

I'd like this community to take hold of its future. I'm the messenger. I can't do anything unless people like you say, *yes!* I agree with him. But if I am quiet and say nothing, what good am I as an elected official?

We are a beautiful community. We could really be something. Our dependency on Sacramento and ordinances about not begging and things like that holds us back. I'd like to sit here and tell you that things are improving, but I'm not sure they are. I do not think the legalization of marijuana, which I oppose, will be the economic salvation we are looking for. I think it's going to inflict more social problems on us as we go deeper into process.

I'll give you another example of the kind of frustrations we have: There's a downed tree on Washington Boulevard. And the tree has fallen into the wires. I requested to have the debris removed and the tree stabilized. Codes, requirements, and complications of government make it hard for Pacific Power to do simple things. The Coastal Commission made it difficult to remove graffiti from Preston Rock because we had to get a specific solvent approved. We need a bypass for Last Chance Grade on Highway 101, *now*. It's eventually going to collapse and fall into the ocean. We just don't know when. And we're supposed to have it done between 2031 and 2039. That time frame is unacceptable. But we have a Congressman who holds a different opinion on replacement. Meanwhile, in Sacramento, a basketball stadium can be completed without a CEQUA (California Environmental Quality Act) study and a NEPA

---

* A nearby nail salon

(National Environmental Protection Act) study. Why? Because Sacramento can get an exemption and we can't.

All these things are issues that rile people who don't want to see growth here. But I'm not one of them. I believe that we have to have managed growth. Otherwise, our community will deteriorate. We live in a magnificent part of North America. Why do we tolerate these things? Crescent City and Del Norte County can be so much more than what citizens expect. Low ceilings of expectation have retarded real, managed growth and true prosperity.

—*September 1, 2017*

# Tyler Harrison

"In the parking lot of the Walmart Super Center,
someone scrawled the words 'Meth Town' in the cement.
It says a lot about the state of things."

*A youth activist woke to the importance of civic participation, Tyler Harrison explains some of the serious challenges faced by Del Norte youth, including drug use, homelessness, and the availability of mental health resources.*

I WASN'T BORN IN DEL NORTE COUNTY. I moved here basically the day after I was born. I was adopted; my adoptive parents were in the room when my biological mom gave birth, and they made arrangements to bring me right back here. I've lived here all my life.

I do feel like I belong here. The air is breathable. You can traverse town easily. It's small enough to be comfortable. You can swing to Dutch Bros (a drive-up coffee place) before you go to class. If you're hungry in the middle of the lunch hour, you can go get something fast. Everyone knows everyone. The environment is beautiful. There are a lot of good things about this place.

Unfortunately, there's a lot of drug use here. In the parking lot of the Walmart Super Center, someone scrawled the words "Meth Town" in the cement. It says a lot about the state of things. And it's not an uncommon occurrence to see people buying or selling drugs in public. It feels like everyone either knows a guy who sells, or knows a guy ho knows a guy.

It tests your own values, you know? With substance use being so common, it can become a really easy trap to fall into. There's not a lot to do here, and whether it be from depression or boredom, lots of people end up on drugs.

A while ago, I had this friend. We would hang out over at his house. I was 12 and naïve, so I didn't know it, but his whole family was on drugs. His sister, brother, mom—maybe even him. As time when on, we hung out less and less, but I'd hear about him or see him on the streets. And it was obvious that he wasn't doing okay. And I'd ask my family about him, and they'd say, "Yeah. Still using." It's not a good situation to live in a place where people fall into that, one by one.

For me, keeping out of that scene is about knowing myself. I don't want to do anything unhealthy or dangerous. I don't want to get addicted, drink and crash my car, or smoke and die of lung cancer. And even if it wasn't a physical health issue for me, I don't think it would be good for the mental health of my family if I was an addict. I think that some substances are worse than others, but for me it has less to do with the actual merits of the substance and what it does for you and more to do with the harm that it might cause to me or to my friends and family.

This is a place of great contrast. People come to retire, live out their lives with money in the bank. And there are people here who have nothing and get by on almost nothing every month.

In addition to drug use, our community has a problem with homelessness. I feel a lot of empathy for these folks, and I wish I could do something for them. But it's frustrating. It's midway through the month. I'm broke. I've got to make my money last, so I go to the cheapest place to shop for food in town, Walmart. And there's a homeless person on the corner with a sign says "Need Money" or "Need Gas" or "Anything Helps, God Bless." And I want to help, but all I can do is just make eye contact. And whatever I can do is not going to make a meaningful difference in that person's life. That experience says so much about the state of things. And the fact that it's always a surprise when there isn't anyone at the corner by Walmart.

When I can afford it, I sit down with a homeless person and buy him a pizza and just talk to him for a minute or two. It makes me feel less like a piece of trash to do at least that, and it makes me feel better getting to know the "person" behind my little acts of charity. To be quite honest, it isn't entirely selfless. I started talking to homeless people because I was depressed. I was talking to a therapist who suggested it. I like to help people, and it made me feel good, so I gave it a shot.

There's also a huge issue either with the services we have available—or people's knowledge of available services. Here's an example: I had a friend who was suicidal. Straight up. I'm not a licensed therapist, but whatever, when a friend tells me he's considering suicide, I'm going to help him. I asked if he had reached out for professional help, and he said yes. But his parents won't take him to a therapist. They can't afford it, and don't believe in mental health practices anyway. I asked if he could do anything at the school. Nope. They don't have mental health counselors. Only academic counselors. His only option is to go to the hospital, where they can refer him to someone he can't afford to see in the first place. This is the state of things for youth struggling with mental health issues in Del Norte.

Another example of our lack of services has to do with gaps in our educational system. I went to a private school until I was fourteen. I then transferred to the high school late in my freshman year. I never had to try with the work. I didn't have to think. It was easy. My junior year, I did get really depressed and stopped trying altogether, but I managed to keep on schedule. But when my senior year came, I found out I was not going to graduate on time. It turned out that, when I switched schools my freshman year, I had almost an entire year of credits that didn't transfer—and only a few weeks to make up the work.

The problem was, I was completely unaware of it. I don't know if the counselors were aware of it either until my final year. No one told me. No one seemed to be making sure I was on track. And I later found that I'm not the only one this has happened to.

I couldn't imagine making up the work in time, so I took the option of graduating a year late. I became dual enrolled at Castle Rock, under an "adult ed" program.

One good thing about that extra year is that I got to take some extra classes, and I took a computer drafting class with a wonderful teacher, Mr. Lauble. Wow. Talk about a healthy support network—having a role, a job to do, and a place you belong. If you did your work and didn't cause trouble, you had unconditional positive regard. There was endless responsibility, but he would let you do things. Play music in class, take a break, or even leave early, as long as you knew you would be responsible for your work.

In Mr. Lauble's class, we got to use a 3D printer. We had to build it ourselves and learn how to use it from scratch. No one had ever done this before, so it was always "Look in the manual" or "Find what we can learn online" to solve problems. Those were lessons in patience and grit. We did everything from the ground up with little outside help. A part broke once, and we 3-D printed a replacement.

Having been in Mr. Laubel's class gave me the sense of what I was missing from all my other classes where it was just fill out worksheets, write papers, repeat. We weren't engaged as a team, learning together. It made me critical of our educational system here. "Sit there alone, do your work alone, get it back alone" is a lazy way of teaching—and it doesn't get students interested in anything except getting out of school.

The poor educational system connects to another challenge we face in this community: isolation. We live in a very tiny place, away from most other places, and the road out is currently crumbling into the ocean. But isolation also affects how we relate to each other. In LA County, you can meet a million people—someone new every single day for the rest of your life. Here, you can't pick and choose. You're friends with Joe from third grade because you were the only two kids who liked Power Rangers. You have to make due even if you have very little in common. And this can make you feel really lonely. You know the same people, and you go to the same places. The range of experiences is very limited.

There's a positive side to isolation. Not everyone is going to be the same as you. And this gives you a chance to learn empathy—to accept people and to make friends you might not make if you lived somewhere else. But maybe it's not enough of a positive to make up for what we're missing.

Del Norte County has its issues. There are a lot of things here that suck, and they can get to you. The weather. The economy. The health care system. The school system. Imagine a clock. It kind of hovers over your head as it's ticking down to zero. How long do you have until you end up on drugs, broke, or homeless? I worry I will end up like that. I do have it better than some people, and I can be grateful for that, but I feel this omnipresent dread.

What stopped that clock for me—and started adding time to it—was getting involved in volunteer work, like with Building Healthy Communities. Even when the work was done and we would just sit around and talk. Having friends and coworkers who understand and care—and making the community better, even just a little bit—being involved in positive things did wonders for me. Good people, good connections. You have to feel like you fit in and that you're contributing. That's what's keeping me sane.

But we live in a place where you feel like, at some point, you have to go. You have to leave. The college here can give you an AA, but you don't want to end there. If you want to make something of yourself, you have to go. And I'm not sure if that's good or bad. But it's part of what it means to live here—to thrive, you have to get out.

*—October 24, 2017*

*Eric L. Norris Jr., son of contributor Cherece Norris,*
*celebrates his high school graduation from*
*Castle Rock Charter School*

# PART III: BELONGING

*When do we feel like outsiders?*
*When do we feel we belong?*

# Deaun Reilly

"Nobody had rain clothes. Children don't use raingear in
Del Norte County. When I got my teaching credential at HSU and
started teaching school, I noticed the kids would be out in the
school yard on a cold day, and they didn't even wear *coats*."

*Deaun Reilly moved to Crescent City just a few weeks before the 1964 tsunami.
Over her lifetime, she's adjusted to more than just the weather. Over and over
again, she has found ways to adapt and fit in to this unusual and isolated place.*

MY FAMILY CAME TO CRESCENT CITY in early March,
1964, from Castro Valley, which was a small town outside of San
Francisco. I drove up with my daughter and my mother in our
Ford T-Bird. My husband came in his pickup with the two boys,
their snakes, and the dog.

We drove up Highway 101, the beautiful redwood coast highway. Leaving the concrete and asphalt freeways to travel miles on
this two lane road with the massive redwood trees on either side
was an unforgettable experience. Most four lane roads were yet
to be built. We noticed the longer we drove the scarcer the towns
became. The highway took us through the town of Klamath which
had a bank, supermarket and other places of business. It was very
quaint and lively. The road narrowed, and it was another half hour
before we saw signs of another city.

Our trip was just a few weeks before the tidal wave devastated
downtown Crescent City, and the same year the Christmas flood
wiped out the bridge over the Klamath River and overwhelmed the

town of Klamath as well as several bridges on Highway 101.

Our destination was the El Patio Motel on H Street. H Street was the main highway at the time until 1958 when Caltrans deeded it back to the City of Crescent City. We'd bought the motel as a great adventure. Little did we know the extent of the adventure. When we arrived, we had to get settled and start looking at the different rooms and the laundry where we would be doing the motel sheets and towels. It was overwhelming, even before the tsunami came.

My husband and I had visited the area previously, just before Christmas. We flew in by plane to look at the property and I figured we'd get a Christmas tree while we were here. You know, from the woods! That was my idea of a souvenir. It turned out Christmas trees weren't that easy to get. But we finally found one and brought it back with us on the plane as checked luggage. Can you imagine? Back then you could do that. When we arrived home, it came out on the conveyer belt with the suitcases.

That first trip when we flew up, we had a real shock. I felt like I would be moving to the Wild West. Some of the streets downtown were gravel and the sidewalks were just boardwalks made from planks. It was a funny coincidence that Wells Fargo was opening their bank that weekend where U.S. Bank is today. And for the celebration, they had a stagecoach and real horses. Another thing I remember was it was misty and wet and muddy, but everyone was commenting on the "beautiful weather" and how lucky we were to have it for the bank celebration. I thought, "This weather doesn't look good to me!" But it didn't take long, living here, to realize that it *was* a beautiful day. There was hardly any rain and the horses only stirred up a little bit of mud on some of the unpaved streets.

After that first visit, we decided that we would go ahead with the move, and we went back to the city with our Christmas tree in with the luggage. We drove up a few months later.

That year, 1964, was a wet year. On the first day of school, I made the mistake of sending my children off with red rain boots and yellow slickers with hoods. Well, it was raining. Where I had just come from, if it even looked like rain, you put rainwear on your children for their walk to school. My kids came home that first day and said, "Mom, do you realize we were the joke of the school?"

Nobody had rain clothes. Children don't use raingear in Del Norte County. When I got my teaching credential at HSU and started teaching school, I noticed the kids would be out in the school yard on a cold day, and they didn't even wear *coats*. They had a sweater if they were lucky. I don't know why. Maybe they just don't like wearing weather protection. It's still true to this day that kids around here, and adults, go without. But maybe it was just hard to find, though we did have Johnson's Men Store, Trehearne's and Daly's Department stores. Johnson's is where Chase Bank now sits today. Daly's was in the Old Ben Franklin building. Trehearne's, where we have government offices today, collapsed during the tidal wave.

A few days after that first day of school, as I was going from room to room trying to keep the fresh linen dry, I remember thinking I ought to get myself an umbrella. I went to look for one in town. The sales people shrugged. They didn't carry them. They asked me, "What would you want that for?" It turns out we don't use umbrellas in Del Norte County because the wind comes with the rain and open umbrellas turn inside out. Ladies did wear those little plastic bonnets tied under their chins to keep their hair dry, though. That was the style at the time even though Crescent City was not fashionable by any means. Another change in my sense of fashion.

A week after my umbrella expedition, on March 27, 1964, the downtown was wiped out with the tidal wave. I was managing the hotel, cleaning rooms, doing the laundry, and getting three children off to school. My husband at the time worked on the units. That was his expertise and he was very good at it, which was good, because the amount of work was overwhelming. We were working hard, but we were young and full of enthusiasm.

There were a lot of motels south of town, but all of them were pretty well wiped out that day. The Thunderbird, now Motel 6, had water up to the second floor. And I know that because the people who came knocking on our door early that morning were coming from there. That's what woke us up—a truckload of people talking about a *tsunami*. I'd never heard that word before. I said, "I have no idea what you're talking about," but here was this truckload full of wet people and they needed a place to stay.

I'd hardly looked at all the rooms; we just started opening the doors and letting people settle in. Before the end of the day we were full and we didn't even know who was in our rooms. It turns out it's very important to know who your guests are. For one thing, the sheriff came looking for missing people. We were new to hotel administration, but we learned fast.

It's a little hard for me to separate the tsunami from the Christmas flood, which came at the end of that year. It was a wet year, a wet introduction to Del Norte County. That fall, after the tsunami, it started raining, it just didn't stop. The tsunami had washed out the downtown, but the Christmas flood wiped out bridges in Klamath and further south, and ultimately, the highway.

The Army came from Fort Lewis, Washington to install temporary bridges on Highway 199. Some of these young soldiers were staying at our motel, and played with our two boys, who were thrilled to horse around with real soldiers. But there was some tension between the tourists and the Army boys, and we got to hear both sides.

These young men had served overseas in the Korean War and were used to army vehicles. They didn't understand the sensitivities people felt towards their cars. For example, in Klamath, they ran a barge to get across the river. But they hadn't perfected it. People would come down from Washington who were used to ferries. They couldn't imagine that this ferry was just a crude, flat barge. People had to get out of their cars and put on lifejackets for the ride across. After what was sometimes a rough crossing, the barge slammed into the opposite bank. The soldiers would use a bulldozer to push dirt over the lip of the barge so that the cars could get off. But if a car hesitated—and often, one did—the breaking action would push the barge back into the river. To keep that from happening, the operators put a hook on the bumpers of the cars, and some cars lost their bumpers in the process. Their drivers were not happy. Those without bumpers would be fuming by the time they got to our motel. We heard about their experiences in no uncertain terms.

Moving as we did from the suburbs into a rural area was quite a journey into the unknown. We were different in many ways from the locals. For example, we brought our piano. My mother insisted that the children have a piano, so it came along with our move. I didn't know many other families with that luxury item!

We had to learn to dress differently, too, and not just when it came to rainwear. I had been PTA president at our little neighborhood school in Castro Valley, and so when things settled down with the hotel, I decided that I would meet local people by getting involved in the PTA again. Of course, I had city clothes. I didn't have the kind of things other mothers here wore. Dresses and skirts just weren't practical in the wind and rain. I soon learned I needed a pair of jeans. And as for how the men dressed, well, Del Norte was a logging and fishing community. The men didn't wear suits.

I didn't really mind these adjustments. This turned out to be a wonderful place. Nature becomes a big part of your life here. You get out and enjoy it. If people were looking for restaurants and shopping malls, they were in short supply. Lighthouse Repertory Theatre and the Community Concert Association provided most of the cultural activities at the time. Each organization had about three or four programs a year. I remember going to see a production of *Carmen* put on by the high school drama and music class under the direction of Gene Petrict. It was in the auditorium of the old high school. Red's Theatre, single screen on G Street, was the only movie theatre in town.

One of the things I love the most here is the ocean. I used to go swimming in it! I guess I didn't realize it was cold. One of my kids got into diving for abalone. He found an untouched abalone bed off Pebble Beach. He made a wetsuit out of plastic bags, and would go down and bring up so many abalone. I still have some of the shells. We had abalone up to our ears, and of course we didn't realize how lucky we were.

One of our guests at the motel would bring us fresh salmon instead of paying rent, and that was quite a treat. I never liked salmon before I came here. I think it was because the salmon we got from the Bay Area was at least two or three days old when it arrived here. But there's nothing like fresh salmon right out of the ocean. At the time we probably would have preferred cash to salmon, but we took whatever we could get. Looking back, I should have appreciated it more.

One of our more interesting guests during the tidal wave was a young homeless woman named Sylvia. I'm not sure she was homeless by our standards today. She lived on the beach, like a few other people did. The sheriff brought her by the motel because he was worried about her. He didn't want her on the beach anymore and so she stayed with us on and off for a long time.

She had some kind of mental illness and had been in a mental institution. It was at the time when the government was letting out patients who were not harmful and not too severely handicapped. She was reluctant to stay with us when she found out that we weren't Catholic. Because we weren't married in a Catholic church, she said we were living in sin. She kept disappearing, and the sheriff kept bringing her back.

I tried to help her. First, I went to the Catholic Church. But because she was so disruptive in mass, and because they didn't really have the facilities for her, it didn't really work out. Then I found out she had parents nearby, in Fort Dick. Her mother had divorced and remarried, so she wouldn't stay with them, on account of her beliefs. She just up and left. Her parents were happy she found a place where she would show up now and then. It gave them some peace of mind. They didn't have much money, but they would give us venison for taking her in.

Sylvia had a strong sense of independence, and she didn't like staying without being able to pay. She didn't have any money or any job, so I offered her work weeding in front of the motel. But that didn't really work out, because in the end, she decided the weeding wasn't a good thing. God put those weeds there for a reason, she said. She didn't want to take them out.

Sylvia was quite well known in town. Somehow, between the tsunami and the Christmas flood, she acquired a bicycle with a basket and a live white rabbit who rode around with her. She peddled around town and got handouts and food. She was happy just to be free and on her own.

There were other homeless folks too, who stayed with us. One fellow came often, especially when there was a tsunami warning. He didn't really like being confined, but he was worried. Sometimes he even showed up before there was a warning, certain that there was going to be one. The tsunami was traumatic for people. It wasn't something they could just get over after a few days.

When I first came here, there were lots of sawmills and we passed many logging trucks on the highway on our drive up from the city. Save the Redwood League was advocating for a National Park. They had hearings at the fairgrounds, and I went and represented the Motel Association. It was a really interesting time because I felt strongly that if you cut all the redwoods, then what do you have here besides the ocean? It's not an area to attract industry. Transportation is too difficult. Why not use our natural industry—these beautiful trees—to support our community? The coastal fog and cool climate is a natural setting for the growth of redwood trees. You shouldn't just cut them all. You cannot grow a 2000 year-old redwood tree in ten years or one hundred years or five hundred years.

The tsunami and the flood put Del Norte County on the map, and so our redwoods trees became better known. A female photographer from National Geographic came to our motel and we struck up a friendship. She invited me to come to fern canyon with her for a photo shoot. She also photographed the way the timber companies had logged the area south of town—leaving a fringe of trees along the highway that hid the empty hills that stretched all the way south. You couldn't really tell, unless you did a fly over, which she did.

Politics were complicated. The logging business employed a lot of people. The mills employed a lot of people. So the economy was really thriving at one point here. And the fishermen were thriving. I think that part of the economy is pretty much finished now. It's sad for the people who live here and depended on it.

Now, we have government offices downtown. We have government supported everything. Our new industry is our maximum security prison. Pelican Bay brought a mix of people. The Correctional Officers (COs) who came had money and time—and many of them had ambition. Some stayed and fixed up run-down properties. That was the good part. The influx of people and cash opened up office jobs which some people in the area filled, and new people came to live here. But many retired people who had moved here to get out of the city sold their homes when they heard the prison was coming. They worried about the families of inmates moving here and changing the culture. That may have happened to some extent.

My own work shifted, too. I left the motel business, and my husband chose a different life. I went back to school to get my degree and my teaching certificate, driving to Humboldt to do it. I can't imagine making that drive today, but surprisingly, the road was in better shape than it is now. It was narrow, yes, and there were slides, but it wasn't falling into the ocean in as many places. Back then, it took about an hour and ten minutes to get to Humboldt State University. Well, it probably should have taken a little longer, but I drove fast.

I was teaching at Crescent Elk in the 1980s when the Hmong population began to arrive. Boy, did those Hmong children come to learn. It didn't take them long to learn English, and pretty soon, when the school gave out awards, most of the students on the stage were Hmong. The Mexican kids, too, came to study and learn. They worked hard. They were not a problem. After both groups had been here a while, they probably accepted some of the ideas and behaviors of the other students here. But to me, these students from elsewhere were an asset.

There was a time I thought I might move away. I did a lot of traveling during the summers, and I really liked it. I traveled to many of the places in our social studies books and brought back pictures and artifacts to share with the students. It made the pages in those books seem more than just print on a page. Some of these kids had never been out of the county. Isolation is one of the challenges, living here.

At one point, I applied to teach in Saudi Arabia because I felt I needed to get out of town. It's not a good place to be single! But I met a wonderful gentleman who became my second husband. I was chair of the City Planning Commission and he was an engineer for Caltrans. He came before us to present a proposal for a highway project. Well, he talked me out of going to Saudi Arabia! I'm not sorry I changed my mind, but I'm sorry that I didn't have that experience. Because of his interest in bicycling, though, we took several trips to Europe on our bicycles. Getting in shape for our trips became a big part of our lives.

Despite the challenges of living in Del Norte, you can do so much here. You can get so involved in the community. And you're sort of *needed*. And as you get older, you need to feel needed. That's one reason I feel I belong here, still, after all these years.

*—September 7, 2017*

# Athena Csutoras

"In Crescent City, I always felt safe, even when alone on the beach or in the forest. I felt like I could trust people because I knew them or was related to them. I realize there is a certain naïve attitude here and it is important to guard oneself, but my background, my experiences, my life ways have proffered an attitude of acceptance of others no matter who they are or where they have come from."

*Born to a prominent family in Crescent City, Athena's "rebellion" in raising mixed-race children out of wedlock strained some relationships within her family. But she drew strength from the love and acceptance of other family members, the natural world, and her strong sense of independence.*

I WAS BORN AND RAISED IN CRESCENT CITY. There's never been a time when I didn't feel I belonged. Both of my parents were from here. My father's family has been in the community the longest, going back to the 1800s. In fact, Joe Hamilton, for whom the elementary school was named, was my great, great uncle. I went to the school named after him and so did my children. My mother's parents were Greek immigrants who moved here as young adults between 1918 and 1920.

Both sets of grandparents lived in town. We had cousins, aunts, uncles, and other close friends of family, it seemed like everywhere. We sat down to dinner as a family every night where we learned the give and take of belonging and responsibility to others. I particularly remember picnics at Jed Smith State Park. All the Greeks in town would come and make a lineup of picnic tables. The long line of tables were covered with cotton tablecloths and topped with all sorts of delicious foods.

A most profound early memory of mine embodies a lesson in belonging, rebellion, perseverance, and independence. It was a Saturday; I was five years old, the third of six girls. My two youngest sisters were both still in diapers with at least one of them taking a bottle. I went to my mother, hairbrush in hand, and presented myself. I was ready for her to brush my long, tangled curly locks as she did every Saturday morning. It was a special time, just me and Mom. On this particular morning, she was busy tending to Sheila and Doris and said, "Tina, do it yourself, I don't have time." Feelings of disappointment quickly arose. I went to the mirror and tried to run the brush through the tangles. It was hard, and I was angry. I soon began to cry and then decided to hide. I hid under Mom and Dad's bed. After about half an hour, I heard Dad calling my name. I heard everyone in our house calling for me, "Tina where are you? Are you here?" I didn't answer. Dad went in one direction around the block and sent Beverly, my older sister, in the opposite direction. I don't remember who found me or how long it took for them to find me, as I wasn't coming out on my own accord. That day I realized I would need to gain some independence and begin to do things on my own. But the fact they took the time to find me gave me a sense of belonging and a brief practice in rebellion and persistence. Both of these traits have served me well in fitting into this community as an adult.

There was a sense of safety and belonging that was prevalent growing up in Crescent City. Family structure and routine were everything. Weekends were family time. In those days, and when our parents worked, we had a "babysitter" who came to our home daily. Beverly, Cheri, and I went to the old high school gymnasium (Recreation Department on H Street) and participated in tumbling, trampoline, archery, fencing, arts and crafts, and basketball as early as seven years old. It was drop-in with no charge and many neighborhood children took advantage of this after school and during the summer months. In this day and age, in many families, both parents work outside the home, and the kind of personal home care we received in the 1950s has changed. In today's world, group child care and family child care homes have taken the place of a parent at home or having someone come to your home to see after the welfare of children. Activities that used to be offered for free are either nonexistent or offered only for a fee.

It wasn't until I was about 10 years old that I began realizing other children's daily lives were different than mine. I spent the night with a nearby neighbor. I asked for a glass of milk before going to sleep. This caused discord between the parents because if I had a glass of milk, every child in the house would want a glass of milk and there wouldn't be any milk for cereal in the morning. In our house there was most always enough milk, and if we ran out, we simply got more.

I never considered our family affluent or wealthy, but we did not want. Our grandparents made sure of that. We got new clothes three times a year. My father's mother, whom we always called "Honey," took us to Daly's department store to choose the latest special fashion dress for school. My mother's mother, whom we called "Grandma," was a seamstress so many of those new clothes were custom made. Saturday night's traditional meal was steak dinner with homemade French fried potatoes. I found out later in life that Honey always bought the steak for us, because it wasn't in my parents' budget to afford it.

Grandparents were my safety net. I remember feeling special and loved by Honey most of all. "What's mine is yours," she would tell me when I asked to use her fingernail polish or browse through her junk drawer. I remember many other friends in those days who also shared the closeness of their grandparents. In current times, there is something missing when grandchildren are distanced from their kin. There is also a kind of strange opposite to this: the prevalence of grandparents raising their grandchildren. Changing times show the effects of single parent families, drug abuse, and poverty—all of which were uncommon or unheard of when I was growing up in Crescent City.

We did have struggles. Dad had various jobs. He worked at the docks. And he worked at the family business, Howe and Hamilton Hometown Hardware, down on Front Street. It got wiped out in the 1964 tidal wave. Dad and my grandfather gave it another go by creating Stowers Hometown Hardware, but the rebuild was unsuccessful. It couldn't compete. Coast-to-Coast Hardware came in, and grocery stores started carrying various hardware items. It was hard to keep the business alive.

After two and a half years feeling disappointed by the community, my father left his hometown to find work and live in Burlingame, California. Two years later, my mother, who had worked for Del Norte County at the Auditor's office and at the Assessor's office, went to join him in Millbrae, California.

This was the year I graduated from High School and began my adventures outside of Del Norte County. Mom took her two youngest daughters while Cheri, a year and a half younger than me, stayed in Crescent City with our grandparents for her senior year of high school.

Within two weeks of graduation, I went to Bakersfield, where my older sister lived. I started college there, but when Beverly's husband came home from Vietnam, they moved to Monterey, so I stayed in Bakersfield on my own for another year, then moved to Long Beach where I had friends. I lived in Long Beach for another year.

In those two short years, I discovered I'm not city girl. I wanted to be where I knew people, where I could trust people. I wanted to be back in my home town where things were predictable and easy and slow. In other places, there were so many strangers, and I had only a few friends and virtually no relatives. I recall going to the beach in Long Beach and finding it was not safe to be there alone as I was propositioned by a strange man. At the age of twenty, I was naïve to the dangers of cities.

In Crescent City, I always felt safe, even when alone on the beach or in the forest. I felt like I could trust people because I knew them or was related to them. I realize there is a certain naïve attitude here and it is important to guard oneself, but my background, my experiences, my life ways have proffered an attitude of acceptance of others no matter who they are or where they have come from.

Over the last forty years, in some aspects our community has changed. The number of people you see on the beaches, rain or shine, has really grown. But if you grew up here, you know the places to go to find solitude. And there's such an abundance of nature here. People are discovering what I've known all my life—and maybe that's what's attracting them. You can go to the river and to the woods and to the ocean all in the same day. There's fresh air. There's abundant food. I have learned to dig for butter clams and gather seaweed and so many other life sustaining foods: crab, fish, eel, and wild berries. I grow a huge garden and put up food for the winter each year. This is a place where people can forage for what they need, and it attracts and sustains people who enjoy that lifestyle.

One memory really stands out for me—one moment of belonging, but also rebellion, was when I was still pretty young. I'd come back to the community from Long Beach, and I moved out of my house and spent five months from the end of May until the first rains came in October at "Camp." Camp was near the confluence of the Middle and South forks of the Smith River, just downstream from Slant Bridge. Larry Matthews, my boyfriend (and the father of my children), and I did this several years in a row. It was his idea. Camp consisted of an old army tent tied down atop wooden pallets. Inside we had a carpet, chest of drawers, and bed. Outside the tent was a rock hearth with brick top and a fire/cooking pit in the middle (a remnant from a homestead of the 1800's). We gathered drift wood, of just the right size to build a good cooking fire, from the beach. I started each meal by heating a large pot of water while the driftwood burned down to a lower heat of embers and coal. When the water was hot, I moved it to the side and cooked whatever food was going to be prepared. The hot water was used to wash dishes after each meal. One year, Larry and some friends brought down a wood cook stove. I was able to bake bread in the woods. During this time, Larry went to work at a local mill. I enjoyed being at camp by myself. I got a job waiting tables at the Rusty Nail Restaurant in Gasquet. Before each shift, I'd jump in the river, change into a dress, and go to wait tables. I was twenty-one and Larry was twenty eight. I loved the freedom, independence, and adventure of my life.

Being with Larry brought a different level of cultural awareness to my life. Larry is Native American; his mother Margaret Charles is from four local tribes: Yurok, Karuk, Tolowa, and Tututni. Margaret was a dental hygienist. She was proud to be an educated Native American woman active in the Business and Professional Woman's Club, United Methodist Church, and Tolowa Nation. Through these organizations, she traveled all over the world giving lectures on what it was like growing up during a time of cultural transition, oppression, and how her family coped with learning "white man's ways." She would recall how her brothers were sent off to boarding school, and how she and her sister were allowed to stay home to be with their mother. Even though Margaret didn't participate in local native ceremonies or basket weaving, she knew how to gather foods and basket materials from the earth, and she shared that information when she traveled and gave her presentations. Her father was born and raised in the village located at the steps on Pebble Beach Drive and Pacific Avenue in Crescent City.

One thing that saddens me is not being privy to traditions of the local tribes when raising my children. I recall a time when Margaret shared with me how one of her Native American friends made fun of me for not placing a life line on the baby basket I carried my children in. If I had known about the tradition of placing a string of shells and beads across the top of the basket (a life line), I would have done so. But I didn't know—and that hurt.

It was fear of persecution that prevented Margaret's family from participating in local native ceremonies and dances. Margaret's parents raised her to become an educated woman and protected their family from being persecuted by whites by not participating in native tradition. So Margaret's sons were raised without those traditions as well. This is one example of how government-supported systematic destruction of native culture affected the personal lives of native families in our community.

Larry and I never got married, but we stayed together for ten years and had two children, Ruben and MarKawShuWa. I had two home births and educated myself on the art of midwifery. During a seven year period, I studied to be an emergency medical technician and attended 65 home births.

Being in my home town, not married, and having birth out of wedlock was challenging for me, but then I was twenty-three, finding my way through life in rebelliousness and independence. The real challenge came in being frowned upon. However, Grandma (my Greek grandmother) was my mentor and accepted me no matter what. She shared with me her knowledge on child rearing and delighted in my company. She understood what it meant to rebel and strike out on her own. Grandma was raised in Istanbul, and left her home town to marry my grandfather without ever meeting him, only corresponding through letters until she traveled across the Atlantic Ocean and across North America to meet him in San Francisco. She used to tell me how terrified she was and how she wanted to turn back, but couldn't because she would be called a coward.

But Honey, my father's mother, was mortified at the choices I was making. I didn't find out until I was a teenager that she was highly bigoted. Growing up, my friends were my friends. People were people. My parents shielded us from prejudice. When I chose a Native American to be my partner, and then when we had children and didn't get married, it shamed Honey. It changed our relationship. That was hard. That was really hard.

I remember a particular time when I was visiting Honey. My first born was two years old, and I told Honey I was pregnant again. And she said, "Without a father?"

My little boy Ruben said, "My daddy's right outside waiting for us," because he was. Larry dropped us off and then came back to get us.

Honey said to me, on that occasion, "Don't bother to come

back."

It may have been easier for Honey to accept if I weren't living in this community where she had to face her friends and answer questions about her granddaughter who she expected would make her proud, not embarrassed.

That hurt. However, I went back. I chose to keep our relationship going. Somehow, I knew she would relent. I went back again and again until Honey finally said, "Come again." And when Honey died, I was the only family member there by her side. I held her hand when she died. I will always remember seeing her in the hospital bed taking deep breaths for over an hour as I watched her holding tight to her physical being. I felt there was enough waiting and when her good friend arrived to join me by her side I said, "Honey, I'm here and Beth is here, let go. It's okay, Honey, let go." Within a minute, she stopped breathing and she passed. For me, a lot was learned from this experience of life, transition, and death— particularly the power of rejection, acceptance, persistence, and loss.

I persevere in knowing I am able to create my own space in life. My struggles are few. I have been fortunate to experience and learn from cultural discord, in this special rural community. I will always call it home. I will always feel I belong.

*—November 19, 2017*

# Frances Ruiz

"This town is a mixed bag. It's not really a good place for
a retired person without a family near-by. But I have forged my
way in it. And I'm going to keep on forging."

*Frances Ruiz is a retired school counselor and sometime-resident of Crescent
City in search of the finer things in life—including a good book club. Here she
tells the story of how she came to live in Del Norte, and she describes the tenu-
ous threads that keep her attached to this part of the world.*

IN THE SUMMER OF 2004, I was living in Las Vegas. I'd lived
there most of my life, although I was born in Burbank, California. One of my lifelong best friends, Cynthia, who, like me, is also
a school counselor, traveled north to meet her friend in Requa,
California. They went for a ride up to Crescent City on a Saturday
in the summer of 2004, and, very impulsively, Cynthia bought a
house. Just like that! The same day. I love her. She's one of my dear-
est friends, but she's very impulsive and crazy as a bed bug.

She came back to Vegas, happy as a lark, and told me all about it.
"You've got to come up with me for the closing," she said.

So we flew up here over Labor Day and stayed at Crescent
Beach Motel. Well, the house wasn't really very nice.

"What have I done!" she said.

"You bought a house in three hours. What do you expect?" I
said.

And then she says, "Let me take you to the neighborhood
where I should have bought." And she takes me to this neighbor-

hood near Peterson Park—7th and C St.

There's a house for sale, a nice house: 1950s California style, very well maintained, walking distance to the ocean. We're mostly desert rats, she and I, but my parents grew up by the ocean, and I have always loved the ocean. It was unbelievable to think of the possibility of living so close to it.

And Cynthia says, "You've got to buy this house! We've got to call the people who own it!"

I said, "I'm not like you. I'm not going to buy a house in one day." But we called the owner, and we saw the inside on Sunday, even though we had to be at the Arcata Airport by 1 pm.

Well, I fell in love with the house. It was perfect. And all through the showing my friend (well intentioned) was pressuring me, "You've got to buy this house!"

But I'm not like her. I went home and did my research first. My partner at the time was a black man. We were together for twenty-three years, and it worried me that there was such a small percentage of racial diversity here. And only 27% of people owned their own homes! The education levels were low, too. Very few people had a college education.

Now, I'm not a snob. My mom was a florist who went to UCLA for just two years. My dad was a card dealer in Las Vegas who never went to college. But education levels do have an effect on a community. When people are educated, they seem to be more likely to develop a love of music and the arts, and I was worried that Del Norte might not have many cultural opportunities.

But it was so beautiful, and so uncrowded. And Las Vegas had been changing. It was becoming so superficial and so much more about the car you drive and the master-planned community you live in. Do you live in Alliante or Summerlin? How about "I just live in a nice house in a nice neighborhood"?

Well, I looked up the crime statistics for 2003. I showed them to my son who is a police officer. It was an annual report, statistics for the whole year. He says, "Wow, Mom. We have this much crime in three days."

I had lots of equity in my Vegas home. So, after not being impulsive, I bought the house. Ironically, Cynthia, to this day, has never lived in her house. And she will never live here. She's been here many times and has stayed at my house, but she's looking in Seattle now. She rents her place out instead.

For thirteen years, I've gone back and forth between Las Vegas and Crescent City. In the summer, I pinch myself that I own a home by the ocean and the redwoods. But I don't live here year round. I never have. I did try the last two winters here, and I don't mind the rain. It gives me a chance to read. But the weather makes traveling out of here difficult. If you want to go anywhere, you've got to check conditions. The highway is sliding into the ocean. If you want to go to Target, or see a good movie, forget it. I've been known to drive to Ashland just to go to the Varsity Theatre. And I have gone alone.

It's a constant push-pull between benefits and challenges.

For example, I was over at Safeway one night in the early years, about 11 o'clock at night, and I bought two or three bags of groceries. There were only a couple cars in the parking lot, and it was pouring down rain. I get in my car, and there's knock on the window. It kinda startled me. It was the grocery checker standing in the rain. I had left a bag at the checkout, and she had brought it out for me. Okay, that would never happen in Las Vegas. Never. That really touched me.

And most of the time, when you're at the grocery store, people are not in a hurry. In Las Vegas, everybody's always in such a hurry. Here, people are friendly. They talk to you. You don't see them making faces or tapping their feet. I've never met anyone here who was rude. Well, only one.

But on the other hand, there are some real limitations. For thirteen years, I've been trying to start a book club here. Honestly, I went to the Chamber of Commerce, the library, and I went to the place here which in Las Vegas we call the "Ed Shed," the school district. The only book group I was indirectly invited to was a Christian book club. Well no offense to anybody, but I don't want to be in a Christian book club. And I asked around, and some people say there are other book clubs here, but they're all closed.

Now, I tried to start my own. I live on a block mostly occupied by single women in their sixties and seventies, all home owners. And they're great folks. I love them. But not one of them wants to be in a book club. So how do I start book club if I don't have the resources, meaning people who want to read? And I'm not intellectual about it. I have three college degrees, but you don't need to talk to me about the protagonist or the antagonist or the quality of the syntax. I'm really at a stage, "Did you like it? Did you not like it?"

I've been in many book clubs in Las Vegas. I still am. One of them included a school librarian. It's a book club in one of these planned communities I talked about earlier. Anyway, we were picking the books for the following year, and one of my friends, a history teacher, said she wanted to read Jonathan Kellerman.

The school librarian says, "I'm not reading a thing that won't stimulate my mind."

I said, "Well, I'm not going to be in a book club that stimulates my mind every month."

So I left and started my own. People didn't even need to read the book to show up to mine. They could just pretend they were there to hear about it, like an NPR book review. And it was great fun.

It's so hard here to make those personal, social connections. But I have learned some things. You have to work your way in. I'm now on the advisory committee of Del Norte Association for Cultural Awareness (DNACA). I'm part of a new group that grew recently out of the January women's march. I also volunteer at the library, and although I'll be gone for the winter, I plan to come back, volunteer, and make a flyer about a book club—so look for it!

Another big challenge living here is getting good health care. In 2013, over the July 4th weekend, I broke my right foot. I went to the walk-in clinic at Sutter Coast after four days. My ankle was really purple. Someone had told me to make sure I went to the walk-in clinic and not directly to the hospital emergency room because of how they might charge my insurance. So, even though I went into the walk-in clinic, they sent me across the street to the hospital to get an x-ray. But they did say, "Make it clear that you are a walk-in from us, and be really clear about how you are billed." So I did.

The person who did my x-ray explained that I had a fracture on my left foot. And I should explain a little wrinkle here: as a baby, I had polio. The toes on the right foot are all paralyzed. There's a reason I'm mentioning this that will come up later. Anyway, I'm here by myself, no children or family near-by, with a broken foot. It was very frustrating.

It was also clear I'd need several appointments for follow-up care from somewhere other than the emergency room. So I call three different orthopedic offices in town. One office never called me back.

One office called me back and said they could see me August 11—more than a month later. And one office was nice enough to call me back and say they just couldn't see me.

I ended up calling a place in Medford, where I got great care. But I had to make many trips. My ex-boyfriend came up to help. My son came up and took me a couple times. My daughter came up one time. And one time, I had to cross my left leg over my right and drive to Medford myself!

In the meantime, I get paperwork and bills from Sutter Coast. Of course they bill me for an Emergency Room visit. They included a report from a Physician's Assistant in the Emergency Room who supposedly checked the mobility in my feet. She claimed all digits on both feet were moving and wiggling perfectly. Well, I haven't been able to move my right toes since I was 11 months old.

So I wrote this long, well written paper, and I presented it to the Head of Nursing at Sutter Coast. She was so impressed she asked if she could share the paper with her nurses. The hospital ripped up a bill they sent me for more than $800 because every step of the way I had said that I was a walk-in and not an ER patient. They also re-imbursed my insurance for another $900. But what if I hadn't been able to advocate for myself? What if I hadn't documented every step of the experience?

My story is not unique, and it's not the only one I want to tell. My neighbor is seventy-six. She had a health issue a while back, and I drove her over to the Sutter Coast walk-in clinic. This was in March. I checked the website first to make sure they were open. The website said they opened at 8 am. We got there at 9 am. The office was dark, but we saw a note on the door saying their regular hours were at 10 am. It was frustrating, but we went home and came back. We saw another piece of paper. I hadn't noticed it the first time. It said, "Due to the inability to staff the clinic, we will be closed for 4-5 days." I drove her up to Brookings to Curry County Medical Center, and they took care of her in a snap. It's a whole different environment and feeling there.

Because of these incidents, I got involved. I went to a Tuesday morning City Board meeting and a Health Care District meeting the same night. And I told these stories. And I asked, "Does Crescent City want people to retire here and help contribute to the economy? I'm representing five retired women on my block, and none of us are going to stay and risk our health unless things get better."

This town is a mixed bag. It's not really a good place for a retired person without a family nearby. But I have forged my way in it. And I'm going to keep on forging. I'm not ready to give up yet.

And I *will* find, or start, a book club, or die trying.

—*October 2, 2017*

# Amy Campbell-Blair

"Our first year here was pretty rough for a variety of reasons.
It was difficult moving to a strange new place and not knowing anyone.
I was at home with a toddler and got pregnant a few months after we
moved. I missed our family and friends and our old life."

*Amy Campbell-Blair describes the shock of the isolation she experienced when
she moved to Crescent City. But she also explains how that isolation led her
toward a deeper understanding about how to build community.*

I WAS BORN AND RAISED in a small town called Ridgecrest in
the California high desert, two and a half hours northeast of Los
Angeles. It's actually a much bigger town than Crescent City—like
30,000 people—and even though we were geographically isolated,
we would visit LA a lot. I grew up loving the city.

We came to Del Norte a few years ago for my husband's job.
We were living down in Pasadena and he had just passed the bar
exam, but he couldn't find any work. There were too many lawyers
competing for too few jobs. I'd just had our first child, so I wasn't
working. We were getting kind of desperate. At one point, I went
to every California county website to look for job postings because
we were ready to go anywhere.

I found a job posting for the county counsel in Del Norte that
Joel had missed. So he applied, and we drove up here for the interview. We'd actually driven through here before. We camped at Mill
Creek State Park on our honeymoon, but we didn't really spend
any time in the area. On our way back down to So-Cal, they called

us and offered us the job.

There were some immediate positives to moving up here. We'd been so stressed about neither of us having a job, so we were really glad for the change. We also just needed some kind of life change in general—some kind of big change—and here it was.

It was dramatic, coming up here for the interview, a twelve-hour drive with a nine-month-old baby. We got here and it was really beautiful. I remember parking near the lighthouse past Front Street where you can look at the ocean, and we looked in the local newspaper for apartments to rent. We had a lot of hope.

After a while, when we started to settle in here, some of the obvious challenges began to stand out. The isolation was huge. Not only were we in a small town, but the nearest large city was two hours away on a winding road. We really missed the availability and diversity of restaurants and other stores. There are very few places here open late.

There are a lot of things you take for granted when you're in a big metropolis. For example, if you need something, if it's not at the one Target, you can just drive to the other one a few miles away. Here, you can shop online, but that doesn't get you out of the house. You start making different decisions when you realize that you don't have the benefits of living in an area that serves a larger population. I taught myself how to make sourdough bread and croissants because I couldn't get those things here as easily. I don't know that I would have done that if we hadn't moved here.

Another big difference is that while people are friendly, it can be hard to make friends. It's hard to get into a group. I've found, in an urban area, there are a lot more transplants, sometimes a lot of people who don't have family—and that motivates them to put together a community. Whereas if you're from here, you have your family or friends that you've known from high school, and you don't need to meet the new person unless you want to. And you might not even know how new people feel, trying to fit in because you have what you need.

Our first year here was pretty rough for a variety of reasons. It was difficult moving to a strange new place and not knowing anyone. I was at home with a toddler and got pregnant a few months after we moved. I missed our family and friends and our old life. I wasn't sure how or where I would be able to meet anyone to be friends with.

We tried a few churches, but we never really found any place where we fit. I liked St Paul's, the Episcopalian church. We went there the most, and they were lovely towards us and our toddler. But going to any church really was hard after our second baby was born.

I was also working through some pretty deep grief. I was still recovering from a really traumatic birth experience when we moved here. I gave birth to my first child in a birthing center. She finally came after more than twenty-four hours which included very painful back labor and a fourth-degree perineal tear. I got to hold her for fifteen minutes, but then I had lost too much blood, and the midwife realized I had torn too much for her to do anything about it, so I was transferred to the hospital for surgery. There's this surreal picture we have of me in the hospital where I'm totally yellow from loss of blood.

We'd taken a birthing class. I knew things could happen we didn't expect. I knew I had to be flexible. But nothing even remotely prepared me to deal with my labor and injury. People say you forget about the pain after it's over. No. If I think about that day even now, I remember, and I'm amazed that I got through it somehow. My body recovered amazingly well, but I needed to do a lot of work emotionally to cope after that.

So I was still working through a lot of emotional trauma when we came up here, and as much as I wanted to have a community, I wasn't really ready to do the emotional work required. We ended up just staying home from church on Sundays and having family time. It was nice. Someday I'd like to go back to the Episcopalian church. I just haven't been ready yet.

We have managed to build some relationships, though, outside of a church community. Eventually we got invited to a book club, and I was able to meet some people that way. From there, I met one woman who's now a really good friend. She has a daughter the same age as mine. They're best friends now. She introduced us to this other couple with a little boy around the same age as our daughters as well. And now these friends have started to feel like family.

My husband's work, in some ways, made us feel a little limited at first in building community because of the nature of his job. There were certain places we thought we couldn't really go as a family because of the type of interactions he had with some people in the community. He's a lawyer for the county, and one main part of the work in his office is representing the social workers who detain children. Part of it was about us feeling uncomfortable, but it was also about not wanting to make others feel uncomfortable. That's not something a person usually worries about in a large urban area. You might have a profound effect on a family and just never know because you'll probably never see them again. That's harder to do here. I think now, we're learning to give space for that in our lives. There's a certain grace you have to learn. It's okay for people to be upset with you and to have encounters be awkward. Having to face the consequences of decisions, whether good or bad, that affect other people is a good thing to wrestle with.

This also connects with political differences because if I'm being totally honest, at the last election, when our county voted for Trump, that's the moment I really felt like I didn't belong here. When I lived in a larger urban area it was easier to avoid people who I disagreed with on fundamental and moral values, particularly related to politics. That's not so easy here.

But there's a part of me that says, "I do need to hear what you have to say because you're a person just like me. You have beliefs and opinions and experiences that have formed you, and maybe I can't change your mind about anything, but we can at least listen to one another and try to understand where the other is coming from." Nothing will ever change unless we're willing to listen to the fears and concerns and values of others we believe are wrong.

I don't want to get stuck in an intractable conflict with people because it's more important to me that I prove a point or make the best argument for my position.

I study peace and conflict issues and really believe that in conflict situations, there are always intersections of belief and commonalities between people who may appear to be polar opposites on an issue. Granted, value conflicts can be the most difficult to navigate because those are the conflicts that people are willing to die for. However, if people can be taught to look beyond the idea that conflict is always negative or that resolving conflict always means compromising one's values, I think more productive dialogue can happen, and that can lead to action.

So as I reflect on feeling like an outsider here, I don't actually think that other people should get to tell me that I don't or can't belong here. They can tell me that I don't get to belong to their circle of family and friends, just like I get to tell them the same thing. But we all belong to the same land. The drama of the ocean is here for all of us to enjoy. The mystery of the forests beckons all of us to seek it out. The beauty of the river has the power to make us all speechless. This particular bit of earth has been here longer than any particular group of people who happen to call Del Norte home.

That being said, I do want to be mindful of the fact that the Yurok and the Tolowa tribes in this area have called this land their home for thousands of years. That gives me some perspective about how to contextualize what it means to belong here. The way these tribes and other tribes throughout California were initially, and even thereafter, treated by the white settlers who came here to the West is reprehensible, and I think all Californians need to grapple with this history because there are very real consequences that still affect the environment, the culture, and the people who live here. This historical context helps give me a sense of the importance of listening and seeking out all the points of view of people here and not just the particular views of those who happen to have political and social power at the moment.

Belonging shouldn't happen through the harm of or at the expense of others. Belonging should be about loving the same piece of earth and letting that form how we live together. I do think part of making this place home for my family means that we do it because we love the land and the people and not because we're exploiting those we disagree with or because we're only advancing our interests by ignoring injustices going on around us.

Diversity of opinion and thought creates resiliency in people if we allow it to change us and make us stronger. With all of this in mind, my family won't ever be able to belong in the way in which people with more history living here belong, but I do think that with time and commitment, we can find our own way of belonging and our own place among everyone else. Because I do love this place and I care about the people here. Del Norte isn't just a place to drive through in order to get to Portland or San Francisco. It's our home now.

—*October 20, 2017*

# Mien Yang

"My sister has a Caucasian husband. My brother
has an African-American wife. It's just who you like and who you
fall in love with. People are more open to this in the big world—
the big city. But people here are more judgmental."

*A first generation Hmong-American from Detroit, Mien Yang can't help com-*
*paring his life in Del Norte to his life back home. Like many people who move*
*here out of necessity, his sense of belonging—and not belonging—connects to*
*what he's lost.*

I'M FROM THE MIDWEST—Detroit, Michigan. But my wife,
Maiv Lo, was born in Crescent City. She was the first Hmong-
American baby born here, in fact.

After my wife and I got married, we lived in Michigan for a
while. I was managing the parts department of a car dealership in
Detroit. But business was slow and we thought the grass might be
greener in California. We moved to Santa Rosa, and then in 2009
to Crescent City, where my wife's family lives.

It turns out the grass is yellow everywhere.

I had some kidney issues a few years back. Maiv's parents offered to help with the kids while I started dialysis. I got a job at
Tolowa Dee-ni' Nation working at the Head Start, which was part
time at first, but then after about a year, it became full time. My
wife worked housekeeping at the hospital. Since then she's been
going to school off and on, too. And we have four kids.

What was medical care like in Crescent City? Well, all my medi-

cal care for my kidney issues was done in Oregon. I had all my ne-
phrology care in Medford. My transplant was in Portland in 2014.

Before the transplant, I did kidney dialysis for two years, from
home. That was tough. You know, there's two types of dialysis:
hemo and peritoneal. Because of our remote location—there is no
dialysis center here—I had to do peritoneal. The only way I could
have done hemo would have been for me to travel three times a
week to Medford and then to spend hours each day recovering. I
couldn't have kept a job that way. I couldn't have kept my insurance, either. And if the roads had closed and I couldn't get to Medford, I could have died.

So I opted for peritoneal dialysis. That meant having a bag of
water inside my abdomen, which drains the toxins out. Then I had
to drain the water. I hooked up to a tube twice a day—once during my lunch hour and then again after I got home from work. I
was tethered to a twenty foot long cord and a machine during the
procedure. It was really hard. I slept on my side for two years with
a big tube coming out of my stomach. If I leaned one way wrong,
the machine would start beeping and wake me up.

Crescent City is a great place to raise your kids and a great place
to retire. But if you're looking for work, it can be very challenging.
It's great if you can work for the prison or the hospital, but otherwise, it's very limited. Where I'm from, you can always find something, even if it's temporary. But not here. My son wants to get his
work permit and start working, but I don't really think there will
be many opportunities for him other than fast food.

I do enjoy a lot that the area has to offer. The scenery is great. I
like the ocean and the woods and the rivers. I like hiking. I fish and
hunt. I'm an outdoors guy. I'm still trying to get used to the hunting terrain, though. There are so many hills here! It was easier back
in Michigan to hunt in tree stands. But I'm adjusting.

Another good thing about this place is that everybody knows
everybody. You tend to watch what you do. And if something happens, you're going to hear about it, like an injury at a local sports
game or something.

The Hmong community in Crescent City is small. It's like a village. It's close knit. There's a "You scratch my back, I'll scratch yours" mindset, and that's common in the culture. That's what your parents teach you when you're young. You're expected to participate in events happening all over, and then when your own family has an event or a ritual, those people will come to yours.

An example of one such ritual is a spirit calling. We believe that when something shocking or frightening happens—like you get hit by a branch of a tree—your spirit jumps out of your body. It might lay there. It might wander off. Then you aren't feeling well. You get sick. The community needs to help call the spirit back to you and your house. We call to our spirits—the person and the spirit—at different times.

But I find I'm less active in Hmong cultural activities here. Back in Detroit, there was something going on every weekend: weddings, funerals, spirit callings. But there's less happening here.

Even though we don't have Hmong cultural events and rituals as often as other communities, I do think there's a lot to do here, especially with kids. This is a good place to raise kids. There's football, basketball, tumbling, and cheer. I try to be an active parent and keep my kids busy.

I have two kids in Del Norte High, one in Bess Maxwell Elementary, and another in Head Start in Smith River. All my kids so far have gone to Bess Maxwell. In the beginning, we lived in the Bess Maxwell district. But even after we moved, we requested to send our kids there. It's where most Hmong families send their kids. There was a Hmong teacher there, Khou Vue, and lots of Hmong kids. It's kind of like a word of mouth thing. When your family and friends like a school, and they talk about it, you feel comfortable sending your kids there. It's also where the Hmong Cultural Center is located.

My older kids understand Hmong, which they spoke often with their grandparents in Michigan. But my two younger kids don't know many words. My wife and I are two different dialects—I'm Green and she's White. We do speak to our kids in Hmong sometimes, but it's hard for White Hmong to speak Green—it's hard to roll the tongue the right way. So our different dialects have an effect on our younger kids' learning and speaking it.

Yes, Crescent City is a good place to raise a family. Whether you're Hmong or not, no matter what your ethnicity is, you want what's best for your kids. But when they get older, their options are limited. We have College of the Redwoods. But if my kids want to go to university, they have to leave town. And if my kids can make it, I don't want to stop them.

There's more diversity in bigger communities, too. We do have people of different ethnicities and races here, but there isn't much intermingling. If I didn't work for the Tolowa, I wouldn't know very much about them. I can research on my own, but what's written online and what's written in books isn't the same as what you experience personally. In bigger cities, there's more to experience. Like back in Michigan, there's more interaction and communication every day between people across cultures. Here, it's more segregated.

In Michigan, we would go to Mexican Town in Southwest Detroit and get tacos. There was always someone to talk to there and cultural events to participate in. I haven't been to any Hispanic events here.

I do get education on Tolowa language and culture, and that's a positive. And Khou Vue and the Hmong community put on events like New Years. But I would like to see us do more. I'd like to see more socializing across ethnicities—and more cultural sharing.

It's just very cliquish here compared to Michigan. You know, it didn't matter to me that I married a Hmong woman. My sister has a Caucasian husband. My brother has an African-American wife. It's just who you like and who you fall in love with. People are more open to this in the big world—the big city. But people here are more judgmental. They tell you not to do these things.

To be honest, I don't see my future here. I like it, but I don't love it. After our kids are grown, my wife and I hope to travel and experience more. We hope to buy a nice house somewhere in a bigger city. We miss the diversity—and the variety of foods. There's not a big selection here—not too many options. And I miss having four seasons. I love the snow. People say it's colder in Michigan, but it doesn't feel as cold. I can shovel snow in a t-shirt there! I miss the snow.

*—January 15, 2018*

# Cherece Norris

"It was so cliquish. It was clear that if you knew
the right people, you could get what you wanted."

*Seeing her child being bullied drove Cherece Norris out of town. But when she
came back, she came back stronger and more determined to make a safe and
happy life for herself and her family.*

I WASN'T BORN HERE. I actually came in 1993, six months be-
fore the end of my senior year in high school. We moved from
Hanford, California when my dad was transferred here to work at
Pelican Bay.

I was so upset about the move. I thought my life was over. "Why
are you moving me now?" I complained. I was very intimidated,
going to a new school and meeting new people. But I ended up
graduating valedictorian through Paragon High, which was an alternative school here at the time.

So I didn't get to meet a lot of people early on. I started working
at Elk Valley Casino and got to meet people then, including my
future husband, who is a member of the Yurok Tribe, but I never
really put myself out in the community. I do feel like I belong here
now, but I didn't at first. With a small town, it's easy to keep to
yourself, to avoid people—gossip and things like that.

I didn't want kids before I met my husband. I was going to be
a criminal psychologist. But when we got together, everything I
thought I wanted changed. I decided I wanted kids, a minivan, the
whole bit. But when we needed daycare for our children, I realized

there wasn't much choice out there. The places available just didn't seem right. That's when I decided I would stay home. And then I made it into a business.

But even though the home daycare was successful, something happened that made us rethink Del Norte County. Our older son has disabilities. In school, right off in kindergarten and first grade, he got bullied. Kids called him "retarded" because he was in special classes. School became a very unhealthy place. And our family—we hadn't had good experiences to begin with—so we started looking at places like USA Charter School* which was a great school. Eventually, we ended up homeschooling because we're so family oriented, and it was hard for our kids to be away—and to be treated badly.

Our oldest son was being bullied on his youth football team. He was Junior Varsity. The coach decided to punish the whole team for the bullying—he made them all run—and then there was peer retaliation. It just got worse. So we called a meeting with the organizers of the league so that they could address the bullying. When we went into the meeting, none of them even looked at us. They all had their heads down. It just showed me right there that things were not going to change. It was so cliquish. It was clear that if you knew the right people, you could get what you wanted. If you knew the right people, you could sweep things under the rug. I ended up leaving that room very angry.

I didn't want our son to feel like he stuck out like a sore thumb. I had family in Idaho, and I thought if we moved, things would be better for them. They both went to public school, and they fit in. There was some bullying, but it was easier to address because it wasn't a small town where everyone had alliances. You know, the attitude, "If you don't like this person, I won't either." I think they needed to experience that, to see that Crescent City wasn't the whole world. They got to see the bigger picture.

And Idaho was our breakaway. We didn't do daycare there. There was no kids' art on the walls. It was a nice break, and it was

---

* Unchartered Shores Academy Charter School.

a chance to learn a lot about ourselves.

When we left, we said the only thing that would bring us back would be if one of our family members got sick. My husband's mom was diagnosed with brain cancer, and it spread very fast. We moved back October 1, 2015, and we lost her shortly afterwards.

I say Crescent City is not the shape of a crescent, it's in the shape of a boomerang. Anyone who moves here, born or raised, is going to come back. And since our parents are getting up in age, it made sense to stay.

The funny thing is that as soon as we moved back, we heard from our friends and neighbors, "When are you going to open up a daycare again?" We never realized how much of an impact we had on others. And that's when I first started feeling I belonged.

We moved back in, and because our kids learned resiliency outside of Crescent City, they were able to find their places. Our older son works at Best Western. He's the breakfast bar host. Both of them are like us—they don't associate much with the outside community. They keep to themselves. But that's the way they like to live.

Our oldest son, Eric Junior, is more culturally interested and more involved than our younger one. He does participate in ceremonies. My husband really hasn't. I've been with him for 21 years, and we've never been to a Brush Dance together. But our son has. He dances and he crochets traditional hats and makes eel hooks. He's learned a lot of these skills in NCIDC (Northern California Indian Development Council) and through Hop Norris' men's group. My younger kid is more into sports.

As far as our business, we decided, if we're going to stay with family daycare, we're going to go big. I feel like we already had high quality daycare the first time around. That's how we built our reputation. But we decided that this time around, we wanted to be more than just a daycare. We'd heard about the Early Head Start program, and we decided we wanted to do it. It would mean transforming our daycare into a certified *program*.

That's what brought me back to college, too. I needed to take four early childhood education classes. We also needed to make modifications to our home.

You know, I've never been much of a reader with my ADHD. I can read a whole page and not know what I've just read. I'm intimidated by books. But I realized that books weren't out and about here, and kids love books. So we made an intentional change. We started doing the program here called Wee Read and infusing reading into our daily routine. And kids have books at the ready to pick up and look at, too.

And that's part of what inspired me to write a children's book. I had this little boy in day care who was very rough with books. He would tear them and chew on them. And with Wee Reads, I had to buy a lot of books, and they were expensive. So I started looking online for a book that would teach kids how to be nice to books.

The main character of my book is Victig, which in Norwegian means *important*. Victig is a little book himself, and he explains to kids that he has arms and a spine just like kids do. I would like to publish it, but I just got it written up. And I went to a Writers' Conference to learn how to make it happen. I'd like everyone in the Wee Reads program to have a copy, too.

We have eighteen kids enrolled—six in the mornings and fourteen at night. And we're doing great. This is what we love to do.

When my husband was younger, he was told that he was the only Native American in his family who would have to pull out his ID to prove he was a tribal member because he looked more white than the rest of his family did. And he is part white. It just shows more. But I think that's maybe one reason why he doesn't participate in ceremony. He hasn't felt like he fits in. And some Native people treat us badly, and that hurts.

You asked about what feels fair or unfair here, and the process of getting tribal affiliation is something that bothers me. Like many people here, we've struggled with where to enroll our kids. My husband is an enrolled member of the Yurok Tribe, but his grandmother was enrolled in Elk Valley, as many Yurok people are.[*] For

---

[*] Natives in our area often face this challenge, since many are of mixed tribal

our kids, Elk Valley was probably the better way to go in terms of benefits. So when our oldest son was born, we enrolled him there.

When our youngest son was born in 2001, we started the process. We had all the blood lines researched and set up, to prove his eligibility. And at that time, because of the casino, a lot of Yurok folks were trying to sell over their rights to become Elk Valley Rancheria tribal members. And then suddenly, they closed enrollment. It's been closed ever since. Our youngest has not yet been placed there He's been waiting and waiting for Elk Valley to open up. Elk Valley Rancheria has 98 members. Yurok Tribe has almost 6000.

Elk Valley Rancheria was really good to him, though. When we go to the Christmas parties, they always have something for him as well as his brother. They give clothing vouchers to both of our kids—not just to one of them.

We ended up enrolling our youngest in the Yurok Tribe because he said he wanted to be a part of something. It's been rumored that Elk Valley might, one night at midnight, open up and take all the people who have applied and close up again. In the meantime, we raised our kids to split their benefits 50/50 with each other. When the oldest became eighteen, he started getting a stipend. And he's been a man of his word. As soon as he got it—he gave half of it to his brother. We found a way to work it out within the family.

I do want to say that my perception of this town has changed since I got back. I'm a little bit more out in the community, but I won't do anything political. I choose how I put myself out there. Like I don't go to the Chamber mixers or the deck party. You see the same people there, and they're usually people in power. I stay away from them. I've heard the stories. I don't want to use personal relationships to leverage my power. And I don't want to be part of things that I don't think are right, especially when people are drinking alcohol and behaving badly. There is corruption in this

ancestry and may be eligible for enrollment in more than one tribe. This challenge is compounded by the fact that Rancherias, created beginning in 1906 as lands reserved for "homeless" local Indians, did not always group people by tribe, nor did they include everyone in the area with Native ancestry. In this sense, tribal *identity* and tribal *enrollment* are not the same thing.

town. Like I said earlier, if you know the right people, things can get swept under the rug.

It's there. I've seen it enough. But you can live here and make a choice not to be part of it. Sometimes that means not associating with certain people. And that's where we are as a family. We're here. We're staying. You only have to partake in what you want to partake in. And I know what I want to be part of: I want to love people. I want to be a ripple, and I want to teach kids to be a ripple, too.

*—October 13, 2017*

# Pang Hona Xiong

"I told my bullies, 'I have the right to stay.
I have the right to have the same educational
opportunities, just like everyone else.'"

*A Hmong refugee from genocide in Laos, Pang Hona Xiong went from teen bride to mother to community leader. In her essay, she describes the joys and challenges of integrating into Del Norte County.*

I CAME TO THE UNITED STATES in 1991 when I was seven years old. I was born in a refugee camp in Thailand call Ban Vinai.

My father was a solider during the Vietnam War. He fought communists in the "secret war" in Laos on the behalf of the Americans. After the war, he escaped to Ban Vinai. They arrested him for not having legal documents to enter the camp. But with luck on his side, one of his cousins just happened to be in the camp, and she heard that someone named Xiong had just arrived and was in the jail. She went to see if it was a relative, and she saved him by identifying him.

I remember a lot about the camps I lived in. In Ban Vinai, I remember attending church with my parents every weekend. The Catholic Church was beautiful and breathtaking. So were the green fields filled with mango trees, rose bushes, daisies, and *lantanan camara* flowers. I remember walking the path up a hill, past a cemetery, past farm fields, and down the hill to get there. The best memory was playing with my siblings and friends. I remember there was a little hilltop filled with clay. Every day after school, we would all get together to see who could make the best art out of clay. The camp was beautiful in a way. We were surrounded by mountains and jungle on one side, rice paddies on the other owned by local Thai families. It was a lot like Crescent City, where there are Redwoods on one side and the blue Pacific Ocean on the other side.

In Ban Vinai, many families didn't have access to the outside world. The closest city was 24 hours away. It was quiet and peaceful. Although farming was very limited, we had a tiny parcel where my dad could plant some pineapples, banana trees, and yams. But for the most part, we depended on outside assistance. The United Nations provided food once a month, which didn't last long. We got rice and a small amount of meat—maybe fish, pork, or chicken every month.

Some families depended on their families from overseas to send them money. Some found ways to sell things at the market so that they had money to buy clothes, shoes, household items, or to send their children to school.

In the camp, my dad was a blacksmith. He had a shop left to him from his cousin when he and his family left for America. We were not rich by any standard, but we were better off than some because of that income.

After living in Ban Vinai for thirteen years, my father decided to bring his wife and children to America for a better life, so we could better ourselves.

My family was sent to another camp called Phanat Nikhom, the one everyone must go through in order to come to America. It was a terrible place, nothing like Ban Vinai. It was loud and frightening. There were watchtowers and barbed wire. Anyone who went near the fence got shot. We heard screaming and gunshots every night.

The camp was filthy. Now, whenever I walk past the sewage treatment facility on Front Street, it always makes me think of the camp and how it smelled. We were there for about a year. In Phanat Nikhom, there's not much for families to do to earn a living. For many families, the women and young girls would do embroidery (called *Paj Ntaub*) and send them to their families overseas to sell them. Everyone in this camp depended on outside assistance.

One of my worst experiences in the camp was when my siblings and I walked to the well to fetch water. We met a group of young officers on their day off, going to play volleyball and Seepak Takraw. One of them had a huge husky dog with him, and he let it go, and it attacked me. I was on the ground struggling to get up. He was screaming at it, shouting for the dog to kill me. He was screaming at me, too, shouting "Go back to where you came from." A group of young men and women surrounded us and finally made the guard take pity on me and pull his dog off.

When we first arrived, we came to Fresno. My biggest challenge was learning the language. I struggled until I was in middle school. There was little support in the schools, and although my parents were usually involved in my education—they attended every Parent-Teacher conference and all school activities. Even though they had trouble understanding the language and what was being said at these functions, they felt they needed to support us to give us a future, so we wouldn't have to suffer like they did. Being present was important to them.

Every day I tried hard to fit in, but the language barrier kept me out of activities and from making friends. Most of the other Hmong kids in Fresno could speak English, so even among them I sometimes felt like an outsider. As far as the school was concerned, I was not allowed to do what other students were doing because I couldn't speak English. I was not even allowed to participate in school activities like sports or dancing.

In 2000 as young newlyweds, my husband and I moved to Crescent City. I enrolled at Del Norte High School. During my junior and senior years, I encountered bullying because I was so different. My junior year, I was pregnant with my daughter, Angelina Khou Vue who is now in high school herself. Some students did not want me to stay at the high school because I was pregnant. I had students come up to me during lunch time, threatening to hurt me if I didn't transfer to Sunset High School. They said I was going to put a bad reputation on the high school if I didn't leave. Some students even threatened to have their parents bring lawsuits if the school let me stay.

But that didn't stop me. I saw graduation as very important to my future, and I didn't want to go to Sunset. I thought the education would be better at the main high school. During that year, there were five Del Norte High students who were pregnant, including me. The other four left for Sunset or dropped out. But I told my bullies, "I have the right to stay. I have the right to have the same educational opportunities, just like everyone else."

Not only did I stay, but I brought my daughter to school with me the next year almost every day. My mother-in-law said she would understand if I wanted to drop out, but dropping out was the last thing on my mind. My husband would remind me to be positive about my schooling. His words of courage and support, along with the thought of setting a good example for my daughter, helped keep me going. Also, the administration and teachers were very supportive. I am grateful for that. I've been told I was the first young mother to graduate from Del Norte High.

What are the shortfalls for Crescent City? What we lack are decent paying jobs, a four-year university, and a shopping mall. In Crescent City, not many young folks stay after graduating from high school. For example, in the Hmong community many students leave to the cities where there are more job opportunities and four-year colleges. For those like myself with a family to support, I would have to commute to Humboldt State University to get a degree. But commuting is not easy for many because it's very time consuming and expensive.

A decent-paying job is hard to find in Crescent City if you don't have a four-year college degree. If a person has a big family, working at a fast food restaurant is not enough to provide for their family. In Crescent City, we either work for the Del Norte Unified School District, the city, the county, the Pelican Bay Prison, or law enforcement. I know many families where the adults have to work two jobs to bring in a decent income.

Finally, it would be wonderful if we could have a shopping mall in town. My kids and I enjoy going shopping, but the long drive makes it difficult during the winter and raining season due to rock slides, and icy or flooded roads. But if we could have a shopping mall that would help our local families and small businesses generate income, it could be a valuable asset to our community.

What are some of the positive things about Crescent City? Right away this place reminded me of home, of Ban Vinai Camp, surrounded by mountains and forest. Crescent City has a lot of great places to see within a short driving distance, too. We have the beaches and restaurants, hiking and walking trails, the Smith River, the piers, the jetty, and beautiful Battery Point Light House.

My family enjoys outdoor activities. Every summer we would spend our summer fishing and crabbing out in the harbor or on the pier. We also enjoy going hiking, camping, and swimming in the majestic Smith River. My family also enjoys going hunting during the hunting season.

Another highlight in Crescent City is having youth sports available to our children year-round. The youth sports bring families and children together. Allowing our children to participate in the youth sports is a fantastic way for them to explore and develop lifelong skills. These sports are available to our children because of the great community members and local businesses donating their time and money to make it possible.

One more positive thing about Crescent City is our high school. Every year the Del Norte High School Scholarship Foundation Committee hands out hundreds and thousands of dollars of scholarships to our high school graduates. These scholarships are made by our generous local families and local businesses. It's wonderful to see that our community appreciates, values, and cares about our children's education and their future.

*—January 25, 2018*

# Stephanie Wenning

"Each hallway was 'owned' by a certain group.
There was the 'Asian hall' where the Hmong kids hung out.
There was the 'Mexican corner.' There was main hall where
all the jocks and cheerleaders hung out, too."

*Now at the head of a local non-profit, Stephanie Wenning explains what it was
like to be the odd-kid out growing up in Del Norte. Here she describes how she
made her way out—and back again.*

I WAS BORN IN RIVERSIDE, CALIFORNIA, but my family
moved here when I was three months old. My dad was hired as
a Correctional Officer (CO) at Pelican Bay State Prison when it
first opened. He transferred from Chino. Both my parents grew up
in Southern California, and they did not want to raise their kids
there. Southern California was too crowded and crime ridden, too
hot. They were ready for a change. So, as soon as this prison was
built, they jumped on board.

Growing up, I often felt I didn't belong. I think nearly every
child here has those feelings at some point—imagining more,
somewhere else. I was very lucky. When I was twelve, I went on
a trip to Finland with my science teacher, Mr. Caldwell. It opened
my eyes to know that the whole world isn't like here, and it made
me want to see more of it.

As a young person here, I struggled to try to find my place. I
was the bookish nerd. I didn't want to hang out with people; I tried
to isolate myself. I was so shy. I had just three friends. I spent all of

my lunch periods in club meetings because I didn't want to try to be part of cafeteria drama.

The school culture was cliquish. Each hallway was "owned" by a certain group. There was the "Asian hall" where the Hmong kids hung out. There was the "Mexican corner." There was main hall where all the jocks and cheerleaders hung out, too. I remember my friend getting pushed down there, and her books flew all over. There was a lot of bullying. My senior year, there were full-on fights with knives.

It was hard to get through high school, but I knew there was more to see—I'd had a taste of it—and I had a plan. I wanted to be an exchange student with Rotary, and I wanted to finish high school in three years so I could go overseas after graduation without having to return to high school. I took lots of classes at College of the Redwoods along with my high school classes. I even stayed active in many clubs and organizations. I managed to finish early—and as salutatorian of my class.

Through Rotary Youth Exchange, I went to France to a town called Besançon, an hour west of Switzerland, just at the top of the Alps. To me, the town was huge—about 120,000 people—surrounded by a bunch of little suburbs and in a region called Franche-Comté. In a strange way, it was reflective of here. The region was full of rural villages and had more cows than people. And, typical of France, people raised there generally had no interest in living anywhere else; they planned to stay.

I had to be an extrovert in France. Otherwise, I wouldn't have had any friends or learned the language. It really helped me develop social skills I didn't develop in Del Norte. It's funny. I couldn't wait to get out of here back then, and yet I came back, years later.

Here's how it happened. After my year in France, I went straight to Oregon State and got my degree in Interior Design. I was planning on staying in Corvallis. I was supposed to work at a furniture store where I'd been interning. Two weeks before graduation, though, they told me they didn't have a place for me. So I was without a job for two months. I started working as a bartender. I loved the area and my partner at the time was happy in his job, so we had no interest in leaving. But then we split up, and I came home. That was in 2012.

My plan had been to save as much money as I could and then move to the Bay Area. I had been offered a job at the San Francisco Design Center as a textile librarian a year or so before. That had been a dream job. Textiles were my passion, which sounds silly, but they're so fascinating. You can change one part of the weave to work for a specific use. So I was hoping to try again there.

But the longer I stayed here, the more that dream receded. As a kid, I'd hated this place. As an adult, I fell in love with it. I worked at several places, including the golf course and the animal clinic in Brookings. Obviously, not using my degree. But I was gradually losing interest in design work, at least the kind that is available. There's often an emphasis on replacing things that aren't necessarily broken, and that's just not my mentality. Also, I have rheumatoid arthritis so I'm not very good at hand drafting, and I hate the computer assisted design software I had to use to counter that disability.

So I began to think less and less about using my degree and more and more about creating my own way—designing my life differently. I did all kinds of work at the animal clinic. After about three years, I started looking for other opportunities in the area. I'd fallen in love with the environment, and I couldn't imagine leaving.

I don't know how to explain it. Del Norte is a magical place. Just this weekend, a good friend came to visit. We only had one day so we went to Point St. George, to Battery Point Lighthouse, up the South Fork to see the Darlingtonia, and then we came back down through the old growth redwoods. We ended the day by watching the seals by the harbor at sunset. In one day, we saw all this amazing stuff with only an hour and a half of driving.

I wasn't a kid who really liked the outdoors. When you go outside, you're always expected to be active, to play sports, to go swimming. But I've had arthritis all my life, and as a kid, I didn't want to be active. I stayed indoors. But now that I'm older, I can be outside and enjoy it knowing how to do what's right for me.

The Executive Director position for the Del Norte Association for Cultural Awareness (DNACA) was posted in April, about three months after I decided I needed to leave the clinic, so the timing was perfect. My mom forwarded me the announcement from the Workforce Center, and it caught my eye. Arts! That sounded cool. I applied, but I didn't expect much to come from it. I'd never worked for a nonprofit. I'd never done budgets before. I'd never done anything remotely related to this before. But I had a degree and met the minimum requirements, and I got a call for an interview. And I was very blunt in the interview: I didn't have experience, but I had the ability to learn.

At the end of the second interview, when it came time for me to ask questions of the panel, I asked, "Is there anything I said today or on my resume that makes you think I'm not right for the position?"

They said no—that I was perfect. So I left feeling pretty confident. The person I was seeing at the time, though, was very negative. I told him I thought I might have gotten it, and he said, "You probably didn't get it. You're not really qualified for it." It was a whirlwind of emotions, waiting to hear back.

Well, I got the job. It was that relationship that didn't work out.

Growing up here, it's a challenge. You've got to find your niche. I admire a lot of people in this community, like Rachel and Jacob Patterson who facilitate Gender Talk to help youth in the LGBTQ+ community find their place. They are trying to be the adults they needed when they were younger because there really isn't much support for young people who don't fit in.

I'm interested in doing that, too, in my own way, by helping people enjoy experiences in the arts, in a sense opening them up to other worlds and possibilities, to catharsis and expression. We need that here, isolated as we are.

*—September 20, 2017*

# Sam Bradshaw

"I tried to avoid being bullied by being incredibly quiet
and passive much of my time in school. I also tried to avoid being
teased by following norms like spending extensive time in the morning
trying to make my hair and makeup perfect. It never was. I would be in
tears before school almost every morning for most of my time in
high school because I didn't feel like I was good enough."

*Coming from a poor family and identifying as gender non-binary, Sam Bradshaw had two strikes against her as she made her way through the school system. In this essay, she recounts some ways school failed her. But her belief in the power of community organizing gives her hope for the future.*

I WAS BORN IN DEL NORTE COUNTY, but when I was two, my grandma made mom and I move with her and grandpa to Redding so that my mom could quit drinking. It would have been much more difficult to do this in Crescent City where Mom was surrounded by her friends who drank. In Redding, she was able to get sober. And she's stayed sober since I was three years old.

Mom has a serious physical disability. She has a broken back and COPD—Chronic Obstructive Pulmonary Disease—from a car crash ten years before I was born. It happened on the road between here and Klamath. She hit a redwood tree and fell ten feet below the car and lay there for hours as her car burned. The accident damaged her lungs and nearly paralyzed her. She wasn't supposed to be able to have kids and I'm her only child. She raised me on the small amount she receives for permanent disability from Social Security—and survivor benefits from my father passing when I was eight. My grandparents were prominent figures in raising me as well.

My grandma, who never wanted anyone to show weakness, had to adjust to mom's disability. She gave my mom a hard time when she used food stamps in the store at first. But Grandma always needed someone to help, and so she often used mom's disability as an excuse to swoop in and save the day whenever there was an opportunity, even if we didn't want help or were too proud to ask for it.

When I was eight, we moved back to Crescent City, following Grandma and Grandpa who were moving back after their divorce. I went to Mary Peacock School because I lived in that district. Mary Peacock is a school where most students come from families with a higher socioeconomic status, and that fact soon became clear to me. I ended up in a class that had thirty kids in it, and all but four were the kids of well-paid Correctional Officers at Pelican Bay State Prison. One of those four was a doctor's kid, so he was still well-off. Meanwhile, my mom's disability was our only source of income. I didn't feel like I fit in at all.

In Redding, I excelled at and enjoyed school. Looking back, I realize the education there was much better. I was learning things there that I wouldn't learn until as late as 7th grade in Crescent City, even though I was only in school up to second grade. We also took field trips to museums, planetariums, and other amazing places. In Del Norte County, I went on two field trips in my entire school career.

In middle school, there were many challenges. I had been a straight A student, and so I always had a good connection with teachers along the way. But at Crescent Elk Middle School, it was impossible to connect with any teacher. That might have been because I was in the "lower partnership" instead of the upper partnership. I swear there was some kind of conspiracy. I believed at the time that if you had any incident on your permanent record, you got put in the lower partnership. But looking back I see that economic status also may have played a role. I remember joking that if your parent came in and asked, "Will my kid have a good teacher?" they automatically bumped the kid into the upper partnership. If somebody was wealthy and well known, or if somebody took an interest, things were skewed to be better for their kid.

Upstairs, they got to go on field trips and they got the best teachers. Downstairs, the teachers would leave the room and the trash can would get lit on fire, or the kids would throw stuff. The downstairs teachers were always exasperated but still tried to quell the chaos through punishment like in-house suspension, but it made the students resent them. The upstairs teachers always seemed peppy, and I heard students talking about how much they loved their teachers up there.

In high school, the lines between low income and higher income students sharpened and mixed. The rich kids wore $60 hoodies, $80 shoes and $100 jeans from the mall over an hour away. The lower income kids wore $5 or $10 clothes from Walmart in the same designs. The kids who got to shop in malls never had the same shirt as someone else. The students largely cliqued based on income level and race. Intermixing between groups was rare. I believe this increased the rate of isolation and depression in the lower income students.

There was also a disproportionate amount of higher income kids in Advanced Placement classes and of lower income kids in remedial classes. Amongst the lower income kids, it was widely considered a bad thing to be good at school. In college, I still flip my test over as I get it back so no one sees the "100%" on it because I was teased so much for getting good grades in middle and high school. Kids who did well got laughed at and called a "try-hard."

There was bullying in both middle and high schools on a widespread and regular basis. Some of what I witnessed was cruel, but there were rarely any repercussions unless there was a physical confrontation, leaving the weakest students vulnerable to continued abuse. There was also sexism in dealing with bullying; a boy I was friends with was physically attacked by his ex-girlfriend several times, and the school did nothing, saying she shouldn't be punished because it was a girl hitting a guy. My freshman year, I told the principal about me and two friends being bullied for weeks. That was after I had told several teachers. We were harassed, threatened and even had rocks thrown at us. He said that it was "good" for the bully to be aggressive because she was in sports.

I tried to avoid being bullied by being incredibly quiet and passive much of my time in school. I also tried to avoid being teased by following norms like spending extensive time in the morning trying to make my hair and makeup perfect. It never was. I would be in tears before school almost every morning for most of my time in high school because I didn't feel like I was good enough.

It was still difficult to connect with teachers at Del Norte High School, though less so than at Crescent Elk. From our community organizing research, we have seen that Sunset's teachers create a much more supportive, community-building atmosphere. Throughout my schooling, I had friend after friend switch to Sunset. I tried to follow them because I heard how good it was, but was heavily discouraged because I still received good grades, which to teachers and administrators seemed to mean I wasn't struggling as much emotionally as students who had let their grades fall. However, this is a dangerous assumption to make because it is often untrue.

Another challenge of living here which seems to be universal for young people is that it's very hard to get mental health services. There's a lack of qualified professionals in the area, widespread stigma, and a long, difficult process of going through person after person before you finally reach a professional who can really help you. It's hard for everyone, but it's much less difficult for higher income individuals as they can more easily afford to travel to Medford or Eureka for services.

I desperately needed mental health help in middle school. My grandma and my grandpa had died, and my best friend switched schools. I felt like I had nothing left. I was able to see someone for my crisis, and it was very helpful to talk to a counselor about my situation. I talked and talked to her. She made another appointment for me a week later. When I came back, I'd had a relatively good day, so she told me I did not need to come back again. Ever.

Now I use what I've learned about self-care in the camps and programs I have attended to take care of my mental health, but I know others are not so fortunate to have been exposed to this information. Depression and mental illness rates are high and our community has suffered from frequent suicide epidemics.

Youth here have a high rate of trauma and need access to counselors. But the school system only offers academic counselors—and not even at every school. Sunset doesn't have a counselor, and the elementary schools only have a counselor one day a week. Work is currently being done to help the mental and social health of the youngest elementary children and for high schoolers, but very little is being done for middle schoolers. This is unfortunate, as middle school is an extremely difficult and vulnerable time for most young people. It can be the start of many people's downward spirals.

In response to this and other issues in our community, I have become involved in many community improvement projects, and I am a founding member of an organization called the Local Youth Organizing Network (LYON). We work on improving mental health care access issues and other issues that are important to young people in our area.

I've also been a part of the first ever all-youth run Candidates Forum. Last year, we asked politicians to come together in a public forum and answer questions about how they would act regarding issues that affect youth in our county.

One candidate for supervisor, Roger Gitlin, disrespected us by using our event as a platform to criticize local youth on their perceived political inactivity. He said if youth wanted to see improvement, then maybe we should actually turn out and vote. He then listed a statistic about how few youth voted in the last election, though many of the youth present were under 18 and unable to vote at that time. This sent the clear message he was not at the event to gain youth support, because he didn't value it.

His dismissive attitude extended to other responses to questions close to the hearts of many youth. One person asked him about the issue of LGBTQ homeless youth, as their families can disown them when they come out, and because our area is rural, conservative attitudes are the majority. This is a notable issue in our area.

His response was, "I have been in the bushes. I have seen the tiny bottles. I have never seen a tranny in the bushes." And about the homeless in general, "They don't want help." The youth section gasped loudly at his lack of compassion.

Unfortunately, this treatment is similar to several other experiences I have had with many decision makers in Del Norte, with them being very dismissive and even ignorant of the issues young people care about. It illustrates the gap between people in power and the people they claim to be representing. It illustrates the need to always involve the people who are and will be affected by decisions in the decision-making process.

But even though our community has serious challenges and many youth, including myself, feel out of place, I do feel like I belong here and that there is hope for the future.

Coming up through the school system, I always heard kids saying, "I can't wait to get out of here," "I want to get out of this horrible town," and "As soon as I turn eighteen..." They don't see jobs. They don't see opportunity. They believe a person has to leave to be successful. To a large degree, they are right. There is a glass ceiling on economic success in Del Norte. There's a limit to what you can achieve without leaving here.

But I've never dreamed of leaving because I feel this is my home, and I see the potential here. I have this dream of transforming Del Norte into a shining utopia, where people have access to things like good mental health resources and a community center. Everybody would have a sense of belonging.

We could make this place like that. It just takes work and community organizing. It also takes the people in power listening to people, especially youth, or else being replaced by others who will listen. Youth know the most about the issues that affect them and they need to have a say in the decisions that will either improve or worsen their quality of life.

I'm only just recently coming to find what I need to make this utopia happen. Through leadership camps, college classes, memberships in groups working for community improvement, and participation in direct action, I am learning so many things about systems of oppression and taking action to create positive change and equality. I'm learning about youth stepping up and adults stepping back. I'm learning about the way socioeconomic status and location affects our life experience. In my experiences with community improvement, I've learned the importance and power of crafting and sharing your story with others. In my sociology class this semester, I learned about the systems, philosophies, and psychology that drive social issues like poverty, delinquency, and class inequality. I've recently decided I want to get my Master's in sociology from Humboldt State University.

I've begun my journey towards achieving this goal by attending the Del Norte Campus of College of the Redwoods. Here, I have felt a personal connection with nearly every teacher. I feel a strong sense of belonging and community on campus. However, many students, especially those of lower income or of color, have expressed difficulty feeling comfortable and developing a sense of belonging here. Because CR has been such a supportive environment for me, I have been working to improve the campus for other students in return—because I want it to be a safe, familiar space for all the students here.

It is nearly universal for youth in Del Norte to struggle in the school system in some way or another, and I and the others who are in community improvement groups share similar experiences. But we have been lucky enough to have been empowered by these groups and programs, so we feel like our voice matters and that we have the power to create positive change.

We want to use our voices, our power, and all that we've learned to make Del Norte a better place so that future youth will have better experiences, less hardship, more opportunity, more support, more hope, and a greater sense of belonging and community.

We want to empower other youth and help them see that their voices matters. We want to help them learn ways to lift themselves and others up, build movements, and demand the positive change so desperately needed here, so that Del Norte becomes a better and better place, generation after generation.

*—October 10 2017*

# De Shawn Mims

"The astounding similarity we share, behind these bars and on
the outside, is that we all have an innate will to survive, maximize
pleasure, and decrease pain. It's in our nature. To quote the famous
words of Maya Angelou, 'We are more alike than we are unalike.'"

*Unlike the other writers in this book, Deshawn Mims didn't sit for an in-person
interview. He neatly printed his essay on lined notebook paper—the kind you
get when you are incarcerated in Pelican Bay State Prison—and mailed it in at
my request. In his cover letter, he wrote, "I hope I can be of assistance with your
search for a voice behind these bars."*

MY CALAMITOUS JOURNEY TO DEL NORTE'S PELICAN BAY
State Prison level four started on an early dark morning from
Deuel Vocational Institution in Tracy, California. It was a twelve
hour bus ride shackled, cuffed, and chained at the waist, the most
uncomfortable ride of my life, to say the least. This road trip was
one I will never forget, the glimpses of freedom sparking down
California's pipeline, Interstate 5.

I was consumed by the surreal feeling associated with being
sent to a prison I wasn't supposed to be going to, but I told myself
everything happens for a reason, and it will be what I make it.

Arriving at one of the most infamous prisons in the state of
California left me asking myself, "How did I get here?" The duplic-
ity of the "Welcome to Pelican Bay" sign at the entrance, as if I was
arriving at the Ritz-Carlton, led me to ask myself more questions:
"How bad will this be?" "Will I survive this?"

Pelican Bay's level four is the only prison in California where inmates go and get trapped for years trying to get transferred to another institution. I never felt like I belonged here, but there have been times when I've felt like I'm right where I'm supposed to be. I've seen things, I've experienced things, and I've met people who have changed the way I view the world. In the end, that's what the journey of life is all about.

Sometimes when people walk a dismal and treacherous path, they become refined. Looking back down that street, I guess I do belong here. It's where I've learned about myself and had an opportunity to reflect on who I want to be. It's all a matter of perspective, how you survive here.

You ask about the benefits of living in Del Norte County? There are enviable essences of this area, I'm told, such as the clean air, clean water, cost of living, and abundance of outdoor leisure activities. I've never lived in Del Norte County outside of Pelican Bay, so I don't know about that. But I did live nearby, in Eureka, California, for a little while when I was younger, so I'm familiar with the environment. The only negative thing I can say about this place is that it could be more culturally diverse. It needs to advance its economy by figuring out ways to generate revenue and become more hospitable towards tourism. I'm on the inside, not on the outside, so I only know what I've heard.

What are some ways I feel connected to the culture of Del Norte County? How are my values similar to the values of others around me? The astounding similarity we share, behind these bars and on the outside, is that we all have an innate will to survive, maximize pleasure, and decrease pain. It's in our nature. To quote the famous words of Maya Angelou, "We are more alike than we are unalike."

I believe the people living outside the gun towers often forget that when they think about us in here.

I have experienced similarities with most of the people who have come to extend a hand to those of us living in bondage. I think the best of us immediately inspire those of the free world. The worst of us remind them how good their worst days actually are out there. When people can put what they hear about prisoners in the back of their minds and actually engage in a conversation with someone inside, I think they start to relate.

Society has stigmatized felons as the scum of the earth. That's certainly a cultural challenge for us, living here. You can see that in the tough-on-crime approach to sentencing. If people could be as supportive of quality rehabilitation as they are supportive of harsh sentencing, there would be more people getting released with skills to survive in the free world, ultimately becoming fully functioning members of society. Without meaningful rehabilitation, we have people returning to the same areas they were convicted, striving to feed that hunger to survive any way they can.

Hopefully, in years to come, when someone reads these words, they will be able to say, "Times have changed" rather than "It's gotten worse."

Change starts from within—and it is always accompanied by action. Everyone should ask themselves, "What can I do to better myself?" And afterwards, "How can I better my community?"

*—January 28, 2018*

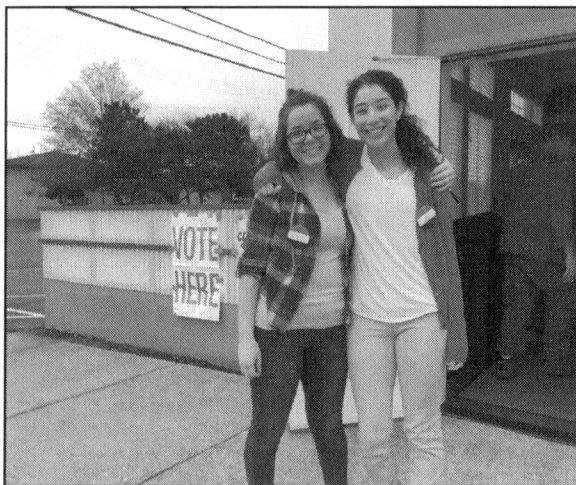

*Saundra De León Mendoza and friend celebrate
exercising their right to vote*

# PART IV:
# VALUES

*When do our values clash with those around us?*
*How do we find common ground?*

# Joan Buhler

"People rallied for Kidtown and came together to build a playground at Beach Front Park, too. Upstanding citizens were pounding nails along with everyone else. It was a great leveler."

*Now in her late eighties, Joan Buhler is a matriarch of Del Norte County. Her life has been unconventional, full of twists and turns bringing her repeatedly back to Crescent City, and may, as she notes, take her away again.*

I CAME HERE WITH MY FAMILY IN 1943. I was only eleven years old. We came up from the south. I remember being so carsick.

We moved here during the war. Crescent City's airport was a strategic spot for bombers if they needed to set down, and my dad had a job with the Department of Defense to beef up their runways. He drove a fleet of trucks.

I was born in western Iowa, but my family moved around a lot. The year we came to Crescent City, I'd already lived in Idaho, Arizona, and two places in California. It was hard to get through school that way. Moving around, you get a little insecure. It was even harder for my brother, who was in high school.

We didn't stay here. We moved to Grass Valley for another job. But in 1945, Dad traded his dump trucks for logging trucks, and we came back. When we came back that time, I really felt like I fit in, like I belonged. It was a nice place to live. I'm glad we stayed.

Dad died that next year, in 1946, in a trucking accident. One of his men had brought a load of logs in, but dad didn't like it just sitting there on the truck. It wasn't good for the vehicle. So he decided he would take it down to the mill in Klamath himself. On the way down, the load shifted. When he took the binder chains off, the load rolled down on him.

I was walking home from the 8th grade graduation when my brother-in-law caught up to me in the car. "Get in," he said. And he told me what happened.

I remember thinking, "I'm an orphan."

That was the beginning of my life with just mom. My two brothers were already in the service, and my sister was living with her husband already.

It was difficult. Mom was left with two or three trucks. She was from Denmark, from the old country. She didn't quite know what to do with the business. My sister helped to take it over at the time, and then my brothers came back to help.

I used to work in the summers in the Del Norte Laundry, where Griffin's Furniture is now. I lived just across the street where Denny's is today. I joke that it was a long commute!

I worked and Mom worked. We worked together at the laundry for a while. Then she worked as a day-time caretaker, looking after older folks in the community.

When I graduated, I didn't know what I wanted to do with myself. I was always musically inclined. I had a music teacher at the high school who was always getting after me about studying music, and so the summer after I graduated in 1949, he arranged for my history teacher, George Berry, to give me a test to go to college. I passed, and I went to Delta College, which later became Stockton Community College.

I was there for a year or so. But I took too many units to be able to work a job, and I ended up withdrawing. I'd met the man who would be my first husband at that point. We moved up together to Crescent City to help my mom. We got married in 1951 and stayed married for twenty-three years. We had four children together.

But we didn't stay in Crescent City. He didn't like it here. We moved back to the East Bay area, to Pittsburgh, where it was so hot and dry and brown. But I had no choice. You go where your husband goes. We lived a lot of different places, including living two years in Maui.

I was in the area for the tsunami, though. We came up to check on my mom. We were stopped on the road. The sheriff wouldn't let us pass through until we explained that we were concerned about my mom. They let us through, my husband, myself, and our four kids. Luckily for her, the water swirled around her house but didn't come in.

One constant in my life is that I've worked. I've always worked. After I got married, I trained to be a clerical worker, and went to work for the Federal Government at the Social Security Office.

What made me come back to Crescent City? Well, my husband passed away, and I was remarried to a man I met at work. Nice guy. One day, I saw a notice on the teletype for a job running the Social Security Office back in Del Norte County, and I applied. I'd been looking for a way to get back to paradise, and this was it. It was 1976. I've been here ever since.

We lived in a house on Glenn Street that the high school boys had built. It's funny—my stepson noticed a plant growing by the tap in the yard. He wanted to know if it was marijuana. I said, "I wouldn't know marijuana from a corn stalk," but it turned out it was. Probably one of the high school boys accidentally dropped some seeds by the tap during the construction process. We called the sheriff, and he took the plant away.

My husband and I ended up getting divorced. I married again, but that marriage didn't last very long either. Then I married Mr. Seligman. We were married only three years until he passed away.

I married Eldon Buhler in 2003. We went to the same church, and his wife passed away about the same time as Mr. Seligman did. Yes, I've had five husbands.

What's been hard about living here? As a kid, the violent storms bothered me. The weather. But I was pretty adaptable. I got over that. But as I grew older, like most of the teenagers, I wanted to get out of here. That trend hasn't changed, I think. I probably also complained that there wasn't anything to do, too. But now, when I hear people say there's nothing to do, I think they just aren't getting involved in things. I'm busier now than I was before I retired.

I've been involved for years with Lighthouse Repertory Theatre Company. That was a big part of my life. And my church has always been important. I'm involved with Community Concerts. So, I'm still in music. That hasn't changed.

What are some other challenges? The drug addiction here really bothers me. And the homelessness. I have a daughter who is recovering from alcoholism. You can only help someone up to a point. They really have to help themselves. My husband's son is battling drug addiction, too. It's true that there isn't a good place to get help here. But it doesn't matter if you're poor or rich, even those with the resources often aren't able to help their loved ones. And drug addiction and alcoholism are challenges everywhere.

One critical challenge for our community is isolation, especially from specialized medical care. Recently, we had to go to Grants Pass for Eldon's eyes, and then to Medford for my care. We had to spend the night. There just aren't enough doctors here—and it's one reason why so many people relocate away from here. You have to wonder, what will happen to us when we get older? What will happen with the highway going south, with Last Chance Grade? It's going to fall into the ocean. Then how do we get south? If we get cut off, it won't just affect people who need medical care. It will affect businesses, too.

I do like the fact that in this community, people pull together. I was a senior in High School when we all pulled together to build Citizen's Dock—we did it for $17,000 when the Federal Government wanted $250,000. Of course, it was weakened by a worm infestation, and then the tsunami really took it out.

People rallied for Kidtown, and came together to build a playground at Beach Front Park, too. Upstanding citizens were pounding nails along with everyone else. It was a great leveler. I brought food to share with the workers, along with a lot of other people.

We couldn't really do that today because of liability. And you're not supposed to bring your food from home. That is a change that erodes community. But that's not just Crescent City.

I do believe that we must pull together now, to make things better.

Things that seemed fair or unfair? Things I noticed about the Native American communities? Well, you can edit this as you see necessary, but when in high school, I guess it seemed to me that there was a big difference between the two Indian tribes. The Tolowa—the Smith River Indians—that's what we called them—were farmers. They were athletic in school and not aggressive. I went to school with Loren Bommelyn's mother, Eunice. She was a year ahead of me. We were friends.

However, the Yuroks—and really anybody from Klamath—just seemed more aggressive and less responsible. Some of them drank. That's one difference I noticed at that time. I don't know if it's changed. But I've never had a problem with any of them. Not a bit. We intermixed. That's my memory from the perspective of a school girl, at least.

Other challenges? I remember in the 1980s being concerned when I heard that many, many Hmong refugee families would be coming to the community from Laos. There was an article in the paper that we would have thousands moving here to Crescent City. Well, I worked at the Social Security Office, and we had a very small staff. I was concerned we wouldn't be able to handle all their needs in terms of paperwork. I actually made a call to the Lutheran pastor who was sponsoring them. I was so relieved that they would come in to the country with all their documentation!

And they did. They came into the community very quietly without a lot of fuss.

What's the appeal of Crescent City? Oh, the beauty of the country. The slow pace. The redwoods. The ocean. When I feel troubled, I just go out to the ocean and I think, how many millions of years have those waves been coming in? They just keep coming and going, and I'm so infinitely small in all this, you know. My troubles are so unimportant.

Or, I'll go to the redwoods, away from all the noise, and just hear the wind blowing through the trees. It's just so comforting to know that you're not the biggest thing in the world.

*—February 2, 2018*

# Dale Fugate

"For one thing, you realize pretty quick that you have
a role to play. At the prison, we're the cops. The inmates
have a role to play, too. They're the robbers."

*A Correctional Officer at Pelican Bay State Prison and a former timber faller,
Dale Fugate describes his life growing up and working in Del Norte County.
One value he holds dear comes up often. As he says, "It's about respect."*

MY TWIN SISTER AND I WERE BORN AT SEASIDE HOSPITAL
in Del Norte County in 1964. We were preemies, so we spent some
time, a month or two, in an incubator there. It saved our lives.

Mom was a homemaker—boy, she knew how to make a home.
My dad was a mechanic for Miller Rellim. He worked on all the
equipment. There was a lot of pride in that. Back in the day, he
could pull apart a D-8 Caterpillar, fix it, and get it back working
in a day. Eventually, his skills led him to doing road construction.
We were blessed because we got to travel in the summers to his job
sites, like Kingsbury Grade, Lake Tahoe, and Woolly Bear Camp—
we went there while they were building the GO Road.* We enjoyed
life in the summers when we went with him.

I grew up in Hiouchi. Life was simple. As kids, we went dirt
biking and hiked up the mountain. That was before you had all
these houses up there. We went swimming when we were a little
bit older. We'd get up early to beat the chores so that we could go
to the Smith River. We had a pool, and the folks across the street

---

* Gasquet-Orleans Road

had a pool, but we never really used either of them. We preferred to swim at Big Rock or just get inner tubes and float the river.

We used to catch salmon in our hands—big ones—fifty pounders. My dad would get mad. "Black salmon," he called them. They're salmon which are no good to eat because they're spawned out. They don't taste good. Dad made us bury them in the garden, but we kept catching them anyway because they still had some fight in them.

The best part of growing up here was the friends I made in the neighborhood and at school. I went to Redwood. Everybody was your friend from day one, even if they were your enemy because it was such a small school.

My eighth grade year, the district decided that kids in Hiouchi had to go to Smith River School instead of Redwood. I was devastated. The school wasn't as nice, and I had to make all new friends. That was rough.

I didn't love high school. I barely graduated. But I had teachers who really cared, who helped me get through. Doris Whalen was one of them. My senior year, I wasn't going to pass her English class. I had an F. She said that if I memorized the Lord's Prayer in Old English, she would give me a D-, which was enough to graduate. I did it. I can still remember the first lines, too. "*Fæder ure þu þe eart on heofonum; Si þin nama gehalgod.*"

Growing up, like most kids, I had all kinds of jobs. There was so much work for kids in those days. I started out mowing lawns. I remember one lady down by the river gave me $5 for mowing her lawn. Another neighbor gave me $20 for about the same amount of work. But we didn't care. Work was work.

I had different jobs all through high school. Most kids did. I worked at Beno's Department Store. I also scuba dived at Undersea Gardens, which is now Ocean World, but at a different location. I washed dishes at Parkway Restaurant, sorted bulbs at Dahlstrom and Watt Lily Bulb Farm, and shoveled fish at Eureka Fisheries.

One story really sticks in my mind when I was working at Dahlstrom and Watt. I was sorting bulbs alongside an older Mexican man. He didn't speak any English. But we stood together on a line for a week or so. There were some other kids there, also working but kind of goofing off. They weren't taking the work seriously. At the end of the week, the old man looked me in the eyes and gave me a kind of nod, as if to say, "I saw you. You worked hard. Well done." That's always meant a lot to me. I was proud to work hard and to earn a man's respect.

Like most loggers, starting out, I set chokers. I worked on old growth redwood for Ziegler Logging. George, Harlan, and Rick Ziegler were awesome people, awesome loggers. I learned a lot from them. Back then, we used a lot of dynamite to split logs and make choker holes. We would always throw in an extra stick for "good luck."

There wasn't anything Rick Ziegler couldn't do. He taught me a lot about working in the woods. Eventually, after working through the various stages of "being" a logger, I decided I wanted to be a faller. I started by bucking logs for my brother Roger on "pull unit" at Simpson Timber Company. It's a big learning curve from logging to timber falling. It was fun and challenging, and the pay was exceptional.

I worked all around the country. I spent a short time in Southeast Alaska, took a couple of trips back to the east coast, went up and down the Sierras, the Coastal Range, and into Washington and Idaho. I even worked a month in Hawaii cutting koa wood on the big island. We worked six days a week, flown in by helicopter every day. That pilot sure liked us. He wouldn't miss a day for anything. Even though we tried hard to get him to call in for weather conditions. After all, we were in Hawaii.

I was one of the last timber fallers on the Biscuit Fire, as a contractor for the Feds. There was standing dead wood along the road, and I cut it down real nice and laid it out so that it was easy to remove, just like I would on any commercial logging operation. I remember this guy overseeing the project coming out and taking a look.

He says, "You know, Dale, that's exactly what I wanted to see."

They're used to seeing crossed up timber and logs that aren't broken down, but I'd done it nice, and clean, and safe. He goes on, "I thought it would take you sixteen days to get that done."

Don't you know it, sixteen days later, I was out of a job.

As timber jobs disappeared, a lot of guys went to work at the new prison in Fort Dick. Larry Bachman went early to Pelican Bay. Mike Coleman and his wife Wendy went there. Gosh, Mike could do anything in the woods, climb and buck, pull and fell. He did that every single day before he became a Correctional Officer. Eric Wilson is another one who went out there. A lot of loggers went out there—a lot of fishermen, too. It's funny, because most of them are retired now, unlike me, who came in late.

These old guys would go, and they'd work ten overtimes a month. That's old school, working as long as they need you to work. Getting the job done. Men's work, you know?

I don't say that to be sexist. Some women work out there, and they do a good job. Maybe what I mean by "men's work" is that a man is tough. He gets up and goes to work every day, even when it's stressful. You don't bitch about it. You're humble, and at the same time, you have dignity because you meet your responsibilities. We learned that in the woods.

It took me a while, but eventually, I applied for a job at Pelican Bay State Prison. I worked for Sierra Helicopters in Walla Walla while I waited to complete my application. But I did have trouble getting hired. For one thing, my background officer didn't want to know about my contract work, just my employment history in terms of companies where I'd been on the payroll. That was frustrating. When he looked at the work I'd done from that perspective, it looked like I didn't do much—or that I did too many different jobs.

But like any logger around here, my job history was incredibly varied. One season it was crabbing, another it was firewood cutting, another it was logging with a helicopter crew.

The background officer didn't get it at first. He was from the city, you see. But when he finally got it, he realized, that's the life here. You shift jobs because the jobs shift. If it's crappy weather, you can't drop trees. You go fishing instead. When the spotted owl was listed, there wasn't logging work, either. So you do something else, like cut firewood. You have to be flexible if you want to survive. Yeah, it took him a while to see what life was like up here in the north.

So, I got hired as a CO at Pelican Bay at the age of forty-two. That was a blessing. I had experience working hard, so I was able to adapt. And having worked as a logger before becoming a CO really helped me.

For one thing, I understood chain of command. I've never been in the military, but from working in the woods on a crew, you knew a sergeant was a sergeant, a lieutenant was a lieutenant, a captain was a captain. You respected people who had experience and authority, and you came in with a willingness to learn. You also understood that while rules were written in stone, what's written—your post orders—it's just the foundation of what you're going to need to know. The rest of it is learned—usually from older guys.

For one thing, you realize pretty quick that you have a role to play. At the prison, we're the cops. The inmates have a role to play, too. They're the robbers. You know, it's like that old cartoon, with the sheep dog and the coyote. They say hello to each other as they clock in to work by the edge of the field. The sheep dog goes about guarding the flock, and the coyote tries to get a sheep every once in a while. There can be respect, but it comes from knowing who we are and doing our duty.

Working with inmates is a lot like working with loggers. They're men, in groups, away from their families. In forestry, I had to deal with guys like that all the time. I'd never really worked with women—although I had a female partner for a while in the administrative segregation unit, and I don't mind it at all—but I came into the job with some good experience.

Another skill set you need is good communication. It's all about talking to your partners. Like, let's say you're on the tier and an inmate asks for a bar of soap. You've got to communicate that to the other COs. You find out, no, we just gave them a bar of soap yesterday, or no, we've got supplies coming in tomorrow.

Just like in the woods, good communication is part of basic safety. That was important when I started at Pelican Bay. It seemed like there was always something going on. Not just stabbings—but other things. Tension. Violence in the yard.

We don't have what they call SNYs here—Special Needs Yards. Child molesters, Rapists. People who need special protection because of what they did. And while we do have gangs and racial segregation, when it gets ugly out there, it's usually because someone's lied or didn't pay a debt. We do have some scenes. We always have.

What I have seen in terms of change that's positive is the effect that comes from education. We're doing more to accommodate inmate education with GED programs and now college classes. I know a lot of COs don't like it. They don't believe it helps. But from what I've seen, it can make a big difference.

This one black kid came in one time, tough as snot, but I watched him pick up a book, and it changed him. The ganglia grows, you know. He's got concepts now. It doesn't help all of them. At that age, they still like to fight. But education in prison can be very beneficial. Even for the lifers—unless they get smarter than we are—they get AA degrees and a lot of us only have high school.

A lot of the new COs coming in today have college degrees. It's funny, though, the old loggers who became COs, even though they have less education, they know how to say "no" and where to draw the line. But these college kids come in, and they don't learn how to say "no" in college. They trained like teachers, you know? They have a different relationship with the inmates, a different mindset about them. You don't exactly learn chain of command, and following orders, and holding the line in college, you know?

Administrators want college-educated people now. I'm not sure why. Some think it might be that they're techies. They think we might be automating the prison industry more, and those skills will be important.

But I worry that these college kids are missing other key skills, and because so many old guards are retiring, they're learning bad habits from each other.

For example, I'm working in the dining hall one day. I got up at 3 am, showed up at 4 am, like always. I get a call from some young CO, somebody I don't even know, for an extra meal tray.

"Well, why do you need it?" I asked.

"Why do I need to tell you?" he said.

I'm like, "I'm not trying to be a hard ass, but I need to account for it, so you need to tell me the reason you need the extra meal tray."

"Are you trying to tell me I need to count every tray?" he said, and he hung up on me.

People used to say that the young guards learned these behaviors from old guards, that these are "old guard tricks." No, they didn't. These young guys are feeding off each other. They come in thinking they're going to be the warden. But after two years, they realize how much is involved in doing a good job. Communication, accountability, and respect.

I worry that our young people today can't learn to have a good work ethic here in Del Norte. Not just in the prison, but everywhere. Because, you know, where's our jobs at? We're going on two generations without an industry that teaches hard work and *makes something.* Our kids are leaving here. My son went into the Marine Corps, and now he's an air traffic controller. My daughter's up north. Her husband works for King County. My other daughter married a firefighter who owns a ranch. They're scattered.

Where's the widget factory they promised us when the logging ran out and the parks came and the mills shut down? We need good paying, private sector jobs for our children who want to stay here and raise families. The prison coming has allowed a lot of us to stay. But we never got any real industries here to replace the ones we lost.

We logged all the wood out of the Forest Service land. I cut one of the last units up in Goose Creek, and it was poor quality timber. It's all been logged. The good stuff was logged in my dad's day. Well, now they turned it into a National Recreation Area, but there wasn't any value left in the timber.

The redwoods are gone. The only old growth left is in the parks, which is a blessing. You look at it, and you say "wow." But I don't think people appreciate how much they've been scammed.

There was a big fight down south for the Headwaters Forest to keep it from getting cut, but that timber wasn't even worth anything. To me, I think corporate did that—created the whole controversy. They fooled these guys. I think Maxxam Corp. funded those protesters, paid them off to protest so that they could save what wasn't worth anything anyway. And those protesters—I won't even call them liberals because they were flat out communists—took money to protest and didn't even realize they were fighting to help Maxxam get rich off the deal. Maxxam wanted the price to go up on that land so they could sell high.

So many court rulings stopped us from falling timber on burned government land. So many court rulings stopped us from cutting one patch of timber or another. But it's ironic, because none of the timber they were fighting over was really anything.

You know, the companies liked to see big sticks of wood rotting from the top down. It meant someone like me could break the top out at twenty-four inches. The only part they wanted was the bottom part anyway. That's the economics of it. We could get a good price for timber that's been rotting for a few years from the top down, because of a fire. They're premium, grade A logs on the bottom. So the logging companies had a vested interest in waiting to log a place. They could log it cheaper, later, but the logs themselves wouldn't lose their value.

You look around and you see manipulations like these in other industries. There's another kind of scam happening with fishing right now. PacChoice owns a lot of the boats up and down the coast and the processing plants. They buy crab and other fish. I think it's racketeering the way they settle on a price per pound for crab. The price of crab started out at $2.25 a pound this year. But all your costs as a fisherman are up. Fuel costs are up. Labor costs are up. And there are fewer crab to catch. This year, it took a while, but they still found a way to control the price.

There are some really good cottage industries here. Look at Alexandre Dairy. They got a great idea to get their kids to sell organic, pastured eggs and put their names on it. Rumiano Cheese not only makes great cheese, but they got this idea to sell whey, which is really big in the health food industry. They were smart about it from day one.

But nothing the government promised us has really come to anything. Social services is growing and growing—just enabling the poor and the homeless. Free phones. Free this, that, and everything else. That machine's being fed from somewhere. It used to be, there were so many jobs that you had to work. If you didn't work, you couldn't get welfare. If you were homeless, we'd just run you out of town, send you down to Eureka.

I know some homeless are dealing with mental issues, and we need to take care of them, but for those who choose not to work, it frustrates me that we incentivize them not to.

It's not just the homeless, though. Our youth don't seem to know how to hustle for work anymore. I've got a young neighbor kid who asked to mow my lawn. So I let him do it once, for $40. He didn't look behind him as he was mowing, and he left a lot of grass uncut. I'm not gonna tell him. His dad should go and look. My dad would have when I was starting out. But his dad didn't. The neighbor lady hired the kid, too, and so did someone else down the street. But he just gave it 10%, so nobody wanted him back again.

I gave him another chance. I wanted these blackberries cut. So I offered him the work, but he didn't want it. I had to do it myself. Some of these kids just don't want to work.

I've seen a few hard workers. Those 4-H and FFA kids know how it's done. But so many of these other kids get cars, and trucks, and tons of rewards from their parents without working. The kid next door has a truck of his own. The only stipulation is that his parent won't get a call from the school about his bad behavior. Really? That's all? And his dad is going to cover the insurance and the repairs. Really?

Back in my day, you got a call from the school, you were getting your ass whipped. When I was a kid, if you walked in front of a car pulling in to Safeway and made it stop, that driver might get out and beat your butt. And by the time you got home, your dad would have heard about it, and he'd beat your butt all over again. It was always about respect. It was demanded from you by your family because that was what was expected in the real world.

Maybe I'm just a fifty-four year-old cranky, man, but it seems to me that things have changed.

Would I ever want to leave? Well, I do miss my kids. They're all scattered, though. So there's no place to move that would bring us all back together.

I might want to live up in Hiouchi again. The weather's good. Not too hot. My wife favors Gasquet, but I don't know. There's a store, and the post office is right there, but Gasquet is too far from town, and in the winter, you can't get up into the mountains because of the snow.

As far as leaving the county, though, you can't get much better than this. No. I'm good right here.

*—April 24, 2018*

# Heidi Hufford Kime

"I would be a rich woman if I had a nickel for every single person who thanked me and Brad for buying an existing building downtown. What got me into local politics was dealing with the city. I started seeing things that were frustrating."

*Heidi Hufford Kime is a member of the "Downtown Divas," a group of Crescent City women who run local businesses and advocate for a vibrant downtown. She runs a physical therapy business and serves on the Crescent City's City Council as Mayor Pro Tem. Heidi's essay ranges over wide territory, like Heidi herself. But in every scene she paints for us, her values dominate the frame.*

I WAS BORN IN EUREKA at Good Samaritan Hospital, and was adopted when I was two months and flown down to Oakland. I was an only adopted child. My father worked for Chevron, and we lived all over the world. We always had a home in California, so we always had a group of very close friends we connected with when we were here—Easter, Fourth of July barbecues—and California has always been home, but we lived in some very exciting places. We lived in London from when I was seven until I was twelve. Midway through eighth grade, we moved to Indonesia. The next year, Singapore. I finished up my high school at a girls' boarding school in Tacoma, Washington while my parents were abroad.

I started college in Diablo Valley, and met a military man who was going to Long Beach State. He'd had experience living in Italy. Cute guy, spoke Italian. He got his degree in physical therapy, and then was accepted to officer training school at Travis Air Force Base. We were married about a year later in 1999.

Travel was in our blood. We both have that adventurous streak. We traveled all over. We went to Mississippi, to Keesler Air Force Base for five years. Then we were off to Japan for three years. We had our son there. Then we were stationed in Las Vegas.

Then Brad did a tour in Iraq. And, you know, being pregnant with our daughter and having a little four-year-old boy crying every night, I was done. Vegas stopped seeming like a great place to live. It was crowded—a city of two million people. I commuted my child thirty minutes to school each way. In Vegas, you have to schedule grocery shopping around the temperature outside because you can't put your baby in the car seat after the car's been sitting in the sun. You have to get the air-conditioning going, and when you unbuckle the car seat, you have to cover the buckles with a towel so that you don't accidentally burn your baby's legs. I mean, stuff that is almost inconceivable. It was just too much, too fast, too busy, too transient, too plastic.

When Brad came back from Iraq, we felt it was time to just be a family and be with our children. We both grew up in the Bay Area, but it had become too expensive to live there. The median home price is like $500,000 to $600,000. We'd both have to work full-time jobs and be slaves to our careers to make that happen. That hadn't been our plan. I was supposed to be drinking wine and cutting roses in my front yard! (It's odd, now, that I'm in politics here, but we have always had a volunteering spirit in my family, and that's how I ended up running for City Council here in Crescent City, but I'll get to that story later.)

Brad's field of physical therapy was in high demand, and he was being recruited pretty hard by a lot of different places. Pretty soon, Brad started giving them my phone number because he was getting interrupted while he was at work with all of these job offers. Somebody with a military background and a lot of experience like him is a very competitive candidate.

Well, he had an opportunity to interview at Sutter Coast Hospital. It was one of those days of clear, blue sky. The Noll Longboard competition was going on. We rented a car, drove around, looked at houses. We were stunned by the sheer beauty. The most pristine place in the world. Sea lions barking at the harbor. Uncluttered beaches. Yes, the town itself looks a little worn, like it's been patched. But looking around, I felt all of my needs could definitely be met. There was a Safeway, a Starbucks, and a few little restaurants. Yes—we could totally live here. I didn't need a shopping mall!

We decided Brad should take the job the minute we landed. We bought a house on Pebble Beach drive, and I love it so much, I tell people I'm going to die in this house. You know, there are river girls and beach girls. I'm a beach girl. Really a mermaid—don't tell anybody. Just this morning I'm sitting by my window, drinking coffee from my big whale mug that says "Go with the Flow," and I see whales out in the water. That's life here. I love it.

I remember one time, in this little cove by our house, seeing a baby whale and a mama whale. My aunt and uncle just happened to have arrived maybe forty minutes before this happened. We were sitting by the window, having a glass of wine, and I'm telling them about where we live, when we see the mama and the baby are separated. The baby is on the other side of this sea stack. The mama started spouting and trumpeting as if to say, "Get your tail out here!" It was absolutely hilarious. I was like, "That's my life! I have a toddler, too!" And I got to share this moment, this connection, with people that I loved.

So, we moved here two months before the 2011 Tsunami. Unfortunately, Brad was miserable working at Sutter. The morale was low. The job was not what he was told it would be. It was so disappointing.

Right when we were closing escrow on the house, we got a call from a friend who is the head physical therapist at a place based in Korea. They needed a contract PT. So—we closed on the house on Pebble Beach and moved to Korea for a year.

My husband loved his job there, but I was taking the kids to school, trapped in traffic that made a twenty-six mile trip two and a half hours long. I found myself sitting in my car, looking at a concrete jungle out the window. People on top of people. Garbage.

I was not happy. I needed my view. I needed my whales.

It wasn't what we had hoped it would be, so we came back after a year, spoke with Mike Zing knowing that he wanted to sell, bought the business, bought a new building in a better location downtown.

I would be a rich woman if I had a nickel for every single person who thanked me and Brad for buying an existing building downtown. What got me into local politics was dealing with the city. I started seeing things that were frustrating.

The Downtown Divas started when I walked into Billie Kay Gavin-Tygart's shop to complain about how hard it was to get good employees. I said we ought to have "Whine and Wine Wednesdays." And that was it. That's how it began.

It was Billie Kay who made it happen. That crafty one invited a bunch of women business owners together. Lots and lots of names were on the list. What you see now is really the core. First and foremost, we took over the Farmers' Market downtown. We grew it and expanded it. We help incubate new businesses there, encourage people and explain things to them. That grew into promoting and growing all the businesses downtown. Now we do a monthly event in the evenings down there, celebrating the abundance we have in our community. We feature artists and musicians. We feature food venders, like Rebecca who does the Filipino food. She's looking at buying one of the empty restaurants downtown.

What's hard about living here? Well, I love to cook. And I've lived all over the world, so I have international tastes. I don't have access to ingredients here, so I have to be a better planner. If there's something I need, like a special seasoning, I have to get organized and make sure I order it in advance. I've got to plan.

As far as the educational system here, I think my daughter is going to be fine. She's at Mary Peacock. But my son is failing at Crescent Elk. I have asked the school repeatedly for tutors. I'm in a position that I can *pay* for tutors. But I don't get calls back. He's never taken seriously. If you're not in organized sports, nobody takes you seriously.

Partly, it's the friends he hangs out with. I say to my son, "When you're hanging out with different kids in school, you need to think, 'Would my mom and dad hang out with their parents? Are they nice people?'" I think he's failing at Crescent Elk because he's mixing with the wrong crowd. He's not motivated at all. He's not motivated to do anything at all.

He did organized sports—he did football for a year—but he was bullied by his own teammates. I said, "Don't worry about it. You're going to be towering over these little losers someday," because he's going to be a tall kid. I said, "You choose to be a good person. If somebody says something crappy to you, don't say something crappy back. Just walk away. If somebody hits you, turn around and punch them as hard as you can, and if that happens, you only have to do it one time to make it count. That will be your reputation. They won't mess with you."

It actually happened, too. In seventh grade, kids were punching each other in the balls—that's seventh grade. He got punched in the balls, so he turned around and punched that kid in the face. They're best friends now.

Why is there so much bullying at Crescent Elk? I don't know. It's hard to talk to a teenager about this. I don't envy the teachers there, hanging out with these rotten little jerks who are twelve and thirteen and fourteen years old. They can be unpleasant human beings at that age! My kid is just not getting his needs met at school. He's highly intelligent, but he's just not captivated by anything at school.

This whole Common Core nonsense happened when he was in first grade here. I had a conversation with a friend of mine who has been a teacher for over twenty-five years. She was able to manipulate her teaching style into the Common Core criteria. But a new teacher without any of that experience—Common Core is dumb! I can't help my kid with math in fourth grade! And now, kids don't have homework. My impression is that they stopped homework because parents can't help their kids with it.

The curriculum is not engaging. I have to chase down teachers for information about my son's poor progress. You have to scream and shout for help. For two years, I've been asking math teachers and the principal for tutors. I'm friends with school administrators. Guess how many tutors they've gotten me? None.

We have kids from Del Norte who go to Berkeley and Stanford and West Point. It's not that we don't have capable kids in this community. Whatever the school district is doing, it's not working for my kid. Education shouldn't be a one-size-fits-all experience. But I can't get anyone to help me. I'm jumping up and down, but nobody is taking the situation seriously.

So this summer, he's going to go down to my parents,' and probably go to the corner store Sylvan Learning Center. But of course we don't have anything like that here.

That's what made me think about this question—what's fair or not fair about the distribution of resources here? Working parents rarely get the support they need here. There's a lot for people who don't work and can't afford things and aren't even interested in enrolling their kids in things, and they are offered so many freebees and scholarships.

Another thing I wish were different—I'd like to see an appreciation for all that we have here. I see a lot of negativity about what we don't have. I want to see a shift in attitude. I feel like when we talk about the positive things we are doing, it creates a message where more people will get involved. There's a lot to do here. Many of them are free, so I don't want to hear "I can't afford to do that." I want to create that recreation mindset. I would love to see surfing camp, archery camp, survival camp. Let's teach these kids how to use a buck knife and start a fire. We've created fear amongst our children and they don't get to do anything.

My kids, though, learn those skills. We go camping. In the summer, we have river days. And when I'm at work, they go to work, too. They fold towels and talk with customers. I want them to understand customer service. These kids coming in for jobs are so unqualified in terms of customer service. They can't answer phones. They're paralyzed. I don't know why they don't have the skills. When the phone rang at home when I was growing up, you answered the phone. If someone wasn't there, you said, "I'm sorry. She's not unavailable right now."

We employed a young woman through TPP* last school year. This young woman did a great job and was very reliable. But she had to learn to answer a phone and talk to people. She never got that experience anywhere.

In school, I had to memorize poetry. I had to give presentations. It didn't matter if you were shy. You were not getting out of it. You had to suck it up, buttercup.

I had this conversation with my son the other day. I said, "I have you for four more years. In four years, you will have to make a choice. You are either going to join the military and go off somewhere else. You will get a job at Dutch Bros and live in a disgusting apartment with three of your guy friends and live paycheck to paycheck. You will live at home and go to College of the Redwoods and have a part-time job. Or you are going to go away to college and I will pay for it. Those are your choices. So, work on setting yourself up for success in case you decide college is what you are going to do. F's in high school are not going to cut it next year."

I hope my son turns it around, but part of the problem in our community is that there is no reality check for other kids here. They will have no marketable skills. They are not going to be in the NBA. They are not going to be YouTube stars. They are not that good.

A friend of my child just tried a marijuana edible! I told my son and all of his friends that I set up an account with North Cost Health Screening, so if any of them are screwing around and doing drugs, I would tell their parents and we would march right down there and they could pee in a cup. Well, when I found out what my son's friend did, my son and I went down there. He was negative. It was the best $45 I ever spent.

He said, "I didn't know you were serious about this."

---

* The Transitional Partnership Program, funded by the State of California, helps disabled, at-risk, and special education youth find and succeed in meaningful work experiences.

Now he knows.

I tell him, he's got to find friends with parents I would hang out with. How would he know which kids? If kids are coming to school hungry, they don't have parents who care about them. If they're not eating all day long, if they're not well-fed, if they don't have to check in, those aren't good parents.

I'm not worried about the Crescent City royalty. I'm not worried about that. I'm not going to tell him who to be friends with. But I want him to make good decisions.

He tells me that everyone's parents are crackheads. I tell him no. They're not.

This has been the first real challenge of living in Crescent City, not being able to connect my son with a good group of friends and positive activities and help in school when he needs it. What I mentioned earlier about the challenge of having to plan for ingredients for a meal doesn't quite rate compared to this one.

One thing that is also challenging here is this Native American facet. It's us versus them, white men versus Indians.

In the political world, we're together. We have tribal members on all of our commissions. The city got a big fat fancy firetruck because we had a grant from the tribes. We worked together. They accepted delivery and didn't have to pay tax. That's $15,000! There are people really looking out for the best interest of spending public money here.

But as a newcomer here—one who had traveled and lived in a lot of different places—I wondered, where's the Native American museum? There's a cultural separation. This goes back to the same things we were just talking about: drugs and poverty.

I wish native history was embraced more. I wish I knew more information about the different tribes. I would love to learn Native American dance.

When I lived in Japan, they dressed me up in a Kimono and I got to learn to do the tea ceremony. They were excited I was joining in and enjoying their culture. We don't have anything like that here.

The buzz word now is "cultural appropriation." I would like to see more opportunities for cultural sharing. My son has been taking Yurok language in Crescent Elk, and he's really liking it. I wish there was more of that. Native American history classes. Handicraft lessons.

How does this connect to cultural appropriation? Let's say I saw this beautiful dentalium necklace. Why can't I own one of those? Someone would definitely criticize me for it. It's so frustrating. It's like, "You can like other cultures, but don't like them too much." I think this fear of political incorrectness is holding us back from understanding each other.

I wanted a simple life. I'm not sure how simple life is for me now. I think I'm busier than I've ever been in this small town, where people claim nothing is going on. It's incredible to me how you can watch movies here, you can be up-to-date on all the latest trends, as though you were not isolated by geography. We leave here to travel and go on vacation, but after about three days, we are ready to come home. In other places, you have a lot more anonymity. Nobody knows you. But the rest of the world is in a hurry. It's crowded out there. There's traffic.

But here, even pushing your shopping cart in the grocery store, people are polite. There's more time to spend with yourself and your family. I live just over one mile from my office. My commute takes me past the ocean. Here, you drive down the street, and somebody waves, "Hi Heidi!" You're out in your yard pulling weeds and someone you know yells out their car window, "Hi Heidi!"

That's why we stay.

—*March 27, 2018*

# Shane Stodola

"People who move here feel isolated. People who've lived here all
their lives feel isolated, too. There is something positive to be said
for isolation and privacy, but it makes us afraid to reach out."

*Shane Stodola recounts how he struggled to build a positive life for himself out
of a chaotic childhood. The values of his grandparents anchored him, and as a
husband and father today, he sees his purpose in the community in a very different light than he once did.*

I WAS BORN IN DEL NORTE COUNTY in Seaside Hospital
in 1974. My grandmother was Anna Leest. She was a reflexolo-
gist here for a long time. She practiced for at least 40 years. My
grandfather was Don Leest, who was a truck driver and a logger.
Both were really amazing people who taught me to be honest,
work hard, and take care of family. They worked full time, but they
also raised their own cows and sheep and goats. They lived healthy
lives, worked on their house, and just generally worked really hard.
My grandma was a Yurok from Klamath and my grandfather was
a Dutchman. The story is that he drove into town, saw my grandmother, and instantly fell in love with her.

Some of my best memories of growing up were playing at my
grandparents' house over on Wonder Stump Road. But most of my
memories of childhood are of my parents fighting, moving from
house to house, and experiencing abuse and neglect because of
drugs and alcohol.

My parents split up when I was in kindergarten. My mom was

an addict. Among other things, she used heroin. My dad tried to work it out, but that didn't happen. I grew up with four sisters, one little sister and later, three half-sisters. I was the oldest. And I did a lot to take care of them, especially to protect them from my mom and the people she brought around. She was dealing drugs and, well, it was a bad place to be.

I bounced around a lot, growing up. I would live with my dad sometimes, and my mom sometimes. Then she would get arrested, and I might be placed in foster care. I was in a lot of foster care homes—never in this county, though. Mom would take us somewhere, like Reno, and then get busted. It would take a while for our family to find us. Nanny and Pop would get us as soon as they found out. And eventually, my dad would take us away from our grandparents.

My dad didn't use drugs, but he was a Jehovah's Witness, and living with him could be very isolating. We didn't see eye to eye about a lot of things, including how we ought to relate to "worldly" people. It was confusing enough as a child to be in so many different homes with different rules. And when I got sent to my dad's, I would lose touch with my mom and my childhood friends from around where she lived, who had essentially become my support system. The separation from those folks was hard on me.

Dad and I had a lot of conflicts over the years. The biggest one was when my sister got pregnant at sixteen, and my dad and my other sisters just kind of cut themselves off from her life. But me, I love my family too much. I couldn't stand that.

I dropped out of school at fifteen and started working full-time. I worked at grocery stores and laborer jobs. At first, I wanted money. But when we lived with my mom, my working became about supporting my sisters. We needed the money to pay bills and buy food. I spent a lot of time making sure nobody touched them, too, making sure my sisters stayed away from most of the people coming around my mom's house. Those people weren't safe to be around.

My coping strategy to survive my childhood was to be mean

and aggressive. I was just an angry person when I was younger. If people mouthed off or looked at me sideways, I'd punch them. I wasn't a bully, but I liked to hurt bullies. If I saw someone thought they were stronger than someone else or picked on people, I beat that guy up. I know that's not the right way to be. I know that now. But at the time, I took a lot of joy in it.

Eventually, when I was almost eighteen, my mom got pinched for a big drug deal. She was going to do prison time. So my sisters went to my dad, and I moved up to my aunt and uncle's in Salem, Oregon. I didn't like being away from them, but Salem was good. I met some of my best friends there, actually, when I tried to go back to high school there.

High school didn't work out, but that's where I met my buddy, Sean. The first time Sean ever saw me, I was coming into the classroom. I must have looked intimidating because he was terrified that I was going to sit next to him. I did. And I asked him if he had a pencil, and he gave me his whole notebook.

I said, "No, I just want a pencil." We started talking and, eventually, we became best friends.

My mom was killed around that time. It was a car accident, although it might have involved foul play. She had been convicted and was about to start serving a long prison sentence. So she knew a lot of things that might have threatened some people. She was traveling with another man, and he says another vehicle veered across a lane and knocked them off the road. She burned to death in the car.

She got off drugs many times before she died, but you know, it's a disease. You have to be really strong to stay off. She went to rehab several times, in different locations. My grandparents spent the majority of their retirement on her rehab, trying to cure it. And she'd be good for a while. She was an amazing mom when she was sober. She was fun and loving. She would have made a great grandmother. She was quite the lady.

So it was rough going to school after that. I met with the Principal of my school. She was an awesome person. She suggested some other routes, and one was to take the GED test. I passed it right away without taking the classes. I started working again at a few places after that. Bon Marche and Waterford Wedgewood, where I was in sales. They'd laugh if they could see me now with my big grey beard! But I was respectable looking there and covered my tattoos. I also worked as a prison guard in Washington State. I wasn't intimidated by the inmates. I felt like I knew that world, so it didn't scare me. But it was a sad place. I found different work as a custodian at an elementary school. I really liked that work.

It was a long journey back to Del Norte County. In Washington, I got married and we had two babies. It was good, but it wasn't exactly what I wanted. My cousin and best friend, who lived in Del Norte, kept calling me, asking me to come back. He was an alcoholic and wasn't doing too well. I wanted to come home to be with my family.

So I convinced my wife at the time to move back. I got a job with Pacific Power, did some landscaping for a buddy of mine, and then got a job doing custodial work at the College of the Redwoods. Now, I'm in charge of maintenance here.

It was here in Del Norte where I met my current wife, Courtney, way back in 1997. I met her when I was dating one of her friends. She came walking out on the deck of her house, and I just fell in love with her. She was so beautiful. We dated for a little while, but she broke up with me. She was afraid I was going to get bored with her. I kind of ran around a lot back then, so she might have been right.

When I came back here, we actually moved in a few houses down from where she lived, and we reconnected. Being so close, it brought up a lot of old feelings. I fell in love with her again. And one day, I decided I had to tell her how I felt. I had a good life before that. It wasn't great. It wasn't what I wanted, but I just took a chance and told her. It turned out, she felt the same.

So we broke hearts. I'm not proud of that. But sometimes you just have to be honest about what you want. We got together after that and eventually got married and had our daughter.

What's good about living in Del Norte? There are so many amazing things here, more than people realize or take advantage of. This college, for one. My mom went here for a time, after one of her rehabs. I was so proud of her. I used to walk the halls with her. Now I work here. And it helps a lot of people pull themselves up.

We have the National Forests and Parks. We have so much natural beauty here. Our family camps most of the summer. We even camp during the work week, and I drive down to work and then drive back to the campsite at the end of the day.

But Del Norte needs more ways to look out for kids. In other places, they have YMCAs and recreation programs that have more than just sports. They have music programs and other programs for kids who aren't athletic. They have Big Brother / Big Sister programs for kids who get sent to foster homes, too. Here, the bowling alley isn't open regular hours, and the movie theatre costs $9 for a ticket. It's a hard place to be a kid, especially if you don't have parents watching out for you.

There's two ways you go when you're growing up hard. You become super-achieving, super-athletic, or super-academic. You feel bad about yourself, but you don't let anyone see that. You cover yourself by becoming strong on the outside. The other way kids go is to close it all in. They don't try to achieve anything. They feel as bad about themselves as the super-achieving kids, but they have nothing to protect themselves. They disconnect.

I think we're missing an opportunity to connect with kids like these, the disconnected ones. The community is broken. We live together, but in isolation. We do come together for a few events a year. Fourth of July is great, but it's mostly for show, for tourists. It doesn't connect people together. It doesn't connect young people with adults who care about them. It's just a parade.

People who move here feel isolated. People who've lived here all their lives feel isolated, too. There is something positive to be said for isolation and privacy, but it makes us afraid to reach out. And so many people around us are hooked on drugs or are homeless, it's hard to trust people you meet.

Because our economy is so bad and finding a job is so hard, a lot of people do turn to dealing drugs. It's an easy way to make money. My mom sold drugs forever: heroin, meth, cocaine, marijuana. Our houses were raided all the time. So drugs perpetuate our problems.

I did a lot of drugs for a while. But you get to a place where, when you've seen what they can do, you just can't stand it anymore. For me, I was about twenty-three or twenty-four when I stopped. It was when I had my first kid. You don't want to be around it. Alcohol, too. It just disgusts you. You come to see people who use drugs as selfish.

But for me, marijuana isn't in this category. I don't use it. I haven't for a long while. But when other people do, it doesn't bother me. Yes, Mom smoked weed, but she was an alcoholic, too, and that was far worse. I wouldn't mind seeing alcohol banned and marijuana made legal. I've never really seen people become violent and aggressive with weed. They say it's a gateway drug, but I think alcohol's a bigger gateway. At least marijuana helps with some medical problems. I have a friend with leukemia, and it was the only thing that helped with her pain.

It also bothers me, all the empty buildings downtown, the new CVS ruining our beautiful land, K-mart and Home Depot where my cousin and I used to run around when we were little. But while we have so many big drugstores, we only have two big grocery stores! And the community doesn't have a good way to help businesses succeed that we really need and really add to our community. It's like our systems of government are designed to keep us down, not lift us up.

Also, there aren't very many cultural experiences here compared to other places I've lived. I'm enrolled in the Yurok Tribe, and Courtney is enrolled through Tolowa Dee Nee Nation. So we go to tribal functions like Dee-ni' Day, food forest activities, and the Salmon Festival.

Our two youngest daughters will dance. Though my boys aren't interested. I do want them to learn basket weaving, though. It's something I'd like us to do together. Traditionally, men learn open weave, and women do closed weave, though I'd like to learn both. My Auntie Lena (Hurd) Carmondy teaches a class. I really want my boys to learn how to make baby baskets, so that when they're older, they can make one for their own kids. All our kids were carried in them when they were little. And they all had rattles, too. It's a very important tradition.

You do get different benefits depending on the tribe you belong to. It does seem to me that the Yurok Tribe does less for families than the Tolowa Tribe. Through the Tolowa, the kids get help with clothes and preschool. The tribe also helped us with buying our first home.

But honestly, the big picture for me is, I'm an American. I don't really want to feel entitled to anything. All of us need to realize that the world owes us nothing. I have a job. I work hard. I bring home a paycheck. If I want to change that, I change it. I'm not entitled to more than that. Wanting money from your tribe, I don't think we should think that way. Our tribe doesn't owe us anything. What we get from them, we need to take as a wonderful gift.

Growing up in Crescent City was a crazy life. But I don't regret any of it. It took me a while to find myself, but I did it. And now I'm back. I feel so lucky to have what I have here. I'm very fortunate.

*—February 5, 2018*

# Krissy Peters

"I have faced many challenges throughout my life, but they have only made me stronger. I am not willing to give up, because my life is worth fighting for. My dreams are worth fighting for."

*Born in Crescent City but raised outside the area in foster care, Krissy Peters understands the ravages of neglect and abuse. But as an adult, she frames her identity and sense of self not by the past, but by her values, one of which is determination.*

I WAS BORN IN CRESCENT CITY at Seaside Hospital in 1973. I have this vision of my mother being in labor, having a view of the ocean, and having this sense of peace. I never spoke to her about it. It's just my own idea.

When I was ten, my mother was in a severely abusive relationship. We left Del Norte County in the middle of the night for Klamath Falls, and I did not return until adulthood, about six years ago.

I was raised in the foster care system in Oregon from the time I was twelve until after I graduated high school. I would not trade that experience for the world. It was one of the best experiences I've had. The family I lived with had strict foundations. There was consistency. I knew what to expect. I was loved. It was a caring environment, and I got to live the life of a normal teenager. I was taken out of a home riddled with abuse and drug addiction. I think it's given me the foundation for who I am today.

I know my foster mom felt like her work hadn't gone in the direction she wanted it to go. We did talk about her successes and

261

her achievements, and she didn't feel like she had very many. There were a lot of girls from her home who turned to drug abuse and were even imprisoned. She felt like she didn't have a good enough impact on their lives. I assured her that she did touch lives. She touched my life. It made all the difference in the world to me. I am one who changed; I am a cycle breaker. I can do a lot of good in this world.

I am not in contact with my foster mother now. She doesn't do a lot of technology stuff like Facebook or Snapchat. And also, because of my past, I have a hard time with emotional connections sometimes. I'm afraid of rejection. But I think she would be very proud of the woman I am today because I stand strong in my values. I have confidence and self-worth, and I'm empowered every day. Sometimes it takes a really strong person to get through normal, daily activities.

My foster mother wasn't the only strong influence in my life. My late Auntie Molie helped to raise my older sister Cassie, who passed away when she was twenty-one. I'm not sure why Auntie didn't raise me, but she was a mothering type for me. I often communicated with her before she died, and in one conversation, when I was young, she told me, "Our people—Yurok people—need help. The way you can help our people is to go away and become educated, gain experience (work experience, life experience) and bring that experience back to our people."

I would love to have a relationship with my remaining family here, but I don't believe that it will happen. It is part of the deep hurt in my life. It's something that I suppress because there's nothing I can do about it. I don't have control over other people's lives and their decisions. They are drug addicted, and they choose to be involved in criminal activity. It's very toxic, and I cannot allow toxic people in my life if I'm going to be successful.

My mother makes poor choices in interacting with her children and grandchildren. Her choices are so disgusting to me that I haven't spoken to her in over four years. One of my siblings committed a serious criminal act that hurt another individual and that person's family, and my family took part in covering it up.

You asked me about my values and how mine might be different from those around me. I believe people need to be held accountable for their actions. I remember when I learned this lesson. One day in foster care, I knocked a knick-knack off a shelf. That was my first lesson in being accountable. I had to do extra chores to pay it off—to make it right.

These people are my family, but at the same time I have my own children to look after. I still am raising my youngest son, and I have to make sure he's protected and that I'm protected as well. I know that loyalty is important. Blood is thicker than water. Snitches belong in ditches. I really am a loyal person. But I am loyal to people who deserve it.

When I first moved back to Del Norte County, my son and I camped out in a tent on the river. It was fishing season. A lot of families do that. My Auntie Molie owned property on Requa Hill. In her will, she left a spot to her brother, my Uncle Merkie, but under the condition that I and my siblings would be able to use it for fishing. Having a place to fish, a place to keep nets and boats, is very important in our tradition. Our family spots—Auntie Molie's and Uncle Merkie's two spots together—are the two deepest and best holes in the river—or so I've heard.

It's the Peters' family that had the allotment on Requa. I'm named after my grandmother, Christina Peters. Growing up, I was Christina Gardner. Gardner was the name of my stepfather. I never met the man who was my biological father, whose name was Doering. But years ago, when I was getting divorced, my divorce decree had a question about what I wanted my last name to be. I pondered that for a long time because my name is important to me. Because I had my grandmother's first name, and I was very proud of her and where she came from, I chose her last name, too, and took back our family name.

When I was young, I was taught our family song. I would stand in the living room of Auntie Flo's house. I would sing our family song, and when I was done, everybody around me, all the adults around me, would cheer and praise me. I felt so proud to be able to sing that song. I didn't know the importance of it. I just knew when I sang it, they liked it, so I did it as often as I could.

I attended the brush dances, but I wasn't allowed to dance. I never understood why back then. None of my family could, other than my older sister Cassie. But I did watch. I was a very perceptive girl. I watched them in their dance regalia. I don't believe that I ever wished I could be them, but I was always curious about what they were doing. Auntie Molie was always really happy and cheered and clapped. I remember sleeping on the ground and eating food with everybody, the same food. I remember people were just gathered together as a family, and it was a happy, peaceful time.

I later learned females can only dance if they are virgins. I couldn't dance because I was raped as a child. My daughter wasn't allowed to dance either. My oldest sister never danced. My brothers didn't dance.*

I am a positive person. And my positive from this is that I have been able to watch my youngest son dance. When he was young, he asked me if he could, and I said yes. I showed him where the men's camp was. I explained that I couldn't go with him, because I'm a female, but I told him he needed to go there, be strong, have courage, and ask if he could dance.

I shed tears of joy seeing him dance. I was so proud. He's now eleven. He's not jumped center yet, but he's getting ready. His confidence is building.

Back in 2012, after my son and I had been camping at the river for a while, the rains came. I knew I had to come up with a plan. I found a motel, then an apartment, and then a job with the Yurok tribe—in that order. It took a lot of faith to believe I could get that job. I was a fiscal clerk. I had twenty-five years of experience from working in Klamath Falls, so it turned out I was a strong candidate.

Since then, I've had a number of jobs. I feel fortunate. I feel

---

* Editor's note: A Yurok elder suggested this rule is interpreted differently by different families. The way it was enforced for this contributor's family should not be viewed by readers as standard practice.

blessed. Recently, I stopped working and became a full-time student at College of the Redwoods. I have a waiver for my tuition. My books are supplied. I get to enjoy the pleasures of an educational experience at no cost to myself, other than my living expenses. Knowledge is power. I know things now that I didn't know before. School is cool.

At the college, I took a history class I enjoyed. I hated history before. Being a Native American, I'd learned that history was bad. The truth was horrific, and the presentation of it wasn't fair. So as a child, I wasn't allowed to celebrate the 4th of July.

But my prejudice against history was simplistic. I never even understood the concept of the holiday. I didn't pay attention in grade school. But when I came to college, I learned about the American Revolution and the Constitution. I was able to form my own opinions and ideas. In a sense, the history I'd learned in grade school was one-sided. There was this presentation of America being a white man's country. But college-level history holds this up to the light, and it also holds people accountable. I enjoy the complexity.

One of the things I struggle with is feeling excluded by my own people. I was working for the tribe, and I had two nieces who passed away. Their funeral was held in the Yurok Tribal Office, where I worked. When Monday came around, I still needed time to heal. I found it so difficult to perform my job duties. And ultimately, I feel like the tribe gave up on me. I felt like I was shunned. People were starting to talk about me and spread rumors that were untrue. That was very hurtful. I developed some medical issues as a result, and so I left the tribe. I don't know if I'll ever work for them again.

Even now, it is a challenge to get the tribe to support me with the higher education grant. They gave me a grant in 2001, but I had to withdraw because of domestic violence issues. So in spring of 2017, I reapplied and was put on probation for that issue more than fifteen years before. I just don't feel like the tribe supports me. I have a lot of compassion, a lot of empathy for people in general, including my people, the tribal members. Why can't they extend that empathy to me?

Sometimes, I fear I may not earn enough in scholarships to finish my education. I had to leave once before to support my family. Will I have to again? More than anything, I want to live my dream: to become a first-generation college graduate and to set an example for future generations. I'm not sure what I will do with my degree, but whatever it is, I want to do work that I am passionate about, and I am passionate about helping others.

I have faced many challenges throughout my life, but they have only made me stronger. I am not willing to give up, because my life is worth fighting for. My dreams are worth fighting for. I am important, too, and I am good enough to receive a higher education.

*—October 11, 2017*

# Blake and Stephanie Alexandre

"There's challenges in every community. I've been
to a lot of places, and I don't want to pretend that this
community has more than any other. Life just hands you
obstacles all day long. How do you handle them?"
—Blake Alexandre

*Stephanie and Blake Alexandre run Alexandre Family Farm. They were inter-
viewed together in their home on their farm on Lower Lake Road.*

Blake (BA):     I WAS BORN AND RAISED IN FERNDALE
in Humboldt County. We moved here at the end of 1992.

Stephanie (SA):  WE HAD BEEN MARRIED FOUR YEARS
already and dairied with my family in Southern California.
When this ranch came up for sale, it was an opportunity go
back to Blake's roots, closer to home. We thought we'd raise
our kids in Ferndale. But once we were here, we realized we
needed to be right on the farm.

BA:    We grew roots here. We didn't spend a lot of time going to
town here. We spent all those early years on the ranch, trying
to make this big mess more organized and make it work like a
functioning, sustainable business. We knew we needed to hire
and employ a lot of people.

This dairy was built with investor-type money, and it was
not really managed by dairymen. It wasn't that old, maybe ten
or twelve years, but I would say it was poorly managed and
somewhat rundown, even though it was new construction.

Most dairies in this area are small, but this one was built to be large, so that brought a lot of challenges.

Dairies here on the north coast have been around for about 150 years. They all started small. That's how everyone did it. Dairying had been existing at that level for a while, until many started joining up or else going out of business. Slowly, what used to be hundreds of dairies became about twenty.

I don't know the reason why. I wasn't here. But I think it was probably the same thing as what's happening today—economies of scale make bigger dairies more profitable. And it's hard work. As the next generation grows up, they may have less interest in the business. Dairying is seven days a week, 365 days a year. It's hard. Some kids see it as a sentence, in terms of the workload. That's a real challenge, and we can see it today.

Also, dairying here in Del Norte means we're a long ways from the consumer markets. We're a long way from the Midwest or another country where the feed is grown for the cattle. It's expensive to be a dairy farmer here.

SA:　So when we moved here, we had a two-year old. We lived on top of the milk barn, right where the office is today. The house on the property was in pretty bad shape, so we just slowly remodeled it. About the time our third child was born, we were moving into this house. We had an opportunity to live in a house just down the road, but we wanted our kids to live right on the dairy. But we were taking a big risk.

BA:　It was a big investment, a big project. A lot of land and a lot of buildings.

SA:　We do love what we do. We believe in it. At one point, in 1999, we identified that we were getting paid the same price for our product as they did in Kansas, where they are milking ten thousand cows right by the feed. At the same time, the organic market started to come in, so we identified that as an opportunity.

As we learned more and more about organics, we just came

to love it. It fit with our area, too. Going organic early on was such a great move. It's expensive to bring in feed, but growing organics here is conducive to our environment. Our average daily temperature difference between summer and winter is just eleven degrees. The grass is just perfect for grazing, so we really have leaned a lot on our grass-based genetics, on our grass-based style of dairying.

That's helped us stay in business. We don't make tons of money, but we can provide for our family and take good care of our employees. We still live in the same house. It's never been about the money for us. It's about our community.

BA:   It's a lot of hard work and perseverance and never giving up. I don't look at our business as a success. We're still struggling. We keep biting off more, and taking on more, and fighting to make it work.

Going organic and pursuing the niche market was a good thing, and a lot of that decision at first was financially moti-vated. Eventually, we came to understand the organic prin-ciples and believe in them. It helped us create a business that was more exciting for our employees, too, especially for the more long-term ones. It motivated them to stay. It also helped our kids feel this was a viable option for them rather than a sacrifice, something that they weren't really interested in. We wanted them to feel it was a good career and a good life.

Everything we do is really about doing the right thing, not about the money. We want to create products we can be proud of, and that people would desire and pay extra for—because it really does cost us extra to make them.

SA:   Look out the kitchen window here. There are two hundred elk out in the field, eating the great feed.

BA:   They're with us every day. [Laughing] They really bought into the organic idea, too.

I think the point I would add about organics being a great fit for us here is something that our son Dalton has pointed out:

Our cows are in their natural setting, in their natural environment, eating the grasses they were meant to eat. These grasses are easy to grow in this climate. We're really, truly working with nature. Our yields and our production keep going up and up every year. We just keep tweaking it to make it better.

SA:   We really see signs all the time that it's working. Fish and Game monitors the stream that comes through our property, and they make comments that those fish are the healthiest salmon in the area. A bald eagle nests on the edge of our property. Aleutian geese that we've fed for years keep coming back. When we go to town on a rainy evening, all these frogs jump on our windows all the way to the property line. As soon as we leave the ranch and cross the property line, there's no more frogs. People often comment that life just flourishes here. It's true.

We have a lot of cheerleaders in the community, too. We've done our best to always be transparent—or as Blake says—translucent. We have a bucket calf project where kids from the community help train and raise a calf. All those families learn about us and become ambassadors for our farm. We want our community to be positive about us.

BA:   Our community has supported us all the way through, even before we came here. They told us we'd be a big employer. I'm like, "You're kidding, right?" But I took that as a big responsibility.

I think we've been fine with the environmentalists here, too, listening to them and trying to help them when we can. We bought the land, own the land, and have to make money off it, so in a way, no one can be bigger environmentalists than we are. We always try to do the right thing.

And it shows. We're a Mecca for more than 250 species of birds on our ranch alone. We have thousands and thousands here every day.

SA:   [Laughing] Not counting the chickens.

BA:　Not counting the chickens.

　　You ask about the local debate about marijuana. In terms of marijuana, I'm on the local ordinance planning group. They asked Stephanie. They asked Vanessa.

　　Finally, I took the job. To be honest, I don't read the newspaper. I quit reading it twenty years ago or more. I like good news, not bad news. I don't like reading other people's opinions about things, either.

　　We had our first meeting. There are nineteen people in the planning group. Everyone took a turn at talking. During my turn, I voiced my opinion that it would be great if we could grow our kids up in a marijuana-free county. I asked if there was anybody on my side. I asked for a show of hands. Eighteen people sat on their hands. Everybody thinks it's a good deal for the county.

　　So, my mission at these meetings is that I'm the guy representing the other side, and I think a lot kids in the future might appreciate this stance.

　　I think there's a lot of faith in pie-in-the-sky dollars and pretend-tax income. Most people have no clue of the real negative side to this issue and where it's really going. I say this coming from Ferndale, which fifty years ago was the marijuana capital of the world. I grew up with marijuana everywhere, and I saw it ruin a lot of lives. It's not a gateway drug, but it's a gateway to a really bad lifestyle. So, I'm generally against it. I see my farmer friends, neighbors, who want to go in that direction, but I think growing organic, healthy food would be a more noble cause.

SA:　I agree with what Blake's saying. I have done some research and know that there are some legitimate medical purposes for marijuana, whether it's kids with seizures or pain therapy. It has its purpose. But for our area, we can get it in three other counties in a very short drive. We care about the kids and their future.

BA:　We're not against medical marijuana.

SA:    I'm all about holistic healing.

BA:    But ninety percent of the marijuana grown on the black market isn't going for medical use. We don't need more. We have to ask ourselves, why are we here? What are we doing? We're trying to grow healthy food that's good for humanity and can make a difference in their lives. We're not just making a commodity. We're trying to grow something special.

SA:    We have a strong faith, and we believe that God has a purpose for us—to help people. Our dream is to get whole milk back in schools. Our job is to persevere and get past the obstacles. For us, success is taking care of those around us.

BA:    You asked about the larger community and the benefits of living here. We raised our kids to be homebodies, to be naïve rednecks, if you will. We consciously said that. Going to town was an experience we didn't take lightly. That's just old-fashioned, conservative values.

So, the benefits of growing up here for our kids were an endless supply of work, and endless supply of groundedness and values. A lot of people might say that was a burden or a challenge for them, but I don't think so.

Our kids participated in 4-H and FFA, sports, and church. That was it. And it was one sport for each kid, not three. Just for a season. We didn't make a big deal about sports. It wasn't about winning. It was about working hard, and participating, and doing your best. I think we really sheltered our kids.

One of the things we realized when we came here was that our kids were the only Ag kids, the only ones from a farm. We really didn't recognize that when we moved up here.

It's tough, when you're a farm kid. You don't often meet people who share your work ethic and values. I think it was harder on our kids when they moved to town school.

SA:    Blake and I were both very social in school and in college, and we found that our kids, when they were in high school, weren't asking to go out on Friday and Saturday nights. One time, we made a comment about it, and they just said, "You don't want us out there on a Friday or Saturday night." So we had family movie night instead. We'd pick up a movie on the way home from school.

Our kids clearly saw the difference, too, between themselves and other kids. Then, in junior high and high school level, they started getting involved and going to different areas of the state with FFA and 4-H, meeting other Ag kids.

By the time they were older and started to look at colleges, we said, "Go anywhere in the country. Everywhere is a day away from here." We'd both gone to Cal Poly, so we didn't encourage them to go there. But they clearly craved an ag community. They wanted to be with other kids, raised in a similar way, those kids who drove tractors and cut thistles and did things on the farm all the time. Those kids they met through 4-H and FFA were going to Cal Poly, so that really influenced them. All five of our kids ended up going there. Our youngest is a freshman this year. The rest have graduated and are all working for us.

Joseph, the oldest, is married to Alexa and works at the dairy in Ferndale. He has an MBA and helps a lot with the financial stuff. He's fifth generation of our family there.

BA:  We really discouraged going to an Ag school. But Agricultural Business was Joseph's interest. Alexa, his wife, is a high school Ag teacher and an FFA advisor. She also does a lot of work for us.

SA:  Our second child is Christian, who has always had an interest in chickens. He also takes care of the shop, irrigation in the summer, silage, and a lot of the trucking.

BA:  He just married Callie. They're still in their first year as newlyweds. His wife, Callie, has an interest in photography but also works in our office. Today, she is in Sacramento-San Leandro doing demos for our new milk product line.

After Christian is Vanessa. She's been out of college for three or four years and lives here at home. She's twenty-four. Out of all the kids, she has the most interest in cows. She loves to hang out with the cows and heifers and all the outside crew. She's always been the sibling secretary for all the brothers and sisters. She does a lot of computer work and is doing our marketing, branding, and social media. She and Christian represent us a lot.

Next is Dalton. He's in San Leandro at our creamery where we're processing the milk. He came on full time with us this year. It's working out well so far. I think he's really buying in and likes it. The fact that we're now processing the milk makes it interesting for him. He is completing his Agricultural Engineering dress at Cal-Poly.

We'd like to process milk in this community someday. It wasn't our wish to go out of the area to do it.

SA:   But we couldn't start from nothing, either. We have no processing facilities here.

BA:   You ask about challenges of the community and about Highway 101 and Last Chance Grade. I don't lose any sleep over that. It's always been hard to get in and out of this area. It always will be. It's like everything in life. We can't dwell on the negative or what could go wrong tomorrow. There will always be challenges. We just meet them when they come.

SA:   So Savanna is going to be nineteen next month. She's ag systems management. She was always outside as a kid, driving equipment. We joke that she wrecked her first car at six years old. She joked that one day she was going to drive the swather (the mowing tractor) to school.

At one point, maybe she was a freshman in high school, we were having a family meeting. I said, "If you have an extra hour, could you come by the office to help me?"

Joseph piped up and said, "Mom, she's the best equipment driver we have. Find somebody else."

That was a big statement. Joseph is quiet and methodical.

That told me a lot.

BA:    You asked what I meant when I said we raised our kids to be "naïve rednecks." It means that in a world dominated by screens and computers and all that, I taught my kids that computers are generally evil. There's a reason there's a bite out of the apple.

I believe that when we drive on family trips, there's no devices in the vehicle. There's no watching movies or anything. We talk about life. We talk about business. We look out the window and talk about what we see.

There was an iPod someone got for Christmas one year. After the first fifty miles, I just got out, threw it on the concrete, and it was done.

So, when I say "naïve," I mean that they were naïve to all that crap and confusion and poor parenting. Our kids could watch all the TV they wanted as long as they did it before 7 am.

SA:    He makes it seem like it was solid and hard, but it was beautiful. We ate dinner around the table as a family. We had breakfast together. And there's a reason they are coming back. They love it—they love family. And all their lives they've found peer groups that supported that, too, and a church. They've grown up happy and confident and never afraid to get in front of people to talk.

BA:    Life was sometimes hard for them when they were going to town school. Both for the boys and the girls. They weren't fully aware of all the nuances of teenage communication. They thought black was black and white was white. They got there and they saw some new values, learned some new words.

Christian saw some kids stealing out of the soda machine and thought it was wrong, so he told on them. Little simple lessons like that, I think were good. They all went through this transition where they had to consciously weigh and balance and discern what they were seeing at school and at home. Eventually, they learned to rise above and to connect with kids from other communities like them.

SA:    They also made some really good friends here, too.

BA:    That's right.

SA:    We started our kids a little early in school, too. My husband and I had both been the youngest in our class. I talked to teachers about this and many of them were against it. They felt that it would be a disadvantage, our kids starting so young. But we believed—with our little study of two—that it would help them work harder. They'd be the underdogs. They'd be challenged.

   We're at home to love them and support them and to help them with their homework. We knew we could do it, and we purposely gave them a disadvantage. We didn't want life to be too easy for them.

BA:    A little saying is, "The degree of satisfaction is directly proportional to the degree of difficulty." That's true with everything, every day in life.

   There's challenges in every community. I've been to a lot of places, and I don't want to pretend that this community has more than any other. Life just hands you obstacles all day long. How do you handle them? Well, it's always half full around here. We try to bring that across with our employees. We try to hire and fire based on character. We raise our kids to be positive, too. We say, "Don't tell me the cow wouldn't let you move her into the field. Just move her. We make the rules."

   I know there's negatives in this area. When we moved here, we looked at the median income. It was the lowest in the state by far. But we can do something about that.

SA:    God calls us to do that.

BA:    That's right. We're here for a reason. We work on that every day.

   It's true that this community, like every community across the county, is not raising people with a work ethic today. Our grade schools and grammar schools, I don't know what the heck they're doing. They're teaching something that doesn't have a lot to do with basic skills, the skills kids need to be able to be good at things. We've embraced technology because it's an easier way to get things done, but basic skills are frowned upon in a sense.

I wish we were teaching kids to set an alarm clock, wake up on time, and then go accomplish something. If we could teach kids to do that, we would have a different community. But the problem is all over the country. We're not that special and unique here.

That's the situation. We want to do what we can to help.

SA:   Sometimes I'll get involved with school systems work, and I'll be shocked by the numbers—that so few kids aren't reading at grade level in third grade, for example. And we need to hear this. We need to be aware of the numbers.

When kids aren't prepared, it all comes back on the community. Those who can't get a job fall on the back on those of us who can. Those of us who have insurance pay the emergency room bills of the last of us who don't have it. We see that. But at the same time, everyone who doesn't have the means shouldn't feel like a victim.

A big part of it is a parenting thing, lack of fathers playing a role in raising their children.

BA:   Teachers are confused about how to handle these kids who had poor parenting. It's a crazy challenge. I feel for them. But the solution is firm, firm, firm.

I've gone to the high school to do job interviews, and it's pathetic, the level of skills the applicants have.

SA:   When you look at old pictures, of teenagers and how they used to be, they look so healthy and happy, robust, and with beautiful teeth.

But look at teenagers today. So many are not healthy. How much of this is tied to nutrition? That alone makes us feel like we have a purpose, to provide nutrient-rich foods to the community and teach people to eat like we did hundreds of years ago. With the green grass, rivers, sea, and hunting all around here, there is no better place on earth to find "nutrient-rich foods" than Del Norte County.

BA:   I would say it like this. We raised five kids to be farm kids. I think it worked really, really well. They're going to come back to this community and make a contribution. I wish there were more parents in town trying to raise farm kids. It's that simple.

*—February 20, 2018*

# Jermaine Brubaker

"Here, when you express yourself, you face judgment.
You don't have a place to just be who you want to be. I see
that in a lot of the young people I work with. I see they feel
like they have to fit in a box. They don't feel physically
or emotionally safe to be themselves."

*Growing up, Jermaine felt like a misfit in Crescent City. She got out of town
fast—only to return later, as a self-described "boomeranger." In this essay, she
focuses on how difficult it is to fit in here when you feel oppressed by a culture
of small-town conformity.*

I WAS BORN IN DEL NORTE COUNTY. It was a home birth.
I was born in a little row house across from Crescent Elk Middle
School. I was raised by my mother. My dad, who was abusive, left
after I was six.

Mom was a local artist who worked at the College of the Redwoods as an art teacher. My childhood involved a lot of time on the
beaches doing art projects. My mom started her own Montessori
preschool over by the senior center—and then a co-op with other
parents. I had a very different kind of childhood experience, which
involved a core group of the hippies and artists who were in this
community in the 1970s. This world included the Condons, the
Neisons, the Mungers, the Selfridges, and the Yarboroughs. We did
so many things: shows, spinning and weaving, screen printing, silk
screening.

The college offered credit-based enrichment classes in all different mediums. It was before the state-wide rules about class repeat-

ability, so there was so much available. Art was a very big part my life here, as a kid, but also for the community as a whole. It's not like that anymore at the college. Now they just offer one or two art classes.

There was a booming economy back then. People would come from out of town and buy art. My mom was able to sell her work on a regular basis. But in the 1980s, when the economy tanked, she couldn't sell much anymore.

My mother came from a small town in Iowa. She knew she wanted to live by the ocean. So as the story goes, she got into a Volkswagen van with my brother, my father, and a cocker spaniel and just started driving.

There are two different versions of the ending, why we came to live in Del Norte County. My mother's version is that she came over the hill and into town, and it was so beautiful, and there was an art community, and she knew it was the place she wanted to stay.

My brother claims she stopped here because we needed an oil change!

I am the only one in my family from California, and so I'm first generation. And I'm the only member of my family still in this community, although I am a boomeranger. I left and then came back. When I was a teen, I couldn't wait to get out of here.

Growing up, I was a radical, a little rebel. I didn't think this town could handle me. I had dreams, and I couldn't realize them here. Why? It was hard to make change here. It was hard to get people to listen.

I've always been one to push boundaries. I staged my first school walk out when I was in eighth grade over a teacher who wasn't good. We got that teacher fired.

That was at Saint Joseph's Catholic School, which is closed down now. I went there through eighth grade. I wasn't Catholic. My mom was New Age, so I was an outsider in a way. I was already learning how to negotiate both worlds. I learned to tell people what they needed to hear so I could get through what I need to get through.

But there was also what I knew to be true on the other side that I learned to keep from certain people.

I also got a lot of slack because people knew my mom. And people saw me as a "good kid" even though I hung out with the whole skater-punk crowd. A lot of my friends were Latino and Native. Cops would harass us. But I was never picked up. The cops would take the other kids in, but they just called my mom. I know I got the pass because they knew who my mom was. But the Jacksons, the Browns…they didn't get a pass.

So early on I was doing "two world negotiation," which served me well at Del Norte High where I didn't actually go to classes and still got straight A's. I could do that because I avoided AP classes, I tested well, and I had good relationships with my teachers. I would go when it was important, but as long as I did the readings, I could pass the tests and turn in my work without attending. I didn't want to go to class because it was so boring. I would rather go to the river or the beach. As soon as it was sunny and I had a car, that's where my friends and I went.

I had a couple of teachers I liked, and I showed up for their classes. They were entertaining. I remember this one class Robin Parker and John Murphy did my junior year. They did it together—a joint English and history class. They targeted a couple of us to enroll because we were obviously hippie kids. So when it came time to study the 1960s, they asked us to bring in music we liked. We did one-on-one work and group work. We played Jeopardy, which is really low-level engagement, but it was more than what other teachers were doing.

There was so much "sit down shut up." Some teachers, like my civics teacher, would just put notes on the board and expect us to memorize and regurgitate them. That was easy for me. But it meant that my education wasn't challenging. Teachers had their routine, and they did it. They were used to kids showing up, sitting down, and doing their work.

Not only was school generally not engaging, for the most part, but some rules seemed arbitrary and the consequences were ridiculous. I failed a geometry class along with half the students because we would come late, and if you weren't in your seat with your book open when the bell rang, you got detention. Of course, it was the class right after lunch, and if you went to detention, you would miss one part of the proof, and you'd be totally lost.

I did get involved in social justice issues. I remember there was an upperclassman handing out pamphlets in the hall about how African Americans were actually gorillas. Nobody was doing anything about it. I remember yelling at this guy in the hallway. He was kind of a big guy, too. A group of us took it to the principal and got it resolved, but the upperclassman didn't suffer any repercussions.

There were a couple of instances like that that made me feel so upset. I remember a group of football players would pretend to be friends with intellectually disabled kids, and then they would encourage them to grab the boobs and butts of different girls in the hallways. Then, of course, the kids with disabilities got in trouble for it.

When I took it to the principal, he said, "Well, boys will be boys." And they were football players, so they got leeway. That was the culture of the school, you know? I didn't feel like I fit in, even though I could roll across cliques and got a lot of slack myself.

I graduated from Del Norte High in 1993 and came to College of the Redwoods next. I knew I couldn't go to a four-year college. I couldn't afford it. My mom had taught here (she'd retired at that point), so it was kind of a safety zone for me. And I knew I needed to get out of here, but I didn't have a plan yet.

I was also working at the *Triplicate*—a job I started when I was 15. I did everything: I was a Jack of all trades. I did the AP wire and ad sales, pay stubs, subscriptions, and design. My mom worked there, too. She did, among other things, political cartoons. She was only part-time at the College of the Redwoods, so she worked other jobs, too. Sometimes three, actually.

At CR, I did well academically, until one semester, I got a severe case of poison oak and had to drop out. Even though my mom had worked at CR, I didn't know about academic renewal for situations like this, so I failed, and I didn't reenroll.

I left town at age nineteen and moved to Sacramento, where I was in a very bad relationship, which I barely got out of alive. I got out of it by working in Yosemite National Park. Then I lived in Chowchilla—for a minute—but ended up back here in less than a year.

When it came to relationships, I made a lot of mistakes. I don't know—I might have escaped some of those if I'd had a better education about the signs of domestic violence and abuse. But that's not something you talk about in Catholic school. At any rate, I knew about domestic violence. In third grade, I helped a friend who was being abused. I ended up testifying in court against her abuser. Also, my mother was a survivor of abuse.

I haven't really delved too deep yet to know what could have been different or how this community could have better supported me, but I do know at nineteen, these abusive relationships start by being addictively intense and wonderful. I remember how my first boyfriend swept me off my feet. It was only after we left town together that things changed.

That relationship also cost me in other ways, too. He took out credit cards in my name and maxed them out. Then he got more of them. I ended up with over $30,000 of debt before I turned twenty. That's something that took a long time to recover from. I knew how to budget, and I knew a little bit about credit, but not enough. To have someone take advantage of you like that, it really screws you up. Helping kids get an education about that might be helpful.

So, I landed back here for a short time. I reconnected with one of my best friends in Eureka. I did the mall work and Sizzler for a little while. That changed when I got offered a management position at the mall. I saw a future in retail flash before me, and it was scary. I was like, "Actually, I'm going back to college." So I enrolled at College of the Redwoods in Eureka.

It was a pretty straight line to Humboldt State University. At CR, they pretty much told me, "You are out of credits here. What do you want to do?"

I said, "Go to HSU?"

They said, "What do you really want to do with your life?"

I said, "Travel and learn?"

They said, "Anthropology is for you!"

So, I got my Anthropology degree from HSU. I had a great time doing it. I had three professors I really loved. I got to study in the West Indies as a senior project. And I use Anthropology in my work today. Working for social change, you have to leave your culture behind and come in to a community ready to absorb and learn and participate as much as possible. So much of social change work is connecting with different cultures and removing your glasses and seeing things from other people's perspectives, with empathy.

I lived in Humboldt County almost twenty years doing all kinds of social change work. I didn't move back until I started working for Building Healthy Communities for the Opportunity Youth Initiative.

Why did I come back? Humboldt County is full of people with degrees and good intensions, and I maxed out at about $13 an hour, competing against hundreds of people with as much experience as me trying to get that next level. Also, I knew how much this community needed experienced people working for social justice. But I knew how hard it would be to come here labeled with "environmentalist" and "liberal," too.

There's so much pushback in Del Norte County—people here don't want to like Humboldt County. I don't know where that comes from or why it's so important to be different. Maybe it's because Humboldt County is known as the place where Grateful Dead fans come to die. It's very progressive and hippie, so maybe that's what people here fear it, but then, it's crazy to go out to dinner in Del Norte County and still get Styrofoam containers. That was a big culture shock coming back into the community. I took for granted that everybody cares about the environment. Many people here don't even recycle. You might get run out of Humboldt for that!

There is a big fear of change here—and an unquestioning attitude that says, "We can't do that here." And there's a resistance to self-expression. There's not really an outlet for people to express themselves. In Humboldt, I did the Kinetic Sculpture Races and was the Rutabaga Queen. I danced Burlesque. Can you imagine me doing that here and also working with youth? Maybe they'd let me bring the Kinetic Sculpture here, but…

Here, when you express yourself, you face judgment. You don't have a place to just be who you want to be. I see that in a lot of the young people I work with. I see that they feel like they have to fit in a box. They don't feel physically or emotionally safe to be themselves. Like, in Gender Talk, where LGBTQ kids and outsiders can be themselves, and then they have to code switch in the outside world and not rock the boat.

We just had our 20th high school reunion recently, and one of my friends who didn't come out as gay in high school still had so much anxiety about being rejected that he walked in the door at the reunion and only lasted 10 minutes. He started having a panic attack.

Not only do we feel we can't be ourselves, but we can't say the things we need to say when it comes to public discourse. We're not honest. There's this fear that you can't rock the boat. If you do, people can shut you down. They can make sure you don't work in this community again.

Part of this is a function of being in a small town. Somewhere else, in a bigger place, burning bridges doesn't have such dire consequences. This is a struggle for me, because I want to shake things up. I want to push people to do better. And they don't always want to listen. In my work doing community development, I have to do a lot of ego massaging, getting people to the table, making them feel safe.

Lots of people here have ideas, but they're afraid to take the risk to share them. If they step out—and they get shut down—there's nowhere else for them to go. It creates an atmosphere of timidity and compliance.

People here take it very personally when you disagree with them. I think it's because they haven't been "shook," and they don't know how to respond to it. The rules of politeness and conformity extend everywhere, and we don't have experience separating the personal from the political. Vigorous disagreement often becomes a personal Facebook attack in the end.

In my work with youth, I see youth voices being silenced at times when boards—often made up of older, wealthy white folks—don't like what youth are saying or how they're saying it. An example that comes to mind is really controversial. But some youth with Redwood Voice did a video about a man in Humboldt County who got shot by police. The youth didn't understand the rules about making the video under an organization with a 501(c)(3). People freaked out, the video got squelched, and it only got released later. A lot of people—youth—were hurt by this because they thought they had a platform for speaking their truth, and they didn't.

Part of the problem is that we have foundations doing social justice work rather than non-profits. I love the Humboldt Area Foundation. I love the Wild Rivers Community Foundation. But their primary purpose as foundations is to raise money and distribute it to good causes. It's really hard to balance that with social change because their primary funders are older white folk in power. You know you need to keep people happy to get money, but if you're then turning around and trying to flip the power structure, that's not going to work.

We have a very "colonized" community. We don't respect indigenous people for the most part. We have people fighting for recognition, trying to get rights. Not long ago, we had the Fish Wars where the federal government pointed guns at native grandmas trying to fish. And we know racism underlies so many things in this community—and I don't just mean individual racist acts, but systemic racism. But our conflicts are so fresh here, so recent, there's so much deep hurt and emotion that it's hard for us to talk about or even recognize it at all.

Until we can really talk about it, and until the people who have benefited from systemic racism for generations can come to recognize it, we won't be speaking honestly. There is such a fear of loss for those in power—if they admit it—they fear they might lose what they have and be seen as a bad person. Maybe they're afraid that what they did to people of color will be done to them.

And the small town mentality extends beyond race, too. That mentality is "If everybody doesn't do what I feel is right, if everybody doesn't share my values, then everything will fall apart."

Only it won't. Or maybe it will, but in a way that benefits us all, because we'll be more honest and open and accepting. Instead of being a big bowl of bright, beautiful, differently colored fish, we're all one color, all goldfish, in this tiny bowl. We could be the vibrant pond of diversity, but it would mean we have to raise our tolerance for each other and for actual dialogue.

*—December 1, 2017*

# William Maffett

"The need for better leadership is not limited to our schools"

*Now retired from a lifetime of service in public education, William Maffett reflects on how values for young people—and adults as well—have changed in Del Norte.*

I WAS BORN IN MINNESOTA, raised and schooled in Oregon, and graduated from the University of Oregon in 1964. I was a history major and a biology minor and made a decision to become a schoolteacher. You could almost literally pick a position and location because the need was so great for teachers in the mid-sixties. I read of a position open in Del Norte County and came to Crescent City right after the tidal wave of 1964 to interview; I received a job offer to teach at Crescent Elk School for the 1964-65 school year.

My plan was to stay a year in Crescent City to get needed experience and then to move on from here. But at the end of the 1964-65 school year, I enjoyed my position so much that I decided to stay a second year. I was teaching and loved working with middle school children. I taught seventh and eighth grade history and reading. Not everyone loves middle-school children, but I did. I had a wonderful principal who was nurturing, supportive, and a fine role model. I don't believe I ever had a better principal with whom to work in my entire career.

Early in my career, achieving tenure after a third successful year was a good thing on your resume. Consequently, I decided to stay for that third year in hopes of achieving my tenure status. That would have been the end of the 1965-66 school year. In the fall of 1966, I began dating the PE teacher at my school, Miss Kathy Mellum. Ironically, she was also from Minnesota and had been raised in North Dakota. We became engaged and then married on June 10, 1967. We both did graduate studies at the University of Oregon in the summers, with lots of sun and warmth, but still returned to the foggy coolness of Crescent City in the fall. Kathy, though she didn't like the coolness, was such a good sport about it; as long as she had warm summers, she put up with the rainy, cool winters.

We bought a nice home on Lake Earl Drive, had a little boy in October of 1972, and continued to grow as community members. We chose to stay in Crescent City and still maintain this community as our home. We now love the drizzly, foggy weather and the rain, as do the redwood trees on our two acres of beautiful property.

After twenty-two years of teaching, and with Kathy's urging, I pursued a California Administrative Credential. I got that credential and immediately became the vice-principal at Crescent Elk School, and some years later the principal of Joe Hamilton Elementary School. I finished my career as the director of Alternative Education for the county and retired in June of 2000 after devoting thirty-seven years to education in Del Norte County.

Kathy took time away from the classroom to raise our son and then returned to teaching at elementary, high school, and junior college levels. She was still teaching at Redwood School when I retired. I still kept very busy after retirement: helping supervise student teachers for Humboldt State University and serving as director of the Del Norte County Library for a short period of time. Shortly after that, I decided to run for the school board and served six years in that position. When Kathy retired from Redwood School in June of 2008, my school board position really took away a lot of time from our traveling. It was then that I met with Superintendent Moorehouse and tendered my resignation; she fully understood my need and desire to resign.

We love this area and have no plans to move away. We do like to travel and we're often gone. We do travel the world, and we talk about our area being a true paradise—pristine waters, beautiful lush forests—but we have to admit that the town doesn't have much to offer. We take advantage of the cultural offerings: Community Concerts, Del Norte Association for Cultural Awareness (DNACA) performances, plays by Lighthouse Repertory Theatre. We support all of them. With events in Brookings, Humboldt, and Ashland, we stay very "culturally fit."

But, there are still challenges. There seems to be a lack of support for the value of education. Parental support seems to be lagging, the causes of which we are not entirely sure nor understand. There is a high percentage, per capita, of unwed teen mothers, and this alarming statistic seems to be persistently high. There's very well documented excessive use of drugs and alcohol also. The downtown business community seems to suffer because of these factors. It's hard for businesses to make it, and flourish, and stay open, so we do see empty buildings in our downtown area. This leads to a lack of small stores and locally owned businesses. The old "mom & pop" grocery stores and meat markets we used to have are all gone. Only Walmart, which does draw lots of customers, much to the detriment of the smaller businesses. We lack any other shopping areas for clothing and other needs. The recent addition of an expanded Wild Rivers Natural Food Market and two new craft beer breweries, Port O'Pints and Seaquake, are a positive addition to our town. But there are other factors to help explain why Del Norte County lags behind.

I came for my interview in the spring of 1964, right after the tidal wave when there was still mud on the streets. But we rebuilt. Things seemed to pick up, although I don't know that it has ever totally recovered to what it might have been prior to the tidal wave. Logging, lumbering, salmon, and crab fishing were flourishing; sport fishing was a large attraction. Most of those industries are basically gone. I think those are contributing factors to our lagging community. I'm pleased that they're not cutting and harvesting the beautiful redwood forests anymore, but I do understand what effect that's had on our community and economy.

It is so sad to think that today an increasing number of young people report that they can't think of a single teacher who seems to care about them. I can see that things have changed in our schools. These kids may have a valid point. My perspective is now limited because I've been away from it for quite some time, but it seems that teaching has principally become about standardized testing and achieving various standards. I think good people are leaving the profession through retirement and for other opportunities and vocations.

Throughout my educational career, I always sought a closeness with my students, and I felt how important it was to give them time and attention and to help work with their unique needs. It really saddens me, but I think it's absolutely correct to say there has been a shift. I know—from what I've heard second hand—that Crescent Elk Middle School, where I worked for so many years, isn't considered safe anymore; there are increased accusations of bullying at school. Crescent Elk has a leadership problem in their administration. It just filters right down from the administration. I know what it used to be like—I know how safe it was. Yes, we had incidents occurring, but that happens in all schools. I am just shocked by what others have told me is going on there. There is an inexcusable lack of monitoring, support, and leadership in our schools today. If it is allowed to continue, or if a blind eye is turned to it, I don't know what it will come to.

A very important side note is that there is a current contractual dispute between the Del Norte Teachers' Association and the Del Norte Unified School District which may influence how the teaching and support staff devote attention to their students before and after class. I don't know if it's compounded by a lack of parental support, or a lack of rigor, or because the district cannot find good applicants. Maybe in the past we had a better cadre from which to select and fill our staffing needs and requirements.

When I was vice-principal at Crescent Elk School, my principal was a lady named Sherry Smith. She was a very skilled leader.

Working with her every day was a joy because of the qualities she had—how she treated the staff and students. That kind of respect and compassion spread throughout the school, and she passed on a feeling that created a non-threatening and safe environment. I worked with all kinds of administrative leaders in my twenty-two years of teaching and then fourteen years as an administrator. Some of them were fabulous, wonderful leaders and mentors with compassion and understanding, who knew how to treat and value people. They knew how to say, "You're doing a wonderful job. I appreciate what I saw in your classroom, and here are the reasons why, and here are some areas where you could do even better." There are a lot of people and current administrators who don't know how to do that, and certainly, I encountered several who bordered on incompetent.

The need for better leadership is not limited to our schools. It's a problem on boards and in government as well. We can't seem to find men and women to serve who have that gift of competence and ability to provide that leadership. It's too simplistic to say that our population is just too small to build a cadre of good leaders. We get a poor leader who then chooses his subordinates in some kind of haphazard fashion, and that allows the problem to continue. The "Peter Principle" is definitely at work in Del Norte County. I might sound jaded, but I've served on a lot of boards, and in a lot of leadership positions, and my perception is that some people are misplaced in leadership roles here. Many people perceive themselves as competent leaders, when in fact they may have gone beyond their abilities, hence the "Peter Principle" effect.

Kathy and I are not users nor growers of marijuana, but we are strong supporters of legalization. It's frustrating to see our city and county leaders dragging their feet about implementing standards and guidelines for the commercial growing, selling, and taxation of cannabis. We are very concerned about the drug and alcohol problems in our community, but we don't see evidence that marijuana is the gateway drug that some people say it is. Control of opioids is a much greater problem. Decriminalizing marijuana, and taking that big responsibility away from law enforcement, seems like a good thing. And it may even contribute to our community's health and economy. There are legitimate benefits—pain relief and relief from insomnia. I'm amazed that our leaders can't get off their tails and do something about providing guidelines for commercialization of the cannabis industry.

In summary, we have called Del Norte County our home for a full 70% of our lives. In spite of what may be considered its drawbacks, we are not leaving our beautiful home in the redwoods, nor are we giving up on contributing to improvements for our county. Perhaps not serving actively on boards, but certainly supporting those that do. And, we will always vote in every election: local, state, and national. There is still lots of hope for Del Norte County, the state of California, and for the United States of America, in spite of current political turmoil.

*—January 8, 2018*

# Saundra De León Mendoza

"My parents want me and my sisters to get a
good education so we don't end up like them. But it's really hard
for us to hear that. We're proud of our parents for working so hard
and taking care of us. We want them to be proud of us. And in a
lot of ways, we want to be like them"

*Saundra de León Mendoza has worked to make a future for herself here, even
though she is undocumented. "Making the best of things" is part of her value
system, one she inherited from her immigrant parents.*

I WAS NOT BORN IN DEL NORTE COUNTY even though I'd
like to say I was. It's a beautiful place. I was born in Jalisco, Mexico.

I was nine months old when my parents brought me to the US,
so I don't have any memory of where I was born. Jalisco has cultural meaning to me, because I'm Hispanic, and I'd like to visit
someday, but Del Norte County is my home.

I remember going to preschool here. And I remember as a
kid going to the beach and the Marine Mammal Center. So many
things here, early on, sparked my interest in nature and the outdoors. And participating in community events like the Farmers'
Market and the Rodeo always make me feel like a real Del Norter.

But there have been times when I've felt like I don't belong.
Growing up, I've come to understand some differences between
Democrats and Republicans. I remember seeing in our last elec-
tion that Del Norte voted more red (Republican) than anything.
And I feel those people don't really like me. When I say "me," I

mean people like me who are undocumented. The current president and his views are really negative towards us. And that hurts me.

I volunteered as a poll worker at the last election, and it really gave me another perspective. The ballots were right there, so close I could reach for one, but voting is something I can't do because I'm undocumented.

But I was happy to be part of it in some way, and I was having a great day as a poll worker. And then someone came in and made a joke when he got out his ID about how he was voting as an "illegal alien." And I get it. It was a joke. But it really hurt. Little did he know, he was joking about *me*—an illegal alien. I don't like to be called that.

I didn't say anything, but that moment made me feel like, here I am, living in this red county, where people hate who I am, even when they've never met me.

I know the feeling of being hated is partly in my head. I feel this way because of what I see in the media and how other people are treated. And a lot of horrible things are happening all over. Some people are getting their whole lives ripped apart when they or their family members get deported.

Maybe it is not happening here, but it could. Knowing that deportation is always a possibility honestly frightens me. I know my whole life, the only one I have ever known, is on the line.

For instance, when I'm driving down the street and something with my car is messed up, I'm afraid I'm going to get pulled over. When I was little, I was really afraid of police officers. Whenever I saw one, it gave me terrible anxiety even though I tried to hide it from my mother. And that anxiety is my reality now.

But I'm thankful for growing up here. I love nature and the outdoors. If we had stayed in Oakland where my parents took us when they first arrived, I don't think I would've had the chance to experience all this.

This summer, through the Youth Training Academy, I got to intern as a tour guide with Redwood Rides, a local adventure outfitter. That really changed my perspective of this place in a lot of different ways. I got to meet people from New York and all over the nation who were in awe of our environment. They'd never seen such beautiful forests and rivers. I got to share this place with them.

In the internship, I learned to train people about water safety—little things like how to get in and out of a boat in different water conditions—and how to pump up the boat if it leaks. I got to go along on the trips, and learned to kayak. And finally, because of the internship, I was hired as a guide. Now on the weekends, I get to lead trips on my own—by myself—for the company!

I always liked the river. Our family came up to swim on the Smith in the summer. We never went in if it was cold. But recently, I learned a lot about the tribes here and how they use the rivers year round. Redwood Rides did a trip for Rios to Rivers, a conservation organization that brings people together from different cultures for a kayaking exchange program focused on river stewardship. I learned a lot about the Klamath River and the effect of dams on rivers, not just here, but in Chile. It showed me just how much we take the health of our rivers for granted and how important they are in so many different ways to so many different people.

Growing up, a lot of my friends called me a "busy bee" because I was always doing something, like attending club meetings and volunteering. Even now, I'm in college, and I'm doing pet sitting and working for Redwood Rides. I just got hired as a dental assistant, too. I'm the person in the back, getting things for the dentist, cleaning instruments, working hard. I love it. Sometimes I think to myself, "Wow, I'm really lucky I have this job." But I know other kids who grew up under different circumstances maybe don't feel the same way. They might think the job sucks.

But I grew up with parents who were always working hard. My dad is a construction worker and my mom cleans houses. They've never really had stable work, and that was always worrisome. Are we going to have enough money for groceries? I never understood, when my dad was sick, why he wouldn't ever go to the doctor. It was because we couldn't afford it. Even as a kid, I worried about these things. I worried that something really serious was going to happen to my dad. But despite—or maybe because of the worry—I learned the value of hard work.

Going to college was always set in my brain. You know, my parents finished middle school, that was all. They never had any more education. But they understood hard work and taught that value to us just by the way they lived. Growing up, I was always trying to do my best, like my parents told me, and so whatever I did, I tried to do it well.

It was weird, in high school, because I knew kids who were involved in clubs and sports, not because they wanted to do well and succeed in those activities, but because they wanted something for their college applications. I remember hearing students say, "I'm only doing this so I can add it to my college application." I was there to meet people and develop leadership skills and do community service. Hearing other kids say that upset and confused me.

My parents want me and my sisters to get a good education so we don't end up like them. But it's really hard for us to hear that. We're proud of our parents for working so hard and taking care of us. We want them to be proud of us. And in a lot of ways, we want to be like them.

I have deeply conflicted feelings about what's happening with Deferred Action for Childhood Arrivals (DACA). I remember when DACA passed, my sister was so excited. She kept telling me how important it was. I was so young. I didn't know what it would mean to be able to work legally. But it was a big deal. We each had to pay almost $500 to get this card. And there was my picture on it. It looked like a license. And my family explained to me I needed it to work.

All because of this card, I gained skills I wouldn't have otherwise gotten. And I was able to get my driver's license so I could take my little sister to school, go to work, or get to the beach. But now that I hear that DACA is ending, all that anxiety I used to feel as a little kid, like when I saw a cop car, is all coming back to me. I've been really sad. I overthink what's going to happen to me and to my little sister, who was born here, unlike the rest of us. I try to be positive. We have a six month period for Congress to do something. So it might be okay.

The feeling of being undocumented now, in this point in history, is like the feeling you get when you think about what it means to live in the Cascadian subduction zone. I don't mean to joke about it, but it makes you feel this impending danger, like an earthquake could happen any time.

My dad's always said, whatever happens, happens. But whatever happens could be the worst thing I've ever experienced. It's hard to live with that. I'll try to make the best of things. But I can't really have a set plan. People like me are in limbo. But people like me will always embrace every second we have.

—*September 12, 2017*

# Don Olson

"I paid my way through college working in
forestry over the summers. Can you imagine that today?
I could make enough money in three months to pay my
expenses the rest of the year at CR and HSU."

*Don Olson spent his professional life as a teacher and administrator in Del
Norte County, retiring from his position as Superintendent in 2015. In this essay, he reflects on cultural changes in education—and his community.*

I WAS RAISED IN DEL NORTE COUNTY. My parents, Donald
and Patricia Olson, moved here from Wahpeton, North Dakota, in
the fall of 1955 when I was not quite two years old.

My mom's two sisters, Mary Jean Johnson and Janet Johnson,
had already moved out here. They'd married two brothers, Bob and
Burt Ames, and they'd offered Dad a job. My parents were tired of
farming in the bitter cold of winter and the heat of summer, so they
came out here. My mother's parents, Albert and Ella Johnson, also
moved here from North Dakota shortly after we arrived.

Dad repaired appliances for the Bob Ames Company. In 1971,
Dad was hired by the City of Crescent City as an electrician, and
later he became the city building inspector. Dad joined the Crescent City Fire Department in 1960 and served as fire chief for
many years as well. He finally retired at age 71.

Mom was a homemaker, but she did work for a while at Daly's
Department Store downtown. It was great having a mom at home
who prepared great meals and was always there for us.

I grew up about three blocks from Joe Hamilton Elementary School. I started Kindergarten in Mrs. Isola's Classroom in the fall of 1959. I went to Crescent Elk after that for grades five through eight, and then on to Del Norte High School.

Throughout the 50s and 60s, the economy in Crescent City was very good. Back then, there was a lot of work. Anyone who was able-bodied had a choice of jobs available. A lot of young families bought houses and lived in the Beresa Tract, which ran from A Street between Indra and 9th Streets towards the ocean. It was a great neighborhood filled with kids. It was like a big family.

I went to school with my friends, and after school, we played together in the neighborhood. In the summers, we would sometimes ride our bikes up and over Howland Hill, swim in Mill Creek, and come back home at the end of the day. In the evenings after school, we made up street games, organizing them ourselves, ball games, one foot over the gutter, and hide-and-go-seek. When it got dark, our moms would call us in.

In my youth, Del Norte County was perceived as a very safe place. But it wasn't without danger. When I was about nine years old, there was a girl my age named Myra Gerling. She lived on Indra Street with her family. She was walking to Pacific Market to get ice cream for a party, and she was murdered on the way. As a kid, hearing about that and knowing the person was very traumatic. Parents did think differently about letting their kids walk around in Del Norte County.

Every community has tragedies, and that was one of ours. However, if the internet had been around in the 1960s, we would have heard more about violence. We would have been more on edge. We just lived a more protected life back then—not from news in general—but from the volume of mass media. Parents weren't as worried and cautious as they are today.

I did well in school. I had very good teachers, though there were a couple who were challenging. I am sure I provided my share of challenges for them as well. But you saw some things done to students you wouldn't get away with today, and for good reason.

For example, students who misbehaved could be swatted with a paddle. I knew that swatting students was never the answer to cure discipline problems. I was the recipient of a few swats in school, and I really did learn that I did not need any more swatting.

I knew I was going to be an educator shortly after high school. My goal was to build students' self-esteem. Taking a positive approach to discipline really served me well as a teacher. I truly enjoyed most of my teachers and vowed to carry on their great practices. It was a good time for education.

One of the things that made me certain that I would be a teacher was an experience I had in high school. I was a cross-age tutor and went down to Klamath, to Margaret Keating School. Helen Tracy was our supervising educator for the project. Margaret Keating was a sizeable school in the 60s and 70s. It probably had 150-200 students. Lots of folks were working in the timber industry, tourism, or at the Air Force Base. While at Margaret Keating, I was able to teach some lessons, and I felt like I was good at it. It was a very positive experience.

How else were things different? There was more respect back then. Partly, it was the way parents felt about their kids' behavior. As a kid, if you had a problem at school, you did not want that information going home. Many parents were going to be hard on you for disrespect or poor behavior. Today, it seems, some students have unconditional support from home. That was always a challenge, working in the school system when this shift happened. But those parents deeply loved their children, too, just like in previous generations. They wanted the best for them. So as a teacher and administrator, I learned to work with the shift in attitudes. The goal of discipline is always to change student behavior. So we had to learn new ways to gain parents' trust and solve problems together.

As a student, I loved going to high school. I started in the fall of 1968. It was fun. We didn't have all AP classes, so there wasn't anywhere near the academic competition you see today for students to get the highest GPA—to the point where students take extra classes just to get ahead of others.

There was competition, but you couldn't get extra. The playing field was very even. You just buckled down and took the same classes as everybody else. For me, it wasn't stressful in an academic way.

In middle and high school, I played all the sports—baseball, football, basketball. When I went to college, I played two years of football and basketball for College of the Redwoods in Eureka. After College of the Redwoods, I transferred to Humboldt State in 1974 as an education major.

I graduated from Humboldt in 1977. There weren't many teaching jobs in the late 70s. Population growth had slowed, and very few teachers were retiring. It was tough all across the country. I applied for teaching jobs from Southern Oregon and all along the I-5 corridor. I applied in Williams, California and at schools across Highway 20. That summer, I was called for three interviews. One was in Williams, and I did not get that job. I next interviewed for a second grade job at Smith River School. I competed against Sherry Smith for the opening. Sherry was chosen for the position, but the principal, Gene Edinger, was impressed with my interview. In the late 70s, it was rare to see a male teacher teaching below third grade.

Finally, near the end of that summer, I got another interview. In August, Bill Blanchard, a third grade teacher at Bess Maxwell School, just up and left. The interview took place in Principal Larry Beam's dining room. I sat at a table and was able to look across at the beautiful Pacific Ocean and Castle Rock. I do not believe that many have interviewed for any job in such a picturesque setting. I finally received my opportunity to teach in Del Norte County as a third grade teacher at Bess Maxwell School.

My brother, Russell, and my sister, Jeannie, moved on to other areas, but I was glad to put down roots here. I always liked it. I never wanted to move. Being an educator, I had a lot of time in the summer to go on long trips to see other places, so I didn't feel trapped. I did a lot of backpacking in the Siskiyous and Marble Mountains. There really wasn't any part of me that wanted that job in Williams. I also liked being near my parents, too, and I know they appreciated that.

I worked at Bess Maxwell eighteen years before moving over to teach at Mary Peacock School. While at Mary Peacock, I went back to HSU on the weekends and earned an Administrative Services Credential. Then I worked for seventeen years in administration in positions from Assistant Principal to Superintendent. After thirty-eight years in education, I retired.

I told my daughters not to go into education. There was a job crunch on at the time they were in college, and teaching jobs were hard to find. You know, these things ebb and flow. But my daughters, Phoebe and Jaden, both received degrees in education and now they are both teachers. And I am most proud of their accomplishments.

I worked my way through college at Del Norte Ice and Cold Storage and Rellim Redwood Company. I worked at Rellim Redwood Company as a forester's technician. We surveyed roads and timber harvest lines all over the Rellim Redwood Company's property. I remember working in the Rock Creek and Morrison Creek drainages before any trees had been logged. It was all old growth fir and redwood. It was quite beautiful.

It is a bit regretful that Miller Redwood Company did not consider working towards more sustainable yield logging practices. It appeared they wanted to cut everything quickly to maximize profits. A piece of property like the one they had may have been logged more sustainably if they'd run one fewer shift. People could have worked many more years. But that wasn't how they operated at the time. Additionally, had there been different planning, that property could have possibly still remained on our tax rolls and continued to provide work for our community in forest industries.

I paid my way through college working in forestry over the summers. Can you imagine that today? I could make enough money in three months to pay my expenses the rest of the year at CR and HSU. Tuition was very low, and because there was no community college in our county at the time, the state paid us a supplement—$750 a year— to travel to College of the Redwoods in Eureka. The tuition at Humboldt was $53 a quarter for all the units you could take. It wasn't hard to find a place to live, either. I rented a small house, a single studio just off campus, for $100 a month.

What were some good things about Del Norte County's educational system through the years I was working? Teachers really cared about their students. I always felt that.

Also, in the 1980s and 1990s, there was a lot of academic freedom. I don't mean teachers could just teach anything they wanted, but they could choose to do different units—like river studies or ocean studies—to tie curriculum into the natural environment. Teaching is much more prescriptive now. Teachers don't have many choices. As an administrator, in the later years, it was my job to observe teachers, to make sure everyone was teaching the standards. That could be disappointing, especially when I knew teachers used to have alternatives and more choices.

The positive effect of a unified curriculum is that wherever you are in Del Norte County—or even the state of California— you know in fifth grade, for example, they're all learning the same thing. So if kids move around, which they often do, they don't miss out. But the negative side is that some of the curriculum isn't all that good.

I'd go into classes and look at the elementary mathematics program, and I'd think, wow the publishers are really missing the boat with that curriculum. I do miss the subject matter projects where teachers would come together in the summer and focus on curriculum and how to improve teaching. Teachers truly had more resources in the 80s and 90s. Units like My Travels with Gulliver (scale of numbers), Family Math, Marilyn Burns Units, CA Math, Project AIMS, and Writing Projects were available to all teachers. Now, it seems that we are all at the mercy of the publishers who make the curriculum. They're in business to make money, not necessarily to create the best education for students. The choices in curriculum are quite limited—sometimes to just a couple of companies. Each publisher has to have their curriculum approved by the state prior to being able to sell their materials.

As a teacher and coach, and then later, an administrator, I did appreciate how the people in this county were outstanding supporters of athletics and music. If you attended a local athletic event or concert, you saw that people were really engaged. The community greatly supports athletics as well as other extra-curricular activities. The key part is, though, how do we build parents' interest in academics?

We tried different things, and sometimes they worked very well. We created Family Math Nights to bring people together for a more academic activity. But it's a continuing challenge to get people to participate. Some families have a hard time being able to attend those activities. Maybe they don't have a vehicle or maybe they work long hours.

We have a high degree of poverty in Del Norte County. But I really believed—and continue to believe—that high quality instruction trumps every disadvantage. We can lift up poor kids and kids of every race to be great students and members of our community and society.

While I was a principal at Redwood School, I gave student success a lot of thought. I started studying test scores. I pulled all this data together, and it wasn't favorable. Our students weren't doing well, and we needed to know why. We needed to take a hard look at our neighbors in Humboldt County and ask why they were scoring so well on standardized tests. We needed to be able to look at the problem in a different way, with a more critical eye.

That wasn't popular. But I kept it up. Eventually, I was hired as the Assistant Superintendent of Curriculum and Instruction. I looked at all the district's data to see areas of need. I found that we needed to be more strategic, to teach to standards where we hadn't focused effectively before. That's how teachers get better. And we did see significant growth in academic performance. By changing how we thought about things, we raised a lot of scores across our district. We rose to a level of similar districts and a few schools met the 800 API benchmark set by the state of California. I am most proud of that work.

We partnered with Sanger Unified School District, a high performing school district outside of Fresno. They taught us that you have to ask four questions: What do we want students to know? How will we know if they know it? What will we do if they do know it? What will we do if they don't?

Not all teachers were in tune with the standards testing movement. Some teachers just didn't want to teach that way. They don't want to feel like they're teaching to the test. But that's not the point. The point is to teach to the standards, to be strategic about it. We did have some resistance, but once we won those teachers over, they began to see success. Then, the movement to increase student achievement was in motion.

One of our community's biggest challenges is how to make sure all our students are truly ready for kindergarten. If we can get that, it's a different game. And Del Norte County is improving in that area through coordinated work between schools and other community groups.

We do need a better means to address issues in our community so that we are going in the same direction. Del Norte County is about evenly split between Democrats and Republicans, which makes us a bit polarized. There's a battle going on to see which direction we're going, and it holds us back. I believe that we need to make decisions, first and foremost, that will benefit our entire community.

Another challenge we have in our school system that you see in the media a lot is bullying. It seems to me that our perception of bullying has changed, though. When I was a kid, bullying was usually physical aggression towards you—and possibly language—but mostly it involved violence or the threat of violence. Now, bullying can be a student simply criticizing another kid for not running fast, or not getting good grades, or being fat. Even though we don't want any of that to happen, it does, and it seems like people are more sensitive to name-calling than they used to be, and they don't know how to cope with small incidents like this.

We have to raise our students to be problem-solvers. You can't always find an adult to solve these kinds of issues for you. So, I believe we need to help kids find language to deflect a bully themselves. Certainly, they should have adults to help them if they're experiencing threats of physical aggression, or overt racism, or sexual harassment, but we need to help them learn the skills to solve those minor incidents themselves. I worry that today, we might be jumping in too soon and creating oversensitivity.

The politics of language has changed for coaches and teachers, too. There used to be a lot of belittling. Someone might have called an athlete a "candy-ass" back in the day. Adults have to be much more strategic and careful about what they say. That's a good thing, really. But it also requires rewriting some scripts we learned or experienced when we were being coached or taught, so it's challenging.

Would I ever leave Del Norte County? I don't think so. I really like my life here. I live in a beautiful home in Hiouchi with my wife, Martha. I have been very fortunate in Del Norte County. I was able to retire at age sixty-one. My dad, worked until he was seventy-one, and, at times, I have felt a bit guilty for retiring so young. My parents taught me the value of a job and a great work ethic.

Del Norte County is paradise. We have unparalleled beauty. The beaches, the rivers, mountains to hike in, great forests to wander through. Best of all, there's also a very strong core of people here who care about the betterment of society. Sometimes we do seem polarized, and we are not always pointing in the same direction. But if we can figure that out and work together, we can really make this wonderful place we call home even better.

*—April 18, 2018*

# Acknowledgments

This book would never have been possible without the contributors who agreed to be interviewed and bravely shared the details of their lives. Thank you all.

I'm especially grateful to the College of the Redwoods for seeing the value in this project and allowing me to take a sabbatical from my teaching assignments to see it through.

I also want to thank the people from The California Endowment's Building Healthy Communities Initiative, the Wild Rivers Community Foundation, Redwood Voice, and my dear friend Melissa Darnell for all providing encouragement and support from the beginning of the project to the end.

Finally, I could never have completed this book without my family firmly behind me. Thanks to my husband Lathrop Leonard, and my children Emily, Lydia, Henry, and Theo. You matter the most to me in all the world. I love you to the edge and back again.

# Index

# About the Editor

RUTH RHODES has lived in Del Norte County since 2003 and teaches English at the College of the Redwoods. She began writing about local culture through two long-running columns in *The Triplicate*. "The Localvore" focused on Del Norte foodways and "The Accidental Family," written by her and other family members, chronicled their family's expansion to include two teen-aged daughters coming out of the foster care system.

Ruth is the author and co-composer of the musical *This is Crescent City*, produced by Lighthouse Repertory Theatre in 2014, and is the writer of a forthcoming graphic novel: *How Did We Get Here?* which tells the fictional story of four young friends struggling to find their place in their community.

In 1998, BBC Radio's show *Short Story* featured "Weaver Bird," a tale Ruth penned while living and working in Kenya as a Peace Corps Volunteer. Her Alaska memoir about living and working in Denali National Park, included in Bona Fide Book's 2015 anthology *Permanent Vacation,* was nominated for a Pushcart Prize.